Martin Köckeritz

Resource Interdependence and Organizational Integration

Material Manifestations of Mergers and Incorporations in Higher Education

The Deutsche Nationalbibliothek lists this publication in the Deutsche Nationalbibliografie; detailed bibliographic data are available on the Internet at http://dnb.d-nb.de

a.t.: Duisburg-Essen, Univ., Diss., 2017

ISBN 978-3-8487-5659-9 (Print)
978-3-8452-9804-7 (ePDF)

British Library Cataloguing-in-Publication Data
A catalogue record for this book is available from the British Library.

ISBN 978-3-8487-5659-9 (Print)
978-3-8452-9804-7 (ePDF)

Library of Congress Cataloging-in-Publication Data
Köckeritz, Martin
Resource Interdependence and Organizational Integration
Material Manifestations of Mergers and Incorporations in Higher Education
Martin Köckeritz
269 p.
Includes bibliographic references.

ISBN 978-3-8487-5659-9 (Print)
978-3-8452-9804-7 (ePDF)

1st Edition 2019

Contents

Figures 9

Tables 11

List of Abbreviations 13

1 Overture, state of affairs, basic approach and study design 14

1.1 What, where and why? Tentative approach to a fuzzy phenomenon 16

1.1.1 Working toward a preliminary definition 16

1.1.2 Where and why? Merger motives and incidence 23

1.1.3 Merger context considerations 26

1.1.4 Research question outline 29

1.2 State of affairs: scientific debates on M&A 31

1.2.1 Business-related M&A research 31

1.2.2 Success factor research ambiguities 35

1.2.3 Organizational integration: conceptualizations and empirical applications 37

1.2.4 M&A research in the field of higher education 43

1.3 Challenges, study aims and design 45

1.3.1 Isolation and fragmentation of extant M&A research 46

1.3.2 Higher education institutions as a specific organization type 49

1.3.3 What a theory should provide (adequacy criteria) 52

1.3.4 Study positioning in the larger meta-theoretical debate 53

1.3.5 Structure of the book, study design and methodological approach 58

2 Theoretical framework: introduction, positioning and assessment of resource dependence theory 62

2.1 RDT as a potential research framework for intraorganizational merger consequences in higher education 62

2.1.1 Introducing RDT: basic concepts and propositions 63

2.1.2 RDT-based merger analysis 66
2.1.3 Opening the black box: RDT as a multilevel approach 69
2.1.4 RDT and institutions of higher education 73

2.2 RDT in the field of organization theory 78
2.2.1 RDT precursors and related approaches 78
2.2.2 Paradigmatic assumptions and positioning 82

2.3 Is RDT an appropriate framework for post-merger integration analysis? 86

3 Resource interdependence and organizational integration: concepts, mechanism and hypotheses 91

3.1 Bridging the gap: meta-theory matters 91
3.1.1 Emergentist materialism: basic terminology and categories 95
3.1.2 Higher education institutions as systems 98
3.1.3 Systemism as a worldview, scientific orientation and research strategy 101

3.2 A systemist perspective on higher education institutions as integrated and distinct social systems 103
3.2.1 HEIs as open allocation systems: from transformation to power 104
3.2.2 HEIs as integrated social systems: from power to control (and back) 106
3.2.3 HEIs as distinct social systems (interior, exterior, boundaries) 109

3.3 General (dis)integration dynamics in the context of interdependence pattern management 113
3.3.1 The dependent variable: organizational integration defined 113
3.3.2 Interdependence patterns and their general relation to organizational (dis)integration 116

3.4 Organizational (dis)integration and mergers in higher education: mechanism and hypotheses 120
3.4.1 The explanatory variables: qualitative (in)consistency and the power relation of interdependence patterns 120

3.4.2 Interdependence pattern relationship and post-merger (dis)integration: hypotheses 124

4 Case study I: the merger of the Universities of Duisburg and Essen 129

4.1 Merging the Universities of Duisburg and Essen: case introduction and research design 130

4.1.1 Background information and time frame 130

4.1.2 Research design 134

4.2 Data analysis and results 140

4.2.1 Scaling and measurement of post-merger intraorganizational power 140

4.2.2 Results of the dimensional analysis 145

4.2.3 Post-merger integration: orientation and level analysis 153

4.3 Exploring the qualitative pattern relations: three chosen fields of integration 162

4.3.1 The integration of physics 164

4.3.2 Educational and social sciences 167

4.3.3 Economics 170

4.4 Résumé and case-specific study limitations 175

5 Case study II: incorporation of the HWP into the University of Hamburg 178

5.1 Case introduction and background 178

5.1.1 Outline of the three merging parties 179

5.1.2 Pre-merger period and political subunit positioning 183

5.1.3 Intraorganizational power distribution 186

5.2 Post-merger integration efforts 190

5.2.1 Basic system structuring—retaining the old parties 193

5.2.2 Homogenization of appointment and endowment policies 194

5.2.3 Education-related integration attempts I: the Graduate School 197

5.2.4 Education-related integration attempts II: teaching exchange and dissertation statute 202

5.2.5 Research and transfer-related integration attempts 205

5.2.6 Administration and support-related integration 208

5.3 Demerger, recapitulation and discussion 210
5.3.1 Recapitulation of integration outcomes 211
5.3.2 Coping with merger demands (and coping consequences) 213

6 Material manifestations of mergers in higher education: conclusion and competing explanations 216

6.1 Recapitulation of the approach and study results 217
6.1.1 What have we done? 217
6.1.2 Recapitulation of the empirical results 219
6.2 Idealism and subjectivism in merger analysis 224
6.2.1 Neo-institutionalist merger analysis 226
6.2.2 Culturalist perspectives on mergers 234
6.3 Conclusion: stuck in the immaterial? 239

Annex A (Interview guide and list) 245

Annex B (Information on documents) 247

Annex C 252

References 253

Figures

Figure 1.1:	Cooperation continuum	18
Figure 1.2:	Organizational linkage continuum	21
Figure 2.1:	Strategic contingencies' theory of intraorganizational power	70
Figure 2.2:	Model of environmental effects in RDT	72
Figure 2.3:	Meta-theoretical classification scheme	83
Figure 4.1:	Steps and objectives of the empirical analysis	139
Figure 4.2:	Adapted SCT scheme	140
Figure 4.3:	Factor-score scatterplot for education immediacy and research centrality	148
Figure 4.4:	Components-score plot	149
Figure 4.5:	Dendrogram of the 9-cluster ward solution	158
Figure 4.6:	Education and Research / Transfer power profiles according to integration and relocation status	161
Figure 5.1:	Pre-restructuring power distribution of the university departments and the HWP	189
Figure 5.2:	Hamburg merger time frame	192

Tables

Table 1.1:	M&A literature reviews and classification attempts	34
Table 4.1:	University of Essen: basic quantitative properties of departments and TRUs in the merger year	136
Table 4.2:	University of Duisburg: basic quantitative properties of departments and TRUs in the merger year	137
Table 4.3:	Rotated factor patterns and intercorrelations	147
Table 4.4:	Cluster means and standard deviations	150
Table 4.5:	Comparison of cluster assignments and validation statistics	153
Table 4.6:	Results of logistic regression analysis	159
Table 5.1:	Hamburg merging parties: basic quantitative properties	188
Table 5.2:	Juxtaposition of chosen dissertation responsibilities	203
Table A:	List of interviews	246
Table B:	List of documents	251
Table C:	Actual faculty organization structure of the University of Duisburg in the merger year	252

Tables

List of Abbreviations

CESM	(C)omposition (E)nvironment (S)tructure (M)echanism model
CGG	Centre for Globalization and Governance
CIS	Center for International Studies
DE	Department of Economics (Hamburg, pre-merger: Dept. 03)
DEP	Department of Economics and Politics (pre-merger: HWP)
DFG	Deutsche Forschungsgemeinschaft (German Research Foundation)
DSS	Department of Social Sciences (Hamburg, pre-merger: Dept. 05)
HEI	higher education institution
HWP	Hamburger Universität für Wirtschaft und Politik
IOR	interorganizational relation
KR	Kleffner report (see Annex B)
M&A	merger & acquisition
RDT	resource dependence theory
SCT	strategic contingencies' theory of intraorganizational power
STEP	Struktur- und Entwicklungsplan (structure and development plan)
TRU	teaching and research unit
UAS	university of applied sciences (Fachhochschule)

1 Overture, state of affairs, basic approach and study design

While they at first glance may appear to be rather specific and infrequently occurring phenomena, full mergers and incorporations have been distinct moments in the overall genesis of organized higher education as well as in the formation of individual institutions. The world's admittedly first and oldest Student University of Bologna, for instance, has from the outset been the result of a successive amalgamation process. It all began with *guilds of scholars* based upon oath, the so-called *Nationes*. These archetypes of organizations in medieval higher education provided the non-Bolognese students with an artificial form of citizenship and protected them from legal disadvantages; the city probably accepted this autonomy as a cost of commercial welfare (Rashdall, 1895: 152ff.). Initially, four larger guilds had emerged, which by the middle of the 13th century had been amalgamated into two cooperating *Universitates*: *Citramontanorum* (Lombards, Tuscans, and Romans) and *Ultramontanorum* (non-Italian students). By the year 1300, both de facto began to act as a unified University of Bologna: they had enacted a common code of statutes, held common congregations, had one seal and were represented by (still) two equitable rectors (*Ibid.*: 178). Mergers and incorporations, nowadays often occurring in larger waves, are to be found in the biography of most institutions and can hence be considered quite regular events.

As will be shown in the following, mergers and incorporations from an intraorganizational perspective can therefore be reduced to several fundamental theoretical concepts like the *integration*, *differentiation*, *centralization* and *demarcation* of organizations. In the context of today's diversified and complex higher education institutions, they also pose concrete explanatory and (normative) management problems, some of which may be briefly listed:

- To what extent are cooperation and / or conflicts between parties to be expected? What drivers have to be accounted for in this respect?
- What changes in structures and processes can / should be effectively realized post-merger and how can these changes be conceptualized and estimated?

- Are realized changes supposed to appear in a homogenous manner across an amalgamated organization? How are possible differences to be explained?
- What factors drive demergers?

To date, such problems have been approached in a surprisingly monothematic manner in both scientific and practitioner debates. Theoretical focus has clearly been placed on the ideational, cognitive and sense-making aspects of organizations: collectively shared and mostly unconscious perceptions have been considered decisive as regards the intraorganizational consequences of mergers. Furthermore, and corresponding to the literature on corporate mergers and acquisitions, the effects of mergers on and contributions to organizational goal achievement (success / performance) have been at the center of interest.

Since many of the above-mentioned questions, however, still remain open and conceptual ambiguities have hardly diminished, we in this book seek to rediscover, further develop and empirically examine resource dependence theory (Pfeffer & Salancik, 1978; Aldrich & Pfeffer, 1976) as an alternative explanatory framework. It is based on the examination of organizational environments, flows of (predominantly) material resources, their control, and the resulting power-exchange relations. I will argue that the study of external interdependence patterns and the resulting subunit power relations are of tremendous significance in the analysis of organizational post-merger (dis)integration.

Our undertaking starts in Chapter 1 by providing important fundamentals. Following some definitional work on mergers and incorporations (1.1.1), existing conceptual contradictions are elaborated in order to substantiate and further explicate our research question (1.1.4). This will be backed by information on the recent empirical incidence of such measures in higher education (1.1.2), as well as political context considerations (1.1.3).

Drawing on the current state of affairs as regards corporate mergers first, this study provides a closer look at basic theoretical approaches and the overall development of the field (1.2.1). It focuses particularly on conceptions of organizational success (1.2.2) and, as it represents our main study aim, post-merger integration (1.2.3).

In building on extant shortcomings in current debates, Chapter 1 determines four adequacy criteria that suitable organization theories should fulfill to approach post-merger integration (1.3.3). Subsequent to considering relevant peculiarities of higher education institutions (HEIs) in Germany

(1.3.2), the chapter closes with a delineation of this study's meta-theoretical positioning (1.3.4), design, and methodology (1.3.5).

1.1 What, where and why? Tentative approach to a fuzzy phenomenon

In order to approach a complex research subject and lay the groundwork for developing concise research questions, a common starting point is to achieve some basic conceptual clarity. Since science is a cumulative endeavor, this first means collating what has become established. As regards many younger and specialized social scientific fields of inquiry, such a shared stock of knowledge will consist of a number of constitutional paradigms and a broad terminological consensus. Hence, what we are looking for is a primary set of concepts to assess existing research, acquire further specifications and introduce ongoing debates. To keep it as open as possible for the moment, we start by considering research on mergers as a form of organizational change.

1.1.1 Working toward a preliminary definition

If we delve into the literature on this subject, a relative lack of attempts at an explicit definition given the large number of empirical studies soon becomes evident, a circumstance that has recently received broader attention in the scientific debate. To examine the conceptual specification and differentiation of terms like *mergers*, *acquisitions* or *takeovers*, Risberg and Meglio (2012; Meglio & Risberg, 2012) conducted several reviews. They analyzed a selection of overall 81 quantitative studies (from seven North American and European management journals, published between 1970 and 2010), which considered merger and acquisition (M&A) performance as the dependent variable. Their results strikingly confirm our first impression: not only are explicit definitions hard to find, scholars generally have rarely discussed the use of different concepts. Instead of explicit conceptualizations, most of the studies reviewed contain more or less implicit demarcations of the research subject, which Meglio & Risberg (2012: 12) have classified according to "features of the merging companies" and "features of the deal". Three fourths of the studies were found to have used complex variations of criteria from both categories to delimit their empirical domain; Risberg and Meglio conclude that "scholars use 'mergers and acquisitions' as a unifying label without any critical reflection over the use of this label" (Risberg & Meglio, 2012: 161).

Are we dealing with an emerging field of study (suggesting a minimum of homogeneity), in which scholars are hesitant to explicitly specify their (field-constituting) research subject? Maybe we got off on the wrong foot. Let us try something else to approach a preliminary definition: Is there something like a consensus about what mergers / acquisitions are *not*? Since they obviously refer to some kind of interaction between at least two organizations, we at once widen our focus to the field of interorganizational relations (IOR), which does conceptually involve a broader range of phenomena like alliances, joint ventures, networks, and several types of more temporary partnerships. The introduction to the *Oxford Handbook of Interorganizational Relations* provides us with a hint:

> In line with the Handbook's focus on longer-term interorganizational relationships we also chose to not include a Chapter on mergers and acquisitions (M&As), as the participating organizations, ex post, become one entity and by definition are no longer capable of sustaining interorganizational relationships (Cropper, Ebers, Huxham & Ring, 2010: 26).

Hence, mergers and acquisitions are considered to mark a transition from inter to intraorganizational relations. Mostly in the heritage of organizational (institutional) economics, such a positioning of various forms of IORs between (neo-classical) markets and centralized structures with unified ownership, including merged organizations, has a relatively longstanding tradition (Galaskiewicz, 1985; Ménard, 2004; Jolink & Niesten, 2012).

Obviously, against the background of insufficient conceptual specifications within the literature on this subject, the *Oxford Handbook on Mergers and Acquisitions* contains a section in its appendix concerned with definitions and defining characteristics:

> To begin with, the differences and similarities between the terms merger vs. acquisitions need to be clarified. A 'merger' refers to the merging of two previously separate organizations and their operations into one. Typically this change is paralleled by the creation of a new joint identity, as in the example of the DaimlerChrysler merger (Faulkner, 2012: 687).

Beyond unified and centralized ownership, two other aspects are thus introduced: a *technical* (often called "task-related") and a *cognitive* defining element, which refer to the unification of value-adding operations and organizational cultures respectively. Subsequent to the specification of the term *acquisition*, which is associated with the general de facto domination of one of the parties in empirical settings (see Singh, 1971; Humpal, 1971; Mangham, 1973), Faulkner (2012) furthermore refers to conceptual differences to other IORs:

> In other words, in alliances, only parts of both organizations cooperate, and sometimes only for a limited period of time. [...] The interorganizational interface in alliances is much more limited than it is in a merger or an acquisition, where by definition every person is somewhat affected (Faulkner, 2012: 689).

Particularly in the second part of the statement, it becomes apparent that the quite common differentiation of M&As against IORs is based on an implied substantial level of intraorganizational change—the complete or majoritarian shift of ownership alone evidently does not suffice as a defining criterion.

Theoretical conceptions and specifications of defining criteria are frequently used in M&A literature as bases of visual display formats like typologies and classifications (see Angwin, 2012). The implicit *a priori* association of M&As with a profound impact on and within the organizations involved, for instance, gives substance to the following well-established continuum:

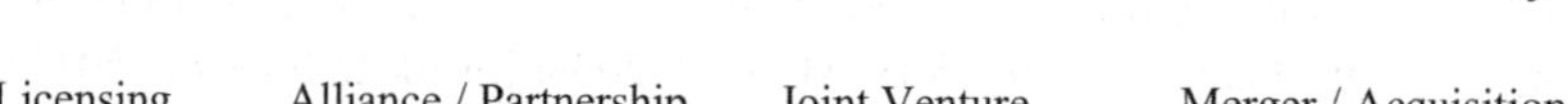

Figure 1.1: Cooperation continuum (Marks & Mirvis, 2010: 11)

Marks and Mirvis (2010), yet without clarifying their meaning in detail, suggested a whole battery of criteria, moving from licensing to acquisition, *investment* and *financial risks*, as well as the *control over* and *impact on the acquired organization* increase. In terms of a definition, the authors stated:

> A merger usually involves the full combination of two previously separate organizations into a third (new) entity. An acquisition typically is the purchase of one organization for incorporation into the parent firm (*Ibid.*: 12).

Remarkably, the "impact" and "pain of separation" criteria indicate that something is supposed to have significantly changed within the organization. Moreover, the association of mergers with considerable intraorganizational impact has not been confined to the M&A research community. In a similar vein, organization sociologist Richard Scott noted:

> No doubt the most drastic tactic used by organizations in relating to critical units of their environment is to absorb these units: two or more independent organizations become a single collective actor (Scott, 2003: 207).

Just as a broader basic consensus begins to appear, it is obviously accompanied by a strange contradiction. Parallel to characterizing M&As as somewhat extreme in comparison to other forms of IORs, it turns out to be equally common sense that M&As on the other hand greatly differ as regards the level of intraorganizational changes. Marks and Mirvis (2010), for instance, only two pages after their impact-continuum, introduced a typology concerning the degree of organizational ("cultural") change that includes a cell with a low level of change in both the acquiring and in the acquired company. Haspeslagh and Jemison (1991: 174), known as important forerunners of the debate on post-merger integration, have evenly discerned a low-impact integration type labeled "holding". Instead of the cultural-cognitive aspects of integration, they have associated sparse integration with a low requirement of organizational and a low level of strategic interdependence. Likewise, Schweiger, Csiszar and Napier (1994) have discussed a respective ideal type of "independence" between the parties, while Birkinshaw, Bresman and Håkanson (2000), in complicating matters further, have equated cases with a low level of technical and cultural integration with "failed acquisitions". In short, the same criterion that is commonly used to distinguish mergers from IORs has been applied to separate different merger settings against each other. This necessarily leads to conceptual ambiguities: mergers can simultaneously on the one hand be drastic full combinations *and* independent / preserving holdings on the other hand.

Specifically, the distinction of merger settings regarding the level of intraorganizational changes realized reflects the experiences of many practitioners. Aside from those mergers that never attempt closer relations between the parties since they are, for instance, undertaken as a form of risk-diversifying investment, many cases turn out to remain en-bloc incorporations without any significant integration of the parties over time. Wasn't the frequently addressed DaimlerChrysler merger, given the enormous hype surrounding its execution, quickly undone without much noise? Following a short negotiation stage, Chrysler, which today belongs to the FI-

AT Group, was divested twelve years after the merger and sold to an investment fund. What interconnecting processes between the two companies had actually to be painfully resolved? What unified production, development, and distribution units had to be disentangled? What percentage of Daimler's workforce really ever had contact to Chrysler employees, and what happened to the characteristic "new joint identity" (Faulkner, 2012) after the split-up? Would we refrain from classifying such a case as a full merger or acquisition in the case of low-level internal changes and easy reversibility?

It is self-evident that employing one and the same criterion to discern mergers from other forms of IORs and to distinguish M&A settings against each other is problematic from a scientific perspective. The use of a continuum implies the existence of one at least ordinal-scaled criterion variable, which allows for stable propositions as to the sequence of phenomena. Any event—to stick with Marks & Mirvis (2010)—that is identified as a merger has consequentially to be associated with a higher level of organizational change than that alliance with the highest impact. However, since conventional wisdom has it that mergers, whether desired or not, do occur in terms of continuing organizational independence, the question arises of how such a (de facto) holding conceptually relates, for instance, to a long-term and capital-intensive joint venture. It therefore stands to reason that a discrimination between different IORs on the basis of intraorganizational impact / unification / integration has to fail.

Since that contradiction concerns rather basic scientific conventions, the broad acknowledgement of such an *impact-myth* in terms of a defining criterion is all the more noteworthy. In another essay fundamental to the integration debate by Borys and Jemison (1989), who in contrast to the above-stated common-sense approach have classified M&As as *hybrids*, the underlying conceptual ambiguity becomes evident. They define hybrids as "organizational arrangements that use resources and / or governance structures from more than one existing organization" (*Ibid.*: 235). Mergers, as one out of five considered hybrid-archetypes (besides acquisitions, joint ventures, license agreements and supplier arrangements), are in the well-known way specified as "the complete unification of two (or more) organizations into a single organization" (*Ibid.*) Just two pages later, the authors again assert that "in contrast to unitary organizations, hybrids are composed of sovereign organizations whose continued existence may or may not depend on the hybrid's performance". This is not quite logical: what else should be the consequence of unifying than a unified, "single" organization? Are merged organizations thus to be considered "unitary" (whatever that means) organizations or are they "composed of sovereign organizations"?

Unfortunately, such widespread ambiguities do not advance our search for a suitable preliminary definition. A constant level of impact / integration / unification is, at least without further distinctions and theoretical considerations, not an appropriate definition criterion. As regards business-related literature, we are therefore left with the criteria of ownership and legal status—any discussion of a potentially developing joint identity between the parties is put on hold for the moment. A common ownership criterion to define the term *acquisition*, for example, is the takeover of more than 50% of the equity of the acquired firm (target) by the acquiring company (Singh, 1971: 27). However, though being much more precise than the measures mentioned before, such standards are of quite limited relevance when it comes to organizations in higher education funded by public means. Ownership has a different meaning, assets and shares are not traded, and mergers are (at least formally) decided on by the public agency responsible. It follows, then, that business-focused M&A research is barely able to provide us with definition criteria we can build on.

How about works specifically focused on mergers in higher education? Though it is much smaller and mostly isolated from business-related M&A research, a respective body of literature exists. Definition approaches have thereby likewise been aimed at differentiating full mergers and acquisitions from several types of IORs. The Australian higher education researcher Grant Harman (1983), in one of the first systematic discussions of concepts and classificatory schemes, presented the following "organizational linkage continuum":

Voluntary Cooperation	Formalised Consortium	Federation	Amalgamation
Cooperation	Coordination		Unitary Structure

Figure 1.2: Organizational linkage continuum (Harman, 1983: 115)

The types of linkage, which Harman illustrates in detail, are arranged according to the degree of liability and the associated loss of organizational autonomy. If we move from the left to the right hand side, arrangements cannot be revoked as easily by one of the parties involved, and it becomes more difficult for the latter "to pursue essentially autonomous directions". Amalgamations or mergers as "the most extreme form of linkage" are defined as:

> [...] a process whereby two or more formerly separate and independent higher education institutions become legally and organisationally a single entity under the managerial responsibility and control of a single governing body and a single chief executive officer. In this process, unless special arrangements are otherwise made, all assets, liabilities and responsibilities of the former institutions are transferred to the single new or continuing institution (Harman, 1983: 114).

Within the specific literature on this subject, this definition has become broadly acknowledged (Goedegebuure, 1992; Lang, 2001). Even though neither the definition nor the continuum is theoretically substantiated, the former is explicit and detailed. It suggests a focus on the legal status of higher education institutions (HEIs)[1] and on the factual technical execution of mergers, which means a shift of responsibilities and control. However, some of the previously discussed ambiguities (some kind of impact-myth) are included as well. Though Harman (1983: 114) admits that in empirical settings "the achievement of a unitary structure is not a necessary characteristic of an amalgamation or merger", some opaque process of becoming "organizationally a single entity" is nonetheless part of his definition.

For the purpose of our study, I propose the following (preliminary) definitions:

> Def. 1: A *merger* is a discrete administrative act, by which all the organizations involved lose their status as separate legal entities, and all the responsibilities of their central level decision-making organs, as well as of their university councils, are transferred to the respective (transitional) organs of a newly founded organization.

> Def. 2: An *incorporation* is a discrete administrative act, by which the respective (transitional) organs of one of the organizations involved assume the responsibilities of the respective central level decision-making organs, as well as of the university councils, of all the other organizations involved. All but the incorporating organization lose their status as a separate legal entity.

Both definitions are somewhat reduced but still close to the one suggested by Harman. They are reduced in that there is a stronger emphasis on the sober fact of what actually happens from a legal perspective. Central level

---

1 In this work, the term *institution* is largely used as a synonym for organization (see Chapter 3 for details).

decision-making organs of existing organizations of higher education in Germany are the *senate* and the *rectorate / presidium* (German: *Rektorat* or *Präsidium*); because of its particular legal status (see Gärditz, 2009: 545ff.), the *university council*, a nouveau type of organ, is mentioned separately. In public higher education, organizational mergers and incorporations have to be executed by the enactment of a law, in which the formal liquidation of the old independent organizations and the formation of a new one is codified (Umbach & Palsherm, 2003). With the enactment of the law, the old central level organs and university councils lose their responsibilities and cease to exist; new (transitional) organs have to be formed immediately. Though there may be a merger process following the execution of a merger, the term *process* is unnecessary for the purposes of a definition. Since they are themselves subject to theorizing, any references to merger-induced organizational impacts like *unifying completely*, *creating a single entity*, *organizationally becoming one*, or *creating joint identities* are avoided. The definitions provided are sufficient to clearly identify our research subject and—though in a nominal fashion—to distinguish it from other types of IORs.

1.1.2 Where and why? Merger motives and incidence

After the search for and discussion of a preliminary definition to build our analysis on, we pause for a moment and turn to the incidence of mergers in higher education, as well as the motives behind them. As concerns the private business sector, the relevance of M&A research is not difficult to justify. This is commonly done by pointing to the frequency and topicality of the phenomenon, as well as to enormous capital flows and allegedly high failure rates. Pablo (2016), for instance, reports estimates of around 40,000 business M&A transactions associated with a capital volume of between 2.4 and 4.6 trillion US dollars conducted in the first decade of the 21st century. Hence, it definitely is a commonplace phenomenon in the corporate world—the larger cases regularly attract considerable public and political interest.

As regards the higher education sector, systematic inquiries, reliable numbers and international comparisons are rare. The literature on this subject is dominated by mostly descriptive accounts of merger waves and policy backgrounds in single nation states or wider regions. Such accounts can, for instance, be found for the huge wave of mergers in Australia in the early 1980s (Harman, 1986; Goedegebuure & Meek, 1991; Meek, 1994), for

China (between 1992 and 2005) (Yang, 2000; Mok, 2005, Wan & Peterson, 2007) and South Africa (since 2000) (Hay & Fourie, 2002; Sehoole, 2005). As regards higher education in Europe, merger activity reviews of varying elaborateness have been provided for the Netherlands (1983–1987) (Goedegebuure, 1992), Norway (Skodvin, 1999; Kyvik, 2002) and Great Britain (Harman & Harman, 2008; Pruisken, 2014). More recently, Estonia has reduced the number of its higher education organizations from 41 to 29 by means of merging; further waves have occurred in France, Finland and Denmark[2]. For Germany, Pruisken (2014), in a detailed account, identifies 70 cases overall (public / private / confessional HEIs) since 1970 and associates them with two larger waves of mergers. Between 1995 and 2009 —the second wave—16 mergers involving 33 organizations (public only) occurred. Therefore, mergers in higher education have been quite regular events in many countries.

Closely linked to the empirical incidence of such phenomena is the *why*-question, concerning the underlying political motives. While in business-related debates motives are generally attributed to the management of at least one of the corporations involved (see Napier, 1989; Trautwein, 1990; Angwin, 2007), in public higher education the interests of the respective governmental funding agency have (sometimes exclusively) to be accounted for. Some authors have provided brief accounts of typical motives or motive categories for higher education mergers (e.g. Harman & Meek, 1988; Skodvin, 1999; Hay & Fourie, 2002; Lang, 2002) such as, for example, the *elimination of double programs, concentration of budgets, realizing economies of scale,* or creating enhanced abilities to *cultivate competitive institutional profiles*. Such motives, however, have rarely been analyzed in a systematic manner; they have frequently, even without naming sources, just been compiled in an intuitionist and cursory manner—to put it another way: they have mostly been conceived of as trivial.

Typical sources of such officially declared motives, if we take Germany (and particularly the latest merger wave) as an example, are principally the reports of governmental evaluation commissions and transcripts of parliamentary debates. The search for motives thus quickly leads to the analysis of political rhetoric. As an illustration, two emblematic official statements shall be given here. The first relates to one of the cases analyzed in this book, the incorporation of the *Hamburger Universität für Wirtschaft und Politik* into the *University of Hamburg* (see Chapter 5). It was made by Jörg

2 http://www.bbc.com/news/business-34902884.

Dräger, Hamburg's former chief administrator for education, in the final parliamentary debate:

> [...] We need the new faculty structure to decidedly promote research foci able to perform, together with innovative research approaches. To achieve competitiveness and excellence, it is indispensable to bundle competences and resources to form a critical mass. This is the only way for us to become internationally acknowledged (CD2|6: 1155D).

The second statement stems from an evaluation commission report concerning the merger of three North German Universities of Applied Science (UAS) in Oldenburg, Ostfriesland and Wilhelmshaven in 2000 (demerger in 2009):

> [...] to recognize the merger as a chance and initial spark for the advancement of the university as a whole and of one's respective own campus site, and in lieu of the fixation on one's own campus site activate the resources of the university to tap and improve possible synergies of the merger, as well as the potentials of the university as a whole (Development recommendations Lower Saxony: 6).

In their emphasis on increased institutional competitiveness, those statements are quite representative as regards goal formulations and merger motives. Though comparable proclamations should possibly be found in most recent cases, they do not, however, provide a proper basis for the analysis of motives—except for a particular research interest in political rhetoric itself. They might indeed point to the actual motives of the deciding public agency but of course do not have to. Concepts are not developed and related to each other in an orderly manner, many claims remain unsubstantiated, and calculations as to cost savings, if existent at all, are often hard to reconstruct. Many official documents do contain only sparse and / or extremely global reasons to justify merging.

Still, such officially announced motives are revealing enough to not be simply dismissed as mere phrase mongering. Due to a lack of systematic inquiries, they are ultimately the only criteria with which to evaluate the activities of the public agencies involved. Furthermore, it becomes obvious that the merger-related impact-myth is reproduced in the debate on public mergers. The advocates of such measures commonly link them to enormous internal and external effects: a qualitative leap in performance indicators, new study program profiles for new target groups, and all kinds of positive outcomes for cities, whole regions, or industries. Moreover, as I browse through a collection of press clippings relating to the Duisburg–Essen case (Chapter 4), merger opponents have repeatedly joined in by complaining about the anticipated complete obliteration of the "old" organizations. Neither grandiose performance effects nor leveling out the merging parties are, however, to be expected without tremendous intraorganizational changes being implied.

Political merger motives and goal achievement are of little interest beyond that assertion for the study at hand. Instead of examining them in more detail, we will now turn to some contextual considerations.

1.1.3 Merger context considerations

Since higher education-specific M&A research hasn't so far generated much organized knowledge as to underlying political motives, and the correlated political rhetoric isn't helpful either, we leave it with a compact account of the greater political impetus associated with the merger wave our two cases belong to. The term *merger wave* thereby relates to an assignment of cases to a certain period and a common macro-level context, which is considered relevant for an observed cumulation of mergers. With regard to the time-related and context-related demarcation of waves in Germany, we follow Pruisken (2014: 149ff.):

(1) The first wave (1970–1995) largely occurred in a context of reorganization due to *scientification* and *massification* in higher education. It comprised the foundation of the Fachhochschulen (UAS) (1969–1972) and, in some German Federal States, the establishment of the integrative *Gesamthochschulen*. The process of German reunification (1990) constituted a further sub-context of the first wave.
(2) The second wave (since 1995) ensued in association with the *neoliberal turn* in German higher education politics (according to Pruisken: the dominance of a market and efficiency logic)

Such general political contexts, though they do not allow for inference on merger motives, provide the advantage of being derived from commonalities between several kinds of political interventions, with mergers just being one of them. It may therefore be assumed that the mergers of each respective wave were at least conceived of as widely consistent with the greater political impetus by the public agencies responsible. Furthermore, the broader context particularly matters for empirical analysis: the considered mergers were not executed in isolation, but were accompanied by and interacted with several other organizational change measures.

The broader impetus relevant to our cases has been characterized by *new managerialism* and *new public management* in higher education (Braun & Merrien, 1999; Braun, 1999; Schimank, 2005; Deem & Brehony, 2007) as aspects of a comprehensive neoliberal turn[3] in German politics. The majority of the change measures induced over the last 20 years have thereby been aimed at convergence of the attributes of public HEIs[4] in line with those of private business firms.

First and foremost, this was attempted by backing the external control of HEIs in combination with an enervation of traditional academic self-government. External control was, for instance, enhanced by the implementation of supervisory boards (university councils / Hochschulräte), which have henceforth granted extensive consultation rights to social actors from outside academia. A considerable proportion of the latter have been business representatives (see Nienhüser & Jacob, 2008). In addition, accreditation systems and numerous temporary semi-governmental evaluation and advisory commissions (see below) have been installed as further external actors; the (failed) intensification of competition in higher education by forwarding private institutions may be added. Increased external control was in a way "activated" by a pullback of public funding together with the coupling of rising shares of funds to performance indicators. The consequence has been an increased dependence on third-party financing, and, in many cases, shrinking state funds.

Enhancement of external control was paralleled on the organizational level of analysis by an incremental reinterpretation of collegial elements and the functional internal differentiation into an attempted hierarchical order (Gärditz, 2009: 33). The withdrawal of state agencies from detailed planning and the introduction of "global budgets" went along with greater discretion for executive organs on the central level (rectorate / presidium) as well as on the level of disciplines (deanery). Furthermore, professionalization of administration through the implementation of full-time faculty managers was advanced in many cases. Hierarchical order has also been fostered by changing academic industrial relations (Wilson, 1991)—since

3 The usage of the term here follows Harvey (2005), who defines *Neoliberalism* as "[…] a theory of political economic practices that proposes that human well-being can best be advanced by liberating individual entrepreneurial freedoms and skills within an institutional framework characterized by strong private property rights, free markets, and free trade" (Harvey, 2005: 2).

4 More detailed information in Subsection 1.3.2.

2007, graduate staff below professor level generally has been employed for a strictly limited period of time.

Furthermore, convergence of organizational characteristics in line with business firms was usually conducted with the implementation of numerous managerial governance, planning and communication instruments. This has, for instance, included SWOT-analyses, management by objectives, the adoption of business IT-solutions, marketing instruments, and HR development units. Accounting has been converted from single-entry to double-entry bookkeeping.

The governmental agencies responsible have discursively framed the development with respective managerial terminology. The state of Baden-Württemberg, to take a case in point, changed the more traditional terms *Rektorat* and *Hochschulrat* into *Vorstand* (board of management) and *Aufsichtsrat* (board of governors) early on. In 2005, the state / city of Hamburg started, in its education budget accounts, to classify HEIs as *Produktbereiche* (product divisions) and education and research as *Produktgruppen* (product families); faculties have had to report on *strategische Entwicklungsfelder* (fields of strategic development). An increasing dislocation of policy formulation processes toward para-constitutional expert commissions, consultancies, and private think tanks has also been characteristic of the broader political context. At least until the consequences of the United States' subprime mortgage crisis in 2008 set in, a virtually hysterical aggrandizement of the problem-solving capacities of business firms and market mechanisms can be recognized in the political discourse relating to higher education.

The intergovernmentally initiated *Bologna Process* (1997–2010) on the Europe-wide harmonization of university degrees, program characteristics, and quality standards also took place during the period under consideration (Olsen & Maassen, 2007; Witte, 2006; Vögtle, 2014). Having started with the official goal of furthering transboundary student mobility, the results of that process have allowed to internationally compare institutional profiles and what they offer in competition with each other. All HEIs in Germany had to face similar challenges during this period of harmonization: they had to decide on the number and basic character of their study programs, the relation of the new to the former programs, administrative responsibilities and much more.

Given the overall intention of this book, merger context aspects have to be discussed in a compressed and rather cursory manner for the sake of brevity. The presentation is neither exhaustive, nor does it account for any implementation differences between the federal states. However, it should have become clear from this brief sketch that the second merger wave has been associated with a period of manifold interventions in German public higher education. The underlying greater political impetus can be described as converging higher education institutions in line with private business firms located in a market setting. We may therefore at least assume that the governments responsible conceived of the mergers under consideration as fitting into the broader collectivity of interventions.

1.1.4 Research question outline

By now, the situation can be described as follows. Common sense seems to dictate that mergers and acquisitions (incorporations) are forms of interorganizational relations, which typically lead to unification of the parties involved. This unification—integration of two or more formerly independent organizations into one—is supposed to be so comprehensive that, as change measures, M&As are usually discussed as a separate category. At the same time, it is broadly acknowledged amongst scholars and practitioners that such change measures frequently result in intraorganizational independence and the local perpetuation of existing structures. Varying levels of organizational integration may occur within the merged organizations: this is realized in some subunits, others remain separate. Consequently, merger cases can be distinguished from each other regarding the level of integration realized. M&A scholars have to date held on to the notion of the inherent, quasi-automatically unfolding high intraorganizational change level (beyond a mere shift of ownership) as the defining characteristic, while simultaneously treating it as a variable.

This “distinctive duality” of M&As (Borys & Jemison, 1989: 235) has also been recognized as characteristic of organizations of higher education, the specific research subject of the study at hand:

> Clearly, when counterpoised to other forms of inter-institutional combination, a defining characteristic of merger is that it involves a loss of autonomy for at least one of the participating institutions. But within mergers there are various organisational arrangements that can allow for considerable degrees of local autonomy for the previously independent institutions (Lang, 2002: 174).

Moreover, it has been found that the a priori association of M&As with a considerable degree of organizational change (impact-myth) is frequently mirrored in political debates. Mergers in higher education are depicted by their proponents as being effective on their own terms; appropriate measures to realize synergies and cost reductions, and to create new profiles in education and research, amongst other things. Their opponents frequently fear the loss of everything that accounted for their old organizations. Save our institution!

Therefore, there is a consistent need to analyze post-merger organizational integration as a variable from a scientific / theoretical as well as from a practitioner perspective. Hence, our research question is: Why do merged organizations (and in particular, HEIs) differ regarding the level of post-merger integration realized within as well as across the cases? More specifically:

Which organizational factors essentially influence the level of post-merger integration realized within merged organizations?

As will be shown in the following, these organizational factors are intraorganizational (subunit level) power relations, which are predominantly rooted in patterns of external resource dependency. Not least because we have not so far discussed any possible construct conceptualizations of post-merger integration—let alone something like a *level of integration*—the explication of our research question is inevitably provisional at present. There is a lack of theoretical considerations, further links, and, in particular, a basic vantage point to approach the phenomenon from, along with a respective embedment within broader scientific controversies. Before reviewing the extant literature on post-merger integration analysis, I shall briefly outline some qualifications as to the research interest here in order to avoid possible misunderstandings and disappointments:

- As already mentioned, there will be no systematic exploration of possible merger causes and their political reasons;
- We will not, in terms of a policymaking perspective, seek to discuss any degree of attainment of such goals—there is no evaluation of overall merger success or failure;
- We will not be concerned with a comparison of different forms of interorganizational relations as possible alternatives to full mergers;
- Even though some concrete means to predict integration feasibility unfold, there will be no emphasis on merger implementation instructions for practitioners.

In fact, we conceive of the mergers examined more in terms of social field experiments with unclear results. We do not primarily seek to analyze the underlying motives of the political institutions involved (i.e. why the mergers were executed). We neither ask how they should be conducted, could be set up in an alternative manner or if the supposed goals behind mergers that have been carried out have been achieved. We rather ask how that mysterious process of "becoming one" and its intensity can be conceptualized, measured, and explained. We ask what happens in terms of organizational integration and which factors it essentially depends on.

1.2 State of affairs: scientific debates on M&A

Up to this point, we have approached this study's research interest on a quite general basis. The need to further explore organizational integration following mergers has been established on grounds of persistent contradictions regarding the conceptual specification of these change measures, related political goal formulations and practical experience. In order to further qualify our research question, in the following we will return to the scientific merger debate briefly touched upon at the outset. What concepts have emerged therefrom and what aspects of the phenomenon have already been covered? We start by introducing business-related M&A research from a bird's eye view—some current general limitations of its use as a frame of reference for our investigation are hinted at. Afterwards, we discuss some theoretical conceptions of integration and extant empirical applications in more detail. This section closes with a compact presentation of relevant writings specifically concerned with mergers in higher education.

1.2.1 Business-related M&A research

Although mergers in the corporate world as empirical phenomena are much older, a broader scientific interest did not occur until the late 1970s. After decades of discipline-related differentiation and growing publication numbers, a huge and—even for the social sciences—confusingly complex body of literature has formed. Cartwright et al. (2012), for instance, in one of the largest recent review approaches, analyzed a choice of 19 top-tier journals from a wide range of disciplines. They identified 416 relevant papers, with 379 of them being empirical studies, which they assigned to three broader categories (strategy, management, and finance) and 11 subthemes. Typically, the multitude of perspectives and research subjects places great demands on classification approaches (Teerikangas & Joseph,

2012); the "comprehensive reviews" sometimes called for (e.g. Haleblian et al., 2009) still do not exist.

In recent times, however, numerous attempts to consolidate M&A research as a field have been undertaken: Table 1.1 presents a collection of reviews. I have decided to arrange them according to their respective *general classification* theme as indicated by their authors. Within the resulting six groups, some information on the *specific review focus*, which points to particular aspects within the broader theme (or the reviewer's interpretation of the broader theme), is provided. Haleblian et al. (2009: 5), for example, consider the overall field-guiding explanation framework, their general classification theme, to consist of *antecedents*, *moderators*, and *outcomes* of acquisition behavior. Empirical studies are grouped by Haleblian et al. according to their focus on one of the three framework elements. Reus et al. (2012: 88), by contrast, conceive of the overall guiding explanation framework (the same general classification theme) in terms of *M&A outcomes* to be the consequence of *contextual factors* and *mediating process factors*—and organize their review accordingly. The last two table columns contain information on the disciplines or fields of inquiry the reviewers consider to have contributed to M&A research as a field, either as explicitly stated or implied through their discipline-related assignment of review sources (last column).

	Specific classification focus	**Statement as to fields of study considered to be involved in M&A research**	**Review sources**
Classification theme I:study focus within the overall M&A explanatory framework			
Haleblian, Devers, McNamara, Carpenter & Davison (2009)	Antecedents / moderators / outcomes (quantitative studies only)	*Economics, finance, management, sociology*	16 top-tier journals subsumed under management, finance, accounting, economics and sociology (167 in all)
Reus, Ellis, Lamont & Ranft (2012)	Context factors and process dimensions	*Strategic management, organization theory, organizational behavior, HR, finance*	Not made explicit
Classification theme II: post-merger integration			
Schweiger & Goulet (2000)	None, micro-level studies excluded	None	Not made explicit
Ranft, Butler & Sexton (2010)	Integration process	None	General ABI/INFORM Global search + 8 top-tier journals (1989 – 2006) classified as strategic management journals
Teerikangas & Joseph (2012)	None	None	Not made explicit
Classification theme III: cultural perspectives in M&A-research			
Teerikangas (2007)	Concepts of culture / culture-performance / impact of national cultures / management of differences	*Economics, strategy, HR-* and *cultural perspectives*	Not made explicit
Stahl & Voigt (2008)	Impact of cultural differences on integration / performance	*Strategic-, finance-, organizational-* and *HR* perspectives	Not made explicit; 56 studies in all (Meta-analysis of 46 studies)
Teerikangas and Véry (2012)	Concepts / culture-performance / cultural change / international aspects	None - the cultural perspective is subsumed under more traditional *social sciences* (e. g. anthropology)	Not made explicit
Classification theme IV: organizational learning and M&A experience			
Barkema & Schijven (2008)	Pre-1990s research / negative experience transfer / deliberate learning mechanisms / experience learning	None	6 top-tier journals (1980 – 2008) classified as management journals
Classification theme V: success, failure, outcomes			
Tichy (2001)	Consumer welfare / shareholder value / regulation implications	*Economics* and *industrial organization*	Not made explicit, 36 studies in all

King, Dalton, Daily & Covin (2004)	Meta-analysis of 93 performance studies; 4 frequently used performance indicators	None	12 top-tier journals (1921 – 2002) classified as accounting, finance, economics and management journals
Risberg & Meglio (2012)	Use of market- and accounting-based performance measures	*Management, organization, finance*	9 Thomson ISI top-tier journals (1980 – 2008), 55 studies in all
Thanos & Papadakis (2012)	Use of accounting-based performance measures	None	28 top-tier and mixed US and European management journals; 4 practitioner periodicals (1961 – 2010); 36 empirical studies in all
Classification theme VI: M&A-research methodology			
Cartwright, Teerikangas, Rouzon & Wilson-Evered (2012)	Distribution of methods and broad disciplines (strategy / management / finance) in top-tier journals	M&A research is considered a discipline within "*management sciences*"; *finance, strategy, managerial* and *human perspective*	19 top-tier journals (1963-2009) subsumed under strategy, finance, organizational behavior, organizational psychology, marketing, and human resource management; 379 studies in all
Bengtsson & Larrsson (2012)	M&A case study research	*Strategic management, finance*	11 heavily cited case studies identified out of the 200 most referenced SSCI publications
Angwin (2012)	Typologies, taxonomies and classifications as means of M&A theorizing	Broadly refers to „*management literature*" and *strategic management*	Not made explicit

Table 1.1: M&A literature reviews and classification attempts

Since many aspects are often pooled in quite global subcategories like *communications* or *leadership*, most of the reviews listed are not mutually exclusive in terms of their objectives. Furthermore, considerable disagreement as to the relevant academic disciplines contributing to the field is striking; some consensus seems to have developed as to the prominence of strategic management. According to Starbuck (2003: 175), who comprehensively traces the historical development of organization and management theories, strategic management has "shown a tendency to split into two domains, one more closely associated with economics and the other more closely associated with sociology or management"—boundaries between disciplines have generally remained blurred. Along the same lines, such development can be said to have taken place regarding the analysis of M&As; the disciplines involved can hence be assigned according to two paradigms:

(1) "hard" strategy paradigm: literature on economics, finance and associated strategic management and organization
(2) "soft" strategy paradigm: comprises approaches inspired by sociology, anthropology, and the field of human relations in business studies

The characterization of both paradigms as "strategic" is due to the fact that the overwhelming majority of approaches are directly or indirectly interested in the improvement of corporate / entrepreneurial target achievement. After all, some focus on success has turned out to be the only true common (and therefore field-generating) orientation so far. M&A research may thus also be designated as *M&A-related success factor research*. As regards the proportions within the field "as a whole", studies associated with the older "hard paradigm" are numerically dominant (Haleblian et al., 2009: 4; Cartwright et al., 2012).

1.2.2 Success factor research ambiguities

We are interested in intraorganizational consequences of mergers in higher education. Specifically, we are searching for a theoretical conceptualization of post-merger integration as well as for essential predictors for the resulting depth of integration. M&A research has, however, largely been seeking anteceding, mediating, and moderating factors pertaining to the explanation and stimulation of post-merger performance (success). What insights from business-related success factor research may be useful for our endeavor? To cut a long story short: little to none. A substantial reason for this lies in the fact that M&A research only appears to be a coherent field of inquiry on the surface; a common stock of knowledge one could relate to hasn't emerged so far. Without going too much into detail, lacking common knowledge can, in turn, be put down to persistent ambiguities of the field's central theoretical concepts and the resulting stark fragmentation of the literature on it. This may be briefly explicated by considering the concept of *organizational success*, which is pivotal to most empirical M&A studies.

In a further review approach, Risberg & Meglio (2012), besides their definition attempts, focused on merger success and particularly on the use of market-based, accounting-based, perception-based or combined performance measures (55 studies were analyzed). With regard to extant approaches to estimating M&A activity outcome on average, they found difficulties identifying the research subjects the suggested measures relate to: references vary between bidders, targets, both of them, or even remain open to interpretation. The different kinds of measures applied themselves turned out to differ enormously (e.g. accounting measures like *return on assets, return on investment, return on equity*, or *cumulative abnormal return*) and were found to unfortunately refer to broadly ranging periods. Some of the metrics are, to take a case in point, reported to relate to future market expectations, while others address changes in past performance (*Ibid.*: 160). For similar reasons, they found it difficult to compare studies that seek to analyze different types of M&As (e.g. related vs. unrelated) according to performance effects or those that try to isolate performance predictors. On the basis of their review, Risberg & Meglio question the validity of the common "taken-for-granted" assertion of high M&A failure rates and reject the existence of a unitary performance concept that could be used for study comparisons.

These findings are in line with other reviews (e.g. Tichy, 2001); King et al (2004: 197) found their meta-analysis failed "to uncover even a single moderator of post-acquisition performance whose significant effect has been replicated across the established minimum of three studies". As regards the widespread use of accounting measures, Thanos & Papadakis (2012: 114) additionally point to the broad variety of accounting standards between countries, which leads to further difficulties in terms of international comparisons and the analysis of cross-boundary mergers.

Reviewers of M&A research have thus confirmed the daunting results of similar earlier debates on success and performance measures in organization studies. Shenhav, Shrum and Alon (1994) evaluated the application of several common goodness concepts like *effectiveness*, *performance*, *productivity*, *outcome*, *efficiency*, and *success* across several fields of study. Their detailed review over a time span of roughly 35 years comprehends 349 articles published in four leading US and European journals (*Academy of Management Review*, *Academy of Management Journal*, *Administrative Science Quarterly* and *Organization Science*). Results show that performance was the dominant criterion (48%), followed by organizational effectiveness (25%) —the latter had been surpassed by the former since the late 1980s. Only one fifth of the studies reviewed used theoretical definitions of the goodness criteria employed. With regard to operational definitions, the authors identified 80 different indicators (which they grouped into 11 distinct categories) displaying a large number of multiple assignments, particularly between performance and effectiveness. Hence, Shenhav et al. (1994) come to similar conclusions as, for instance, Steers (1975), who in a comparison of forms of operationalization of effectiveness found fundamental validation problems. The scientific usefulness of effectiveness in terms of a universal organizational success criterion has been challenged repeatedly (Steers, 1975; 1977; Kanter & Brinkerhoff, 1981; Goodman, Atkin & Schoorman, 1983; Cameron, 1978 (for HEIs); 1986).

In sum then, ambiguous and noncumulative findings are by no means a problem exclusive to M&A research. Nonetheless, it should have become clear that success factor research, not least because of its fragmentation, currently does not provide a promising starting point. What remains to be done? After looking at M&A definition approaches (1.1.1) and the state of knowledge regarding post-merger organizational success as the preferred explanation focus (1.2.2), we will conclude by attending to the mediating mechanism(s) in between the two. Therefore, the state of affairs as concerns post-merger organizational integration will be explored in the following.

1.2.3 Organizational integration: conceptualizations and empirical applications

In the course of discussing possible basic definitions of mergers, we have asserted that organizational integration is somewhat of a prima facie concept of M&A research. Scholars have obviously been unwilling to leave the idea of merging to a mere unification of ownership, or some loss of legal independence: there must be something more to it. Merging as a unifying process is (implicitly) considered to refer to becoming one organization with a common identity, shared goals and processes. Integration conceptually relates to what is supposed to change within the partaking organizations. We have identified a strange contradiction in the scientific debate insofar as integration is, on the one hand, usually set as a defining constant but is understood, on the other, as a typifying variable.

Notable differences as to the visibility and handling of this contradiction exist in the literature on this subject. Some writers, such as the ones introduced at the outset, make it evident or even discuss the "distinctive duality" of mergers yielding "organizational hybrids" (Borys & Jemison, 1989: 235). However, the majority of those M&A approaches, which belong to the "hard" economics / finance and strategic fit paradigm, in terms of a silent ceteris paribus condition tends to implicitly abstract from the concept of post-merger integration[5]. Amongst those studies that do not adhere to such a black box perspective and treat the concept explicitly instead, a broad consensus on considering integration the single most important moderator between acquisition behavior and overall success has become established (Datta, 1991; Larsson & Finkelstein, 1999; Barkema & Schijven, 2008; Haleblian et al., 2009).

Enthusiasm as to the overall explanatory potential of organizational integration has, however, not been paralleled by conceptual agreement. The frequently used term in most writings seems to (loosely) relate to "some form of combining of assets and people", is rarely defined explicitly, and is hardly used as a dependent variable (Schweiger & Goulet, 2000: 63). The degree of integration has often served as a basis of typologies. It is striking that extant defining and paraphrasing statements are circuitous and can barely serve to identify concrete measures. Accordingly, Napier (1989: 277) associated more deeply integrated M&A types with blending or compromising on "major operational and managerial functions" as well as with knowledge and technology transfer or "the widespread adoption of policies and practices of one firm by the other". Haspeslagh and Jemison (1991) see the highest level of integration connected with the complete consolidation of activities, organization, and corporate cultures over time. According to Pablo (1994: 806), organizational integration is "defined as the making of changes in the functional activity arrangements, organizational structures and systems, and cultures of combining organizations to facilitate their consolidation into a functioning whole". Under the label of post-merger integration besides acquirer interventions, Schweiger and Very (2003: 6) refer to several different activities like physically consolidating, standardizing, or coordinating the functions and activities of each party. Larsson and Finkelstein (1999: 6) define it "as the degree of interaction and coordination between the two firms involved in a merger or acquisition".

This choice of defining statements reveals a noticeable proximity to quite global descriptions of what is commonly supposed to constitute organizations *in general*. Most of the statements could be used to discern formal organizations (of whatever type) as distinct social phenomena from non-organized parts of the society. We, in contrast to the latter, would probably consider organizations as (maybe functional) discernible wholes. We would also associate them with some coordination and interaction

5 Merging in economic modeling approaches is sometimes just equated with *perfect cooperation* between organizations; see for example Huck, Konrad, Müller & Norman (2006).

amongst their members. We may also assume some kind of standardization, homogenization, physical consolidation, as well as somebody's interventions in something. And we would also identify formal organizations as social phenomena with a greater degree of coherence against the rest. To form some non-organized part of the society into what we would call an "organization" would probably be associated with the same measures that apply in a merger situation. The term organizational integration in the current debate hence seems to be a synonym for "getting organized"—it is just that what is getting organized are complete, formerly distinct organizations instead of individuals or small groups. This, in turn, corresponds to the classic conception of integration and differentiation (segmentation) as antonyms in organization theory, which may analytically apply to individuals as well as to larger sociological entities (Lawrence & Lorsch, 1967: 3ff.).

As we have gained some information on common conceptualizations of post-merger integration, the question arises as to how they have been employed in empirical studies. In line with Teerikangas and Joseph (2012) and Angwin (2012), three strands of argumentation with strongly varying popularity have emerged:

(1) A *strategic fit perspective* that is largely equivalent to those strands within the (above-stated) "hard" strategic management paradigm, which treats integration as an explicit concept instead of an implicit ceteris-paribus background process;
(2) A sparsely frequented *organizational fit perspective* that perceives of integration and its implementation process as formable and critical moments; the relation between the merging parties' task and process characteristics are focused on;
(3) A clearly dominant *culture perspective* (belongs to the "soft" paradigm) that emphasizes the *cognitive basis* of organizations and their management during the post-merger stage.

A frequently cited work that is representative of the strategic fit strand is Amy Pablo's (1994) decision-making perspective on "determinants of acquisition integration level". According to this, the empirical level of post-merger integration realized (low – medium – high) is exclusively and completely a consequence of conscious choices made by the acquiring company's management. As possible determinants of these choices, Pablo initially discusses the task-oriented requirements of acquisitions. The two interacting forms of these requirements, based on Haspeslagh and Jemison (1991), reflect on the one hand the necessity of connecting value chains for synergy realization (*strategic task requirements*) and on the other hand the need to protect specific capacities of the acquired organization (*organizational task requirement*). Pablo suggests the first to increase the level of integration and the latter to have the reverse effect. As further possible determinants, she accounts for the cultural and political characteristics of acquisitions. The cultural characteristics refer to the acquirers' "routine approach to the management of culture", which means the integration-lowering acceptance of different cultures (*multiculturalism*). Political characteristics relate to the (merely functional) exertion of power differentials to overcome divergent "strategic visions"—power is deemed to further integration if entrepreneurial visions are incompatible.

Empirical examination was carried out on the basis of hypothetical written case studies, in which the explanatory variables were coded according to an experimental design. An overall 57, preferably high-ranking, administrators with variable experience of acquisitions had to work on the case studies and documented their decisions. As regards the results, Pablo reported all the supposed determinants to be effective in principle, with both kinds of task requirements, and particularly the need to protect the acquired capabilities, having the strongest impact on decision-making.

Pablo's work to date has remained one of the few meso-level studies focusing on integration level as the dependent variable. It is, however, guided by some precarious, implicit assumptions:

- ready-made, available and complete strategies: a high level of managerial consciousness, close to perfect rationality;
- comprehensive control of the acquirer's top administrators over strategy formulation;
- disregard of integration implementation: it appears as a mundane and quasi-automatic task; no differentiation between the levels of integration decided on and realized.

Particularly in consideration of the terminology used, her study (and with it actually the entire relevant strategic fit debate) can, within strategic management literature, be assigned to the planning-school, which is critically discussed by Mintzberg (1990).

The second strand of argumentation—the organizational fit debate—is best explicated by a closer examination of Larsson and Finkelstein's (1999) foundational case-survey study. Differing from Pablo (1994), they maintain that organizational integration is not the main dependent variable but is, together with *combination potential* and *employee resistance*, conceived of as one of three major antecedents of synergy realization ("net-benefits"). They hypothesize level of integration, which is not further operationalized on a theoretical basis, to be determined by the organizational fit of the merging parties in terms of their combination potential and management style similarity. They introduce a conceptual novelty by conceptualizing combination potential not only as a *strategic similarity*, but also in terms of the *complementarity* of value chains. Larsson and Finkelstein deem high levels of integration as well as high combination potentials to further employee resistance, pointing to disturbed career patterns, mobility requirements, and cultural conflicts (1999: 6). They suggest that employee resistance in turn hampers synergy realization and therefore success.

A collection of 112 published and unpublished merger case studies represents the basis of their empirical analysis. Sixteen raters (study-authors / M&A researchers / doctoral students) coded the cases; structural equation modeling was used to test the hypotheses. Larsson and Finkelstein report a strong isolated effect of value chain complementarity; organizational integration turned out to be the strongest predictor of synergy realization. Based on their results, the authors emphasize that post-merger integration is not an automatism: a low level of integration was realized in 40% of the cases that displayed a high combination potential. In comparison with the strategic fit argument, the analytical focus hence shifts away from the rational choice and passive insight of top administrators toward a stronger awareness of active integration management. In this regard, those studies dealing with integration implementation speed may be subsumed under the organizational fit label as well (e.g. Jemison & Sitkin, 1986; Greenwood, Hinings & Brown, 1994; Gerpott, 1995; Ranft & Lord, 2002; Homburg & Bucerius, 2006).

Nevertheless, the dominating stream of literature regarding aspects of post-merger integration is neither part of the strategic nor the organizational but the cultural fit debate. Teerikangas and Joseph (2012: 365) conclude their literature review in this respect as follows: "Moreover, the present understanding has defined organizational fit purely through a cultural lens, thereby omitting its other, e.g. structural, operational, dimensions". In the context of the widespread recognition of integration as the most important success factor and through the equation of the accomplishment of integration with achieving a cultural fit between the parties, the cultural perspective has become established as the core of a "soft" paradigm in M&A research.

The cultural perspective[6] claims that organizations are essentially to be conceived of as socially meaningful, norm-regulating and therefore uncertainty-reducing communities. They in the course of their genesis, so goes the argument, generate collective cognitive frames of reference, which are shaped, shared, and reproduced by individual members. These cognitive frames, which are somehow unique but may also display similarities across a larger number of organizations, are deemed to manifest themselves in varying aspects and on different levels of organizational life. They not only relate to the degree of individual autonomy, forms of interaction, communication, problem-solving, as well as leadership styles, but also the shape / use of technology and physical settings, to name a few. By bringing together at least two such tribes, mergers and acquisitions, it is said, do lead to a collision of their cultures (Buono, Bowditch & Lewis, 1985; Buono & Bowditch, 1989; Cartwright & Cooper, 1993). From this perspective, the resulting cultural dynamics have to be managed in order to prevent detrimental effects on both an individual and a collective level.

In contrast to the strategic and organizational fit approaches to post-merger integration, the analytical focus thus changes from strategic relatedness and technical / task-oriented aspects toward the alleged cognitive basis of organizations—determinants of integration (level) on the one hand and overall success on the other are almost exclusively to be found inside the merging organizations. Accordingly, the preeminent managerial task is not so much deemed to be the choice of an appropriate level of integration or the implementation of "structural and processual changes" (Larsson & Finkelstein, 1999: 16) but the identification and handling of cognitive (in)complementarities. Organizational integration becomes "acculturation" (Nahavandi & Malekzadeh, 1988; Elsass & Veiga, 1994; Larsson & Lubatkin, 2001): in their much quoted acculturation typology, Nahavandi and Malekzadeh, for example, denominate higher levels of integration as "assimilation" (a voluntary complete adoption of the acquirer's culture) and "integration" (some degree of change in the structure of both groups). Types displaying a lower depth of integration are labeled "separation" (the acquired company's culture and processes remain separate) and "deculturation" (disintegration as a cultural entity). On the analytical micro-level, all studies that consider socio-psychological consequences (like

6 Instead of discussing this vast and diverse literature in detail, we just leave it with a brief sketch of the basic logic underlying most of the works found within it. An exemplificative study referring to higher education mergers will be introduced in the next section.

identity problems) for employees (e.g. Schweiger, Ivancevich & Power, 1987; Cartwright & Cooper, 1992; Hubbard, 2001; Mirvis & Marks, 1992) can also be subsumed under the cultural perspective.

A further important difference between the cultural fit perspective and the two other strands of debate, besides its dominance in the scientific literature on integration, which is taken for granted (see Riad, 2005), lies in its outstanding acceptance by practitioners. Strictly speaking, the idea of cultural fit is the only theoretical concept that, regardless of inconsistent empirical evidence, (Stahl & Voigt, 2008; Teerikangas & Very, 2012) has—at least as a language framework—found its way into workaday organizational merger discourse.

1.2.4 M&A research in the field of higher education

As indicated above, a limited body of literature specifically concerned with mergers in higher education has developed. Respective analyses are mostly to be found in periodicals that focus on a broader range of higher education issues; the debate is nonexistent in top-tier strategic management and organization journals. A noticeable detachment from the far larger business-related M&A literature is also recognizable: the latter doesn't usually consider organization types other than business firms, and HEI-specific inquiries have, for their part, mostly shown limited explicit interest in identifying parallel debates. Reasons for separation are rarely given on either side; possible peculiarities of HEIs which might justify such separation are either omitted, neglected (e.g. Harman & Harman, 2008: 104, HEIs as "producers"), or discussed in terms of the widespread *loose-coupling* criterion (e.g. Norgard & Skodvin, 2002: 76).

Despite its somewhat artificial detachment, specialized literature has nonetheless transferred conceptions, which are broadly accepted in business-related M&A research as well, by largely drawing on the idea of organizational culture. Grant Harman (2002) discusses institutional amalgamations in terms of merging different "campus cultures"—cultural differences between colleges and universities in particular were analyzed. Appropriate leadership (styles) and communication, as further classic culturalist issues, have been pointed to as a basis for merger success (Locke, 2007; Harman & Harman, 2003; 2008). Kavanagh and Ashkanasy (2006) highlighted the importance of several leadership aspects and change management approaches to fostering merger acceptance and cultural shift. Norgard and Skodvin (2002) combined network theory and a cultural approach to investigate the merger of four Norwegian colleges.

Cultural fit within this specific collection of literature has overall remained the only perspective on mergers and post-merger integration. Analyses that correspond to the strategic and organizational fit arguments in business-related M&A research are rare[7]. A broader perspective on the phenomenon is typical of this research domain; most studies combine descriptive and system-level aspects (e.g. political reasons) with case study elements of selected mergers. In doing so, the cases are in fact usually interpreted in a largely idiographic manner, with theoretical considerations being used more as a loose frame of reference than in terms of an analytical basis. This impression is often reinforced by a tendency to quickly arrive at practitioner implications or even whole process frameworks (e.g. Hay & Fourie, 2002; Eastman & Lang, 2001).

An exception is represented by Kavanagh and Ashkanasy's (2006; 2012[8]) large longitudinal study of three Australian universities that were merged with smaller colleges during the large merger wave of 1983–1987. Interviews and a paper-and-pencil survey conducted on three occasions over four years were combined to analyze changes in individual values and organizational culture, as well as the preferred method of organizational acculturation. In a first step, principal axis factoring was employed to extract five domains of individual values out of 56 survey items (e.g. *discipline of self* and *accomplishment*). While the authors report general congruence within and differences across institutions as regards individual values, changing values during merger processes were not found to have occurred. Varying weightings of different culture types by respondents were used to trace shifting organizational cultures (collective level) over time. In particular, and this is interesting for us, the authors find an increasing emphasis on power as mergers proceeded. In line with Cartwright and Cooper (1996), power is thereby conceptualized as one of four types of organizational cultures, which vary from extreme individual autonomy to the constraining use of power. Drawing on Nahavandi and Malekzadeh (1988), the authors identify integration depth as different modes of acculturation,

7 A limited number of works on economies of scale and scope in higher education merger contexts (Abbott, 1996; Llloyd, Morgan & Williamson, 1993; Green & Johnes, 2009; Klumpp & Zelewski, 2012) should be mentioned here. They have mostly rejected a clear association between mergers and cost reduction. Since those economic studies commonly assume the realization of an appropriate (fixed) level of post-merger integration, we will refrain from any more detailed examination.

8 The data of the 2006 study was reinterpreted.

which Kavanagh and Ashkanasy accordingly hypothesize to be a consequence of individual-level appreciation of the respondent's own university's organizational culture, and the culture of the other merging party. The interview data in this regard provides supporting evidence of the respective hypotheses (but varies from institution to institution).

1.3 Challenges, study aims and design

In Subsection 1.1.1, a preliminary definition of mergers and incorporations was worked out. While doing so, I pointed to a remarkable and persistent contradiction. On the one hand, radical internal changes are commonly attributed to these measures. They are, on the other hand, acknowledged to frequently result in poorly integrated variations, with previous subsystems and structures being largely perpetuated. During the course of outlining merger incidence in higher education, this a priori association with inward radicalness was found to be typically reflected in the far-reaching political goals commonly announced by decision-makers (1.1.2). Such hardly reliable case-specific motives had to be complemented by a brief delineation of the greater political impetus underlying numerous parallel interventions (including mergers) in German higher education (1.1.3). Accordingly, the central research question was laid out:

Which organizational factors do essentially influence the level of post-merger integration realized within merged organizations?

Subsequently, the existing literature on this subject was examined in order to shed some light on possible post-merger integration conceptualizations. Following a sketchy general review of the business-related state-of-the-art (1.2.1), the research into dominating success factors was found to be unhelpful by and large (1.2.2). First of all, this was ascribed to the field's theoretical narrowing on performance explanations and the conceptual ambiguities associated therewith. The initial impression of a vague definitional basis and considerable research fragmentation has thus been fortified. We have afterwards moved from the broader literature toward approaches that consider post-merger integration in terms of an outcome or as a mediating process. With the strategic, organizational, and cultural *fit approaches*, three basic strands of argumentation were identified. The idea of organizational culture thereby turned out to have become dominant within theory and practice (1.2.3). It has also come to prevail in the merger debate being specialized on higher education institutions (1.2.4).

The remainder of this chapter is used to further systemize the previous findings and to reveal the design of the study at hand. Much has been written on the current state of business-related M&A research. In 1.3.1, its deficits are put down to a general lack of theory and the ensuing isolation of studies. A further issue relates to the particular character of organizations in public higher education; in 1.3.2 some of their differences (and similarities) to business firms are briefly sketched. Since a discussion of deficits in the literature on this subject does not suffice, in 1.3.3 we will compile a set of requirements which an organization theory should fulfill to appropriately analyze post-merger integration in higher education.

Subsection 1.3.4 serves to complement the research question and to state the requirements of approaching it theoretically from a fundamental metatheoretical perspective. Initially, therefore, the idea of organizational culture relates to the study at hand and is identified as the main theoretical opponent in explaining post-merger integration. Some of its basic philosophical assumptions will be criticized from the antithetical perspective of scientific materialism / realism, which in turn is introduced as the foundation to build on. In 1.3.5, the chapter closes with a description of the organization of the book and a brief methodological outline.

1.3.1 Isolation and fragmentation of extant M&A research

Lately, it has become common sense that business-related M&A research is in a condition of crisis-laden stagnation, or, put more optimistically, in a stage of consolidation and orientation. On a general level, the field's deficits have been associated with a lack of theory. Cartwright et al. (2012) put persistent shortcomings in a broader context of management studies not having been able to come up with original theories for decades. Reus et al. (2012), in line with Schweiger & Goulet (2000), find fault with missing links between antecedents and context factors. Haleblian et al. (2009: 21), in commenting on the state of knowledge as to M&A antecedents and motives, criticize "that even the most basic questions remain unanswered" and call for a deeper understanding of "contingency conditions". In a similar vein, Reus et al (2012: 99) conclude by declaring there is an absence of a "comprehensive theory of mergers and acquisitions".

As regards possible remedies, some authors have discussed ways to overcome methodological monotony. Demands have been raised to complement the dominating large scale, quantitative and archival data-based studies with simulations, experiments, grounded theorizing and longitudinal case studies (Ranft et al., 2010; Meglio & Risberg, 2010; Risberg, 2016; Bengtsson & Larsson, 2012). Other scholars have suggested to improve theories by refining existing causal models further (King et al., 2004) or fostering cross-disciplinary integration (Haleblian et al., 2009).

Teerikangas and Joseph (2012) also challenge the self-referentiality of the field and in particular its steady segregation from organization studies; they conclude by asking: "Is it now time for M&A integration researchers to go beyond their own discipline to develop new concepts and lenses from which to view integration?" (*Ibid*.: 367).

Although I totally agree that isolation from organization theory has turned out to be a major obstacle to knowledge generation, I still insist that expanding and refining established organization theories instead of developing "new lenses" is the way to go.

Adding to the argument of the self-referentiality of extant M&A research, I would go so far as to suggest isolation from organization theory to be the main source of its deficits. Despite numerous parallels regarding research questions, M&A scholars have been quite reluctant to (even formally) refer to classic organization theory. This notion is supported by the above-stated disagreement concerning the disciplines responsible—after all, no review based on theoretical approaches as a major classification theme could be found. Central works on transaction cost economics (e.g. Williamson, 1975; 1985; 1991; Williamson & Ouchi, 1980), to take a case in point, are, in the reference list of the 199 papers which had been included by Haleblian et al. (2009), referred to by only fifteen percent of the contributions; the value for central resource dependence contributions (Pfeffer, 1972; Pfeffer & Salancik, 1978) is just below five percent. Since the classic works of both streams are must-citations in case of any reference to merger discourse in organization theory, this is a clear indicator that the latter has been largely ignored within M&A research. If at all, the assumptions of agency theory (Jensen & Meckling, 1976; Eisenhardt, 1989) as well as the contingency approach to (see Donaldson, 2001) and the resource-based view of organizations (Wernerfelt, 1984; Peteraf, 1993) have been referred to (Haleblian et al., 2009; Angwin, 2012).

Isolation from organization theory or the "silo-based approach" (Geraldi & Teerikangas, 2015) to M&A research in general and the analysis of integration in particular is threefold:

1) Studies are isolated against each other. We already elaborated on this point during the discussion on definition attempts and (foremost) the conceptual ambiguities regarding success / performance / outcome measures. Due to the broad variance of concepts and measures, only a

small percentage of inquiries can be placed in relation to each other—instead of a coherent field of study, a plethora of unique and narrow-ranging explanations has accumulated.

2) Current M&A literature is isolated from findings regarding other research subjects pertaining to organizations. Organization theory seeks to generate systems of hypotheses, definitions, and axioms to allow for a deduction of valid assertions concerning multiple classes of phenomena. The generation of knowledge concerning a specific (sub)class of phenomena should benefit from a particular theories' (non-)achievements in explaining other phenomena related to the same broader research subject. As illustrated by its artificial isolation from other forms of organizational cooperation (1.1.1), M&A research is, however, largely driven by single phenomena; the implications of extant explanations for other phenomena are rarely discussed.
3) Consequently, current M&A literature is isolated from meta-theoretical debates concerning organization theory. To the present day, nothing like a larger narrative that generates and guides the field has emerged—paradigmatic assumptions have mostly remained implicit and not open to contest. Meta-theory is important for staying in contact, not only with the study of organizations in particular, but ultimately with the development of all factual sciences (we will get back to this in Chapter 3).

Most readers will agree that isolation from organization theory is therefore more than a secondary deficit—it fundamentally impairs the actual prospects of scientific advances in examining mergers and acquisitions. Without a (meta)theoretical basis, it remains unclear how a basic shared understanding of concepts is to be achieved, and how explanations should be classified, compared, converted, refined or refuted.

The second part of the question brought up by Teerikangas and Joseph (2012), which relates to the potential of "new concepts and lenses" to examine post-merger integration, is thus to be answered in the negative. The development of new theories does not solve most of the field's isolation problems, notably if respective appeals again refer to new phenomenon-specific theories (e.g. Cartwright et al., 2012; Reus et al., 2012). Furthermore, such demands falsely imply that the potential of extant organization theories as to merger and integration analysis has been sufficiently explored. On balance, the problem has never been a failure to develop new specific theories but rather to thoroughly connect with existing knowledge. Attempts to constitute M&A research as a distinct area of inquiry searching for a distinct M&A theory have fostered isolation and have turned out fruitless by and large.

The upshot of all this for the study at hand is that isolation of merger analysis needs to be overcome. This became strikingly clear during the delineation of some extant post-merger integration conceptions in 1.2.3.: the question of *what* post-merger actually changes regarding organizational arrangements, processes and other features of the merging parties cannot be separated from what generally constitutes organizations as distinct phenomena, what generates and delimits them against each other and from the non-organized parts of society. No isolated phenomenon-driven explanation will ever provide an answer to these questions. The analysis of post-merger integration should therefore be at the heart of organization theory —and this is exactly where we are going to take it.

1.3.2 Higher education institutions as a specific organization type

Argumentation has hitherto largely drawn on mergers of business firms. This is due to it being our access point to the research problem: private business corporations in organization theory have been the organizational archetype of reference par excellence throughout (Ortmann, 2004: 2), not only as regards the extant M&A literature. Issue-specific literature (1.2.4) has largely sought to transfer and apply conceptions from the business-related M&A research; discussions of system-level or institution-level organizational peculiarities in higher education have remained scarce.

It is, however, important to notice that HEIs are neither to be conceptually equated with business corporations nor with state bureaucracies. Many of their essential features are (at least in Germany) still not regulated by business economists or social scientists, but have to follow legal restrictions codified in the federal *Hochschulrahmengesetz* (HRG) and the corresponding 16 federal state (*Länder*) laws related to higher education. Consequently, the most detailed and well-reasoned accounts of organizational characteristics are to be found in legal discourse, within laws and judgments. Focusing on the situation in Germany, I shall subsequently delineate some respective idiosyncrasies. Similarly to the discussion on the political merger context, this again is carried out in a compact and rather cursory manner for the sake of brevity. In doing so, I will mostly draw on the outstanding and comprehensive account by Klaus Ferdinand Gärditz (2009), as well as a relevant judgment by Germany's Federal Constitutional Court (*Bundesverfassungsgericht* 1973; BVerfG 35 79).

Let us begin with the specific legal status of HEIs in Germany. They are regularly corporations of public law and at the same time state-owned and self-administered (§ 58 HRG). Being state-owned does not imply state control; their organizational status is considerably different from more immediate bureaucracies, like health authorities or the military.

Though there are no specific organizational forms legally implied (BVerfG 35 79: 143), *self-governance* is usually considered the appropriate form of organizational decision-making to protect individual, constitutional science-related freedoms (Gärditz, 2009: 555). The legitimacy of decisions is, in comparison to state-controlled bureaucracies, not drawn from the population as a whole, but from organization members (*Ibid*.: 403). The elective population in HEIs is divided into four groups: professors, non-professorial staff, students, and non-academic (other) staff (§ 37 HRG). Self-administered decision-making happens on two basic system levels: the central level collegial organ is the *senate*, the corresponding governing body on a disciplinary level is the *department* or *faculty council*. According to the legal ideal, collegial organs should be characterized by discursive negotiations and the surrender of ultimate truth claims; they are constituted by elections at regular intervals. Furthermore, as regards many core decisions (e.g. appointments), collegial organs have to be dominated by professors as the main addressees of the aforementioned freedoms (BVerf 35 79: 204).

Public higher education organizations are *Janus-faced*; they comprise elements of state-controlled bureaucracy as well. Self-governance and bureaucracy thereby follow contradictory forms of logic: the former relates to the bottom-up realization and protection of person-bound freedoms; the latter is characterized by a monocratic and depersonalized top-down order. Both are based on different sources of legitimacy, which in the case of bureaucracy is the *Landtag* (state parliament) instead of the community of organization members. Bureaucratic units are consigned with sovereign responsibilities like supervising non-professorial staff, issuing certificates, or administrating organizational resources. Examples of administrative organs are the central level executives: the rector (or president), function-specific co-(pro-)rectors, and the chancellor (or vice-president). They execute state or senate decisions, externally represent the organization, and run administrative operations (Gärditz, 2009: 536ff.). On the disciplinary (faculty) level, the members of deaneries fulfill these functions. The responsibilities of self-governance and state bureaucracy are kept largely separate; the two different logics are buffered against each other to prevent the reciprocal impairment of functions (*Ibid*.: 530ff.).

A general legal ideal in organizing higher education lies in keeping the hierarchical order as marginal as possible in the science-related parts of the organization. The protection of individual science-related rights is the main legal adequacy criterion for assessing organizational regulations (Gärditz, 2009: 439ff.). Organizational differentiation should follow functional (professional) criteria instead of hierarchies. Responsibilities should be shifted to higher levels only where lower level organs lack the necessary decision-making distance and representatives of individual rights start impeding each other. In this regard, in 1973 the Federal Constitutional Court acknowledged an imminent and growing tension. The ideal of pure, coercion-free, and purposeless science confronts the demands of a technologically organized society: higher education has become increasingly resource-intensive, specialized, and massified (BVerfG 35 79: 121).

Being internally constituted in an anti-hierarchical manner should ideally be paralleled by shielding the organization against (external) social interests and economic-utilitarian considerations. External influences on research and education by non-disciplinary interests (though in some respects being common practice) are hard to legitimate – they should be reconnected effectively and permanently to the preferences of the scientists affected (Gärditz, 2009: 509ff.). The state is legally obligated to provide financial and organizational capacities to render the conduct of science possible: without a sufficient material basis, individual science-related freedoms would be hollowed out (BVerfG 35 79: 132). The Federal Constitutional Court has hence acknowledged a link between the provision of resources and organizational dependence.

Finally, it is insightful to contrast these legal considerations to the collectivity of interventions which have accompanied the merger cases under scrutiny (1.1.3). Enhancing external control in combination with enervating self-governance (by strengthening administrative functions) and rolling back state funding both counteract many legal principles of organizing higher education. Having neither been *neo* nor particularly *liberal*, the guiding dictum of the neoliberal turn in higher education politics hence becomes all the more apparent. The artificial organizational vacuum protecting freedoms, which has largely been created through state funding *without* direct state control, was to a greater extent filled with private funding and private control. Not least, therefore, the legal considerations accounting for many characteristics of German HEIs should be kept in mind. In the coming chapters, they will prove to be largely consistent with the materialist resource exchange-based and power-based explanations of organizational structures and behavior that this study provides.

1.3.3 What a theory should provide (adequacy criteria)

To this point, an insistent need to no longer surrender the analysis of post-merger integration to explanations driven by single phenomena has been argued for. Alternatively, such analysis should be approached and developed on the basis of extant organization theory. Persistent isolation has been identified as the main source of research deficits.

During the course of this chapter, enough aspects have been collected to evaluate the eligibility of potential candidates within the realm of organization theory. In terms of an intermediate conclusion, they will now be compiled to wrap up the preliminary delineation of the research problem (1.1), as well as the discussion of the existing literature on this subject (1.2 / 1.3). An appropriate organization theory should meet the following requirements:

1) It should be concerned with mergers and various forms of interorganizational relations. Comprehensive explanations and predictions focusing on such phenomena should be deducible.
2) Since we are interested in intraorganizational aspects of mergers, such a theory should explicitly allow for or be based on multilevel explanations. Bluntly put, it should, first of all, not conceptualize organizations as black boxes, i.e. ignore their internal mechanisms or conceptualize them as some kind of constant. Hence, it should neither treat them as individuals nor as (unanalyzable) wholes. As has, for instance, been demonstrated in connection with the strategic fit approaches (1.2.3), the fulfillment of this criterion is anything but trivial.
3) The theory should involve a concept of organizational integration and should allow it to be used as a variable. Because the very notion of integration of two formerly separate organizations is deeply interwoven with the question of what generally discerns such systems from other organizations as well as from non-organized parts of society, the first cannot be answered without the latter. What gives rise to and constitutes organizations as discernible entities? Whoever asks for the unity and integrity of social structures always asks for their distinctiveness and differentiation at the same.
4) Finally, a potential theory should have a record of applications on organization types other than private enterprises. It would be beneficial if, in the context of higher education, the theory had been applied to multiple organizational phenomena and to interorganizational relations in particular.

The specific organization theory chosen for this study is resource dependence theory (RDT) (Pfeffer & Salancik, 1978). Although appropriateness according to the criteria needs to be discussed (Chapter 2), some predisposition appears on the face of it. The resource dependence perspective as a classic open systems approach to the study of organizations has involved a focus on mergers throughout (Pfeffer, 2003). Moreover, according to criterion 4, many of its empirical applications have been conducted in a context of non-profit organizations in general, and HEIs in particular.

1.3.4 Study positioning in the larger meta-theoretical debate

The derivation of our research problem has hitherto had to remain provisional. Due to conceptual ambiguities, we have determined a continuing requirement to analyze organizational integration as a variable. Furthermore and in respect thereof, a general need to connect the scientific merger debate with extant organization theory has been stated—the field's deficits have been attributed to the persistent isolation of extant studies against each other, against other relevant organizational phenomena, as well as against meta-theoretical considerations. Therefrom, a set of appropriateness criteria for specific organization theories regarding their potential to analyze post-merger integration has been deduced. In order to prepare the discussion of RDT as a possible specific framework, we will, in the following, first widen our focus to delineate this book's core argument and embed it in a central ("classic"), broader socio-scientific debate.

Yet, of course, many will probably disagree with the assertion that a theory is lacking and point to the plentiful works of the "soft" strategy paradigm, which we, after all, have introduced as the dominating perspective in post-merger integration analysis. And, indeed, the "culture metaphor" of organizations (Morgan, 2006), though not usually treated as an organization theory in its own right, has in M&A literature to this day de facto remained the only theoretical perspective concerning intraorganizational aspects. Even the proponents of the strategic and organizational fit approaches to integration, as reviewed in 1.2.3, have mostly included it as an active part of their explanations. Riad (2005) asserts organizational culture has reached a status of quasi-naturalization and being taken for granted in scholarly and practitioner integration debates. During my own field research, many of my interviewees expected questions on cultural differences and the cultural fit between the merging parties, had prepared statements accordingly, or actively introduced culturalist terminology. There is no question that the idea of culture is dominant and any integration explanation needs to take some stance on it.

The conceptual dominance of organizational culture in empirically analyzing intraorganizational aspects is necessarily attended by the preeminence of particular meta-theoretical orientations. These in turn are the fundament of what has been called the *linguistic or cultural turn* (Reed, 2005; 2009), a broad intellectual movement that, far beyond our specific research subject and the analysis of organizations has become established in the social sciences and humanities. While that movement involves a myriad of different approaches, and even within the realm of organizational culture, numerous and sometimes hard-to-classify perspectives exist (Alvesson, 2013: 23), some common basic orientations materialize:

- Social systems like families or universities are conceptualized as social constructions that assume the form of collectively shared cognitions (the collectives may be subunits, particular groups or whole organizations);
- The analytical relevance of the observer-independent reality of organizations as social facts is belittled.

Since the ontological status of social structures is deemed "circumscribed by the inter-subjectively constituted meanings and interpretations" (Reed, 2009: 434), ontology and epistemology are largely conflated, yet with a focus on the latter. The question then becomes how those meaningful social constructions of the different organizational tribes can be assessed by researchers and manipulated by practitioners: through a detailed reconstruction of sense and discursive practices.

As regards its own meta-theoretical orientation, the study at hand turns against the linguistic / cultural turn and consequentially against the theoretical primacy of the cultural perspective in explaining the intraorganizational effects of mergers. The general meta-theoretical position adopted here, by contrast, is characterized by *materialism* and *realism*, and is reflected in the title of the book:

"*Resource Interdependence and Organizational Integration: Material Manifestations of Mergers and Incorporations in Higher Education*"

The first part indicates a suggested causal link between external resource interdependence and post-merger *organizational integration*. The latter, conceived of in terms of a material manifestation of merger processes, is the main research subject. Let us for the moment simplify matters by equating manifestations with consequences and focus on the qualification of being *material*. In contrast to most social constructionist works, distinct ontological qualities of the possible consequences of mergers are stressed—only material entities like stones, persons and supermarkets are existents; immaterial entities like numbers, myths, constructs (representations) and discourses have no own existence apart from brain processes (Bunge, 1996). Post-merger (dis-)integration is analyzed in reference to the materiality of organizations as social systems: it is conceptualized as shifting and thereby concentrating or dispersing intraorganizational resource control. Hence, this book is about merger-induced variations in the relations of concrete (material) entities to each other. Immaterial entities, like shared cognitions or identities that may potentially develop post-merger, are not analyzed. It is important in this context to prevent two likely misunderstandings early on: a) being *material* doesn't necessarily equal being *tangible*. Neither a specific HEI nor its resource-related exchange relations are sufficiently accessible to the human sensorium. b) Being *immaterial* neither means being *nonexistent* in the common use of the word, nor does it mean *not being objectively traceable*. The material / immaterial distinction as the essence of all materialist doctrines is about different *ontological* qualities—and immaterial entities are not analyzed here as merger consequences.

The underlying core argument of this book therefore claims the source of the material merger consequences analyzed to be essentially found in the material conditions within and outside the merging organizations. At this point, the term *manifestation* comes into play, which according to the *Oxford Dictionary* is defined as "An event, action, or object that clearly shows or embodies something abstract or theoretical". According to the majority of proponents of the culture perspective, material aspects of organizations are manifestations of organizational culture—and therefore of immaterial entities. Reviewing the central writings of the field (e.g. Deal & Kennedy, 1985; Schein, 1985; Frost et al., 1985), this criticism is, for example, brought forward by Mats Alvesson, a distinguished contemporary advocate of organizational culture perspectives:

> When, for example, such physical aspects of organizations as architecture are considered, they are often viewed not as sociomaterial situations—the materialization of former activities, functioning at present to restrict or provide opportunity for action or to influence ideas and meanings—but as clues to values and assumptions (Alvesson, 2013: 129).

This way of treating sociomaterial conditions as epiphenomena exactly demonstrates the above-stated widespread indifference of the *linguistic / cultural turn* as regards the ontological objective nature of organizations. In a similar vein, Joanne Martin (2002: 56ff.), in her culture concept overview under the label of "materialist approaches to culture" (though they are mostly not materialist at all), subsumes approaches that implicitly or explicitly refer to material aspects of work in organizations as "materialist manifestations" of *culture* instead of material conditions.

When it comes to the analysis of mergers, changes in material entities are attributed to cultural dynamics within and between the merging organizations, and therefore to immaterial aspects, by the proponents of culture. Buono, Bowditch and Lewis (1985), in one of the most frequently cited works of the M&A soft-paradigm conceptualized material manifestations of mergers as "objective organizational culture", which "refers to various material products or artifacts created by organizations which are symbolic elements of their cultural traditions, beliefs, and value patterns" (*Ibid.*: 481). Organizations are hence treated as mere cognitive enterprises that have to be studied in terms of collectively shared cognitive frames of reference, and, in the case of mergers, the collision of at least two of them.

Ultimately, my goal is, by contrast, to demonstrate that material manifestations of mergers are mainly to be explained by the material conditions both within and outside the merging organizations. As an alternative to the supposed contact between / clash of cultures, the role of external resource-interdependence patterns of organizations will be discussed. I hypothesize that level and orientation of post-merger integration depend on the character of the relationship of such patterns. In particular, I claim the level of post-merger integration to be a function of the relative resource weight of those external interests, which are potentially impaired by organizational integration. Instead of campus cultures, symbols, management styles, and communication as precursors of integration, we will hence talk about student numbers, appointment regulations, office space, and intraorganizational power relations. Since such power relations and the material conditions which give rise to them—just like a possibly present organizational culture—are not sufficiently perceptible, a central task in the empirical parts of this study will be to make them tangible.

In sum then, post-merger *organizational integration* is a) analyzed in terms of changes in organizations as concrete social systems—"changes[9]" of immaterial entities are not considered—and is b) hypothesized (as an aspect of organizational materiality) to be a manifestation of merger-induced

9 Since immaterial entities have no existence on their own, they cannot change. More precisely, being unchangeable makes them immaterial (Bunge & Mahner, 2004).

changes in sociomaterial conditions rather than of immaterial collective cognitions.

The basic meta-theoretical position adopted here is associated with a philosophic debate, which is much older than the social sciences: the dispute between *idealism* and *materialism*. According to the prominent Argentinian science philosopher Mario Bunge, idealism (or spiritualism)

> [...] asserts that all social facts are either ideas or embodiments of ideas, by contrast with materialism, which holds that all social facts are states or changes of state of concrete entities, from persons to social systems (Bunge, 1996: 282).

Without going too much into detail here, parallels to the above-mentioned perspective adopted by many students of organizational culture are evident. Ideas (or corporate cultures) are deemed to have an existence on their own or are even equated with organizations outright. Post-merger (dis)integration, if not conceptually treated as an immaterial outcome itself, is largely considered an embodiment of immaterial frames of reference and their ("managed") relation to each other.

The broader idealism vs. realism cleavage has always accompanied the social sciences. Hinings and Tolbert (2008), to take a case in point, in reflecting on the origins of neo-institutionalism, a close relative of the cultural perspective, associate the former with a long tradition of ideational explanations going back to the grand theories of Emile Durkheim and Max Weber. Ideational approaches have emphasized norms, meanings, and cultural forces to explain the stability of and changes to social structures; they have been in opposition to a sociology of material interests, power, and domination throughout, with the works of Herbert Spencer and Karl Marx as central precursors (*Ibid.*). To further illustrate this aspect, the following prominent quote from Marx and Engel's preamble to his (historical) materialist critique on German Idealism may provide an impression of the debate's ancient, or rather up-to-date nature:

> Once upon a time a valiant fellow had the idea that men were drowned in water only because they were possessed with the idea of gravity. If they were to knock this notion out of their heads, say by stating it to be a superstition, a religious concept, they would be sublimely proof against any danger from water (Marx & Engels, 1970 [1932/1947]: 37).

Instead of the "valiant" Young Hegelian philosophers addressed by Marx, one can easily imagine putting in a contemporary scholarly proponent of organizational culture, a consultant selling "cultural due diligences", an executive chairman of two merging companies or a policymaker in higher education. The cultural perspective on organizations suggests that to manage mergers successfully, extant perceptions (instead of the "idea of gravity") have to be overcome, different leadership styles have to be brought together and a "single coherent culture" (Cartwright & Cooper, 1994: 38) has to be created. The answer of materialism (though not necessarily Marx's historical materialism) to the advocates of the cultural-linguist turn today must be the same as it was back in the day: there is no sound analysis of sociomateriality without carefully considering sociomaterial conditions.

1.3.5 Structure of the book, study design and methodological approach

Following the criteria worked out in Subsection 1.3.3., Chapter 2 discusses the adequacy of resource dependence theory (RDT) regarding the analysis of post-merger organizational integration in higher education. Accordingly, the first section (2.1) of Chapter 2 starts by briefly delineating basic RDT positions concerning mergers / incorporations and IORs. This is followed by an outline of RDT's capacities to provide multilevel explanations as well as of existing applications in the study field of higher education organizations. The explication of the theory in Section 2.1 is augmented in 2.2 by a consideration of some pivotal forerunners. To elucidate its relation to those and other approaches, the meta-theoretical positioning of RDT within an established paradigm classification scheme (Burrell & Morgan, 1979) is examined. Section 2.3 ultimately ties it all together: RDT's potential and weaknesses are inspected against the background of the goals of the study at hand.

The objectives of Chapter 3 are fourfold. First of all (3.1), by introducing the general scientific orientation of *systemism*, it fleshes out the materialist-realist meta-theoretical perspective adopted in this study. Second (3.2), by taking up some of RDT's shortcomings, namely its lacking conception of organizational structure, I in turn apply this perspective to derive a conception of organizational integration / differentiation as a variable. In doing so, I use RDT as a system-specific theory against the background of the underlying materialist ontology. Organizations in higher education are conceived of as being integrated, since their components are linked through functional and power-exchange relationships (coalitional model) on the one hand, and shifts of responsibilities into their political system on the other. In a similar vein to Bunge (1992), a complementing formal model of organizational boundaries (their distinctiveness) is suggested in 3.3.2. Thirdly (3.3), essential influence factors and a causal mechanism to explain post-merger integration are clarified. The explanation provided builds on considering organizational (dis)integration dynamics as a general phenomenon, with integrative and disintegrative forces being present all the time. These antipodal forces, it is argued, gain their force and directionality from the qualitative and power aspects of the unique patterns of external resource dependencies all organizations necessarily confront. Finally (3.4), this general explanation is conveyed to mergers as particular trigger situations and testable hypotheses are deduced. In particular, it is proposed that the level and orientation of integration following mergers depend on the relationship of the respective interdependence patterns of the merging organizations.

The empirical part consists of two case studies with emphases on different parts of the explanation. Germany's largest case so far, the merger between the *Universities of Duisburg and Essen* in 2003, is the subject of Chapter 4. The second case (Chapter 5) is the incorporation of the *Hamburger Universität für Wirtschaft und Politik* into thc *University of Hamburg* in 2005. In case study one, the analytical focus is placed on the intraorganizational power aspect of resource-interdependence patterns. A quantitative birdseye perspective on the connection between resource interdependencies and integration realization is provided. The second case study, by contrast, has a stronger emphasis on the qualitative aspect of interdependence patterns: the multiplicity of subunit interests, integration measures and intraorganizational coping strategies come to the fore. This is largely enabled by an important difference between the cases: while integration options in Duisburg–Essen were often constrained by spatial distance, the merging parties in Hamburg have always been located on the same campus. Therefore, in the Hamburg case, a broader spectrum of integration attempts and reactions was able to be observed; it complements the first case because it helps us to analyze the causal mechanism more assiduously.

Chapter 4 starts by giving background information on the merging parties in Duisburg and Essen, the pre-merger stage and the overall time frame of the merger; research design and steps of analysis are introduced (4.1). Section 4.2 explicates subunit power scaling and measurement procedures—post-merger subunit power profiles were determined by employing principal axis factoring on quantitative archival data. Clusters of units with similar profiles were detected and checked to identify systematically related integration patterns. The third part of Chapter 4 consists of three comparative sub-case studies, which consider post-merger integration attempts with varying outcomes in selected parts of the overall organization. Thus, a more comprehensive perspective on the (intended) establishment of the common faculties of physics, social sciences, and economics is provided.

Chapter 5 attends to the second merger case. In 2005, the Hamburger Universität für Wirtschaft und Politik together with the social sciences and economics departments of the University of Hamburg formed one large faculty within the latter. Subsequent to providing a compact overview of the merging parties and the pre-merger stage (3.1), the chapter elaborates on the post-merger negotiations and the implementation of integration measures. Moving from those efforts with an associated high level of integration toward those with a low level, this study scrutinizes subunit interests, conflicts, and coping strategies (3.2). Before ultimately discussing and theorizing the results, Section 3.3 examines the (partial) breakup of the merged faculty in 2013.

Research strategy and design hence largely follow a *critical realist approach* to the study of organizations (Reed, 2009). This shall be signified sketchily with two key aspects of social explanations in a critical realist fashion: Firstly, a critical realist social explanation demands a focus "on the underlying generative mechanisms that account for surface-level relations, processes and events" (*Ibid.*: 436). As regards the study at hand, these generative mechanisms are resource transformation processes and the power-exchange relations they establish. As mentioned before, these are not sufficiently tangible; they are abstract, yet material (and therefore real). Making intraorganizational power relations on the subunit level visible is a central aim of case study one (Chapter 4). Organizational integration in terms of a concrete, material merger is traced back to these abstract (but material-based) mechanisms. Secondly, these underlying generative mechanisms have to be conceptualized as being effective across different levels of analysis. This anti-reductionist transformative model of social explanation (which is mirrored in the second adequacy criterion in 1.3.3) is represented by RDT's coalitional model of organizations in the study at hand. The latter both allows for and includes individual and subunit level propositions and also regards the macro level of analysis (pairs or groups of organizations).

From a methodological standpoint, a *mixed-methods approach* to the study of organizations is employed. My field research started with qualitative methods: expert interviews were conducted to attain context and in-depth information on subunit dependencies, resources, and political positions toward integration measures. Numerous internal documents were scrutinized. As data collection proceeded, quantitative methods (dimensional and regression analysis) were applied to make power relations visible and provide some evidence of the connection between the weight of specific external interests and the realization of integration measures. Bryman (2009: 520), in reference to Greene (1989), discusses five rationales for mixed-methods organizational research; three of them apply to the study at hand:

1) *Triangulation* to pursue corroboration between qualitative and quantitative data analysis results: in the current study, this is particularly sought after in the context of analyzing the link between important external resource dependencies and the realization of associated integration measures. Quantitative results pertaining to specific clear-cut dependencies were, for instance, able to be compared to interview statements or internal strategy papers.
2) *Complementarity*: parts of the explanation that are implied by quantitatively checked hypotheses were able to be examined more comprehensively on the basis of qualitative data. Consider, for example, the connection between a certain quality of organizational requirements which a subunit confronted and that unit's supportive positioning toward a certain integration measure. Another case in point is the exploration of coping tactics in Chapter 5: qualitative data helped to explore what blocking or furthering integration measures actually means. Hence, the causal mechanism was able to be illustrated and understood in greater detail.
3) *Development*: needless to say, qualitative research was indispensable regarding the development of concepts and hypotheses. As already mentioned, field access and data collection developed successively; quantitative analyses would have been impossible without data provided by interview partners.

This book closes with a recapitulation and discussion in Chapter 6. The empirical results of the study are summarized against the suggested theoretical background; central findings are reflected from the resource dependence perspective. Building on the outlined adequacy criteria, the explanatory potential of the competing culturalist and neo-institutionalist approaches to post-merger integration is subsequently examined. In conclusion, a stronger realist focus on the sociomaterial power aspects of mergers as against the dominating idealist and subjectivist explanations is advocated.

2 Theoretical framework: introduction, positioning and assessment of resource dependence theory

In Chapter 1, four criteria to identify organization theories being appropriate as to the analysis of post-merger integration in HEIs have been determined. Such a theory should first of all (1) display a theoretical and empirical focus on mergers and IORs. To permit the examination of causal mechanisms and intraorganizational merger consequences, it should (2) be able to provide for multilevel explanations. Furthermore, it should (3) allow to approach the complex concept of organizational integration and, finally, (4) be acquainted to HEIs as a specific class of organizations.

Since it seems at first sight to fulfill some of these criteria, resource dependence theory (RDT) shall be considered in the following as a possible framework. In emphasizing the roots and overall positioning of RDT in organization theory, Chapter 2 breaks down into three larger sections. Section 2.1 attends to the presentation of the main work (Pfeffer & Salancik, 1978) and is largely guided by the identified adequacy criteria. This is in Section 2.2 supplemented by a) a comparative positioning of RDT within the collectivity of some of its precursors and close relatives (2.2.1) as well as by b) the review of a more abstract positioning within the field of organization theory according to meta-theoretical criteria (2.2.2). A comprehensive discussion concerning RDT's issue-specific applicability (2.3) tops the chapter off.

2.1 RDT as a potential research framework for intraorganizational merger consequences in higher education

In 2.1.1, we begin by briefly outlining *The External Control of Organizations* (Pfeffer & Salancik, 1978), while subsequently focusing on its merger-related propositions (2.1.2). The multilevel perspective on organizations, which within the RDT framework is closely linked to the *strategic contingencies' theory of intraorganizational power* (Hickson, Hining, Lee, Schneck & Pennings, 1971), is introduced in 2.1.3. The section in 2.1.4 closes with a review of central empirical studies that have been conducted in the context of HEIs.

2.1.1 Introducing RDT: basic concepts and propositions

Pfeffer and Salancik comprehensively presented the *Resource Dependence Perspective* on organizations in their 1978 volume, which has become one of the most cited classics in the field. It was set up by challenging the focus on internal organizational aspects that had until then been prevalent in scientific management, human relations, and structural contingency approaches to organization theory. Following Pfeffer and Salancik (1978), this *internal perspective* was mainly expressed in a) emphasizing the seemingly apolitical input–output ratio assessment (*efficiency*) as well as in b) an overestimation of individual discretion and autonomy. By stressing *external constraints* on individual and collective behavior in general and on executive decision-making in particular (1978: 14ff.), the *contextual perspective* was hence developed in contrast to vast parts of the literature on this subject. Organizational *effectiveness*, specifying to what extent external demands are met, was featured as the decisive evaluation criterion against the by far narrower efficiency concept.

Because of their lacking ability to generate resources autonomously, organizations as true *open systems* are dependent on continuous transactions with other groups and social actors. In allusion to James Thompson (1967: 30), the organizational environment was therefore claimed to be the main source of resource-related contingencies and constraints. The survival of such open system depends on their capacity to "maintain a coalition of parties who contribute the resources and support necessary for it to continue its activities" (Pfeffer & Salancik, 1978: 26). The conceptualization of organizations as coalitions, borrowed chiefly from Cyert and March (1963) was supplemented with power-dependence theory (Emerson, 1962; Blau, 1964), and therefore the notion of organizations as *political systems* was focused on (Morgan, 2006). Power-dependence relations characterize resource exchange between a focal organization and its environment, as well as regards internal coalitions.

Acquiring the resources necessary for survival requires the handling of external demands that are competing to varying degrees and, hence, usually cannot be met simultaneously. Resource dependence is the reason for external control, and Pfeffer and Salancik (1978: 44ff.) identified a number of conditions that affect the probability of successful external influence on a focal organization. In line with Hickson et al. (1971), three main factors were singled out:

1) *Resource Importance,* referring to a) the magnitude of an exchange relative to the total resource input or output of the focal organization and b) the functional criticality of the respective resource;
2) The extent of a social actor's discretion over a resource;
3) *Concentration of resource control,* which captures the availability of substitutes.

Since they determine the dependence of a focal organization and, accordingly, the relative power of external actors, these factors are the basis of explanations and predictions regarding organizational decision-making and behavior. Asymmetries in exchange relations, which necessarily turn up within and between organizations, lead to the emergence of countervailing power (Pfeffer & Salancik, 1978: 52ff.). Hence, in terms of power-dependence theory, organizations and their environments are commonly structured by reciprocal power-balancing dynamics.

Prior to their considerations regarding the multiplicity of coping activities, Pfeffer and Salancik complemented their general introduction of concepts and mechanisms with a chapter that is mainly concerned with organizational information processing: "The enactment process, we would argue, is largely determined by the existing organizational and informational structure of the organization" (*Ibid*.: 89). Drawing partly on social psychologist Karl Weick (1969), they asserted that organizational perceptions of environments are due to retrospective attributions of meanings, which are largely shaped by organizational *information systems,* "conceptualized as the reports, statistics, facts or information that are regularly collected and their pattern of transmission through the organization" (Pfeffer & Salancik, 1978: 74). Information search and processing are thus prone to complexity reduction and, primarily, the exertion of power, as coalitions try to bolster those information system configurations that yield interpretations in their own favor. Consequentially, they identified misconceptions of relevant environmental groups regarding their relative power as well as the very nature of demands as key antecedents of organizational failure.

The core of the volume consists of four chapters (5–8) that address numerous strategies to manage interdependencies with external groups and social actors. It comprises extensive empirical results, some of them previously published (Pfeffer, 1972; 1973; 1974a; 1974b; Pfeffer & Leblebici, 1974; Pfeffer & Nowak, 1976). To begin with Chapter 5, *adoption* and *avoidance* are initially introduced as basic organizational response categories. Adaption, which has been the central mechanism of contingency, population ecology, and economic models of organization, is modified regarding its conceptual relevance: complying with external demands engenders more demands and thus tends to threaten long-term organizational survival (Pfeffer & Salancik, 1978: 95).

Two interconnected classification criteria that loosely structure the sequence of the strategies of demand avoidance and management which are subsequently examined can be recognized (Chapters 6–8): *directness of control* and the *level of the environment* involved. Firstly, the argument moves from tight and direct control of uncertainty sources toward more flexible and indirect measures. Pfeffer and Salancik present mergers (see below) as a means of direct control via ownership in Chapter 6. Normative coordination, joint ventures and interlocking boards are subsumed under *informal mechanisms and semiformal interorganizational linkages* (*Ibid.*: 143; Chapter 7). They serve to set up what has been labeled "the negotiated environment" as an alternative to direct context control. Board cooptation is deemed one of the most flexible coordination measures (*Ibid.*: 161). In Chapter 8, attempted uncertainty control by influencing state regulations is discussed in terms of its own class of strategies. There are practically no clearly identifiable parties involved in those activities that are directed at achieving conformity with (or at the manipulation of) wider social norms and values (*Ibid.*: 193ff.).

Secondly, and accordingly, the strategies are arranged according to the *levels of environment* involved. While mergers regularly apply to dyads (frequently of direct exchange partners), or at least a very small number of organizations, the "usual" number of participants rises when it comes to joint ventures and cooptation networks. With cartels and associations, one moves even farther away from what has been called the *organization-set* (Blau & Scott, 1962; Evan, 1966), which corresponds to a focal organization. Concluding with the larger social and political environment as a source of legitimacy, the authors extend their argument toward what has become known as the new institutional approach. With an increasing distance and number of social actors, the focal organization's control is watered down and its active influence options diminish.

After the examination of the mechanism that mediates between the environment and organizational behavior and structure—which we will refer to separately (2.1.3)—the study closes in Chapter 10 with a repetition of practical implications regarding organizational design.

2.1.2 RDT-based merger analysis

As laid out above, mergers are portrayed within the resource dependence framework as one possible subtype of organizational activities which can be used to restructure interdependence with the environment. Pfeffer (1972) hence adopts an argument originally developed by Thompson (1967), who applied power-dependence theory (Emerson, 1962; 1976) to organizational dependency management activities. Three basic pre-merger forms of interorganizational relations are implicitly associated by Pfeffer (1972) with the following two of Emerson's (1962: 36–38) four generic power balancing operations:

a) Operation 4: the relevant power network, "defined as two or more connected power-dependence relations" (*Ibid.*: 36) is reduced by the emergence of a collective actor → organizational management of *symbiotic* and *competitive* interdependence
b) Operation 2: the relevant power network is extended through a diffusion of dependency toward new alternatives → *lateral* relationship (independence) between organizations

The three forms of relations are identified with the well-known three archetypes of mergers:

(1) *Vertical mergers* refer to organizations that are symbiotically related within the same production or turnover process, commonly in a supplier / purchaser relationship;
(2) *Horizontal mergers* apply to organizations that are competitively related within the same production or turnover process and
(3) *Diversification* or *conglomerate mergers* concern organizations that are not related within the same production or turnover process.

As regards vertical mergers, Pfeffer (1972) empirically examined the hypothesis that cross-industry merger activity level is a function of inter-industry transactions in terms of relative common sales and purchase magnitude. Pfeffer tests against three possible alternative explanations: mergers occurring on a *random basis*; attractiveness through *profitability*, and *industry concentration* as a cooperation-narrowing entry barrier. The analysis of 854 mergers between 1948 and 1969 for 18 selected manufacturing industries reveals a correlation pattern in support of the exchange dependency argument (*Ibid.*: 389). Pfeffer and Salancik (1978: 121) further hone the original study by convincingly testing against the assertion that companies merge with transaction partners because of *previous familiarity*. Focusing on the direction of merging and asset acquisition (forward / backward in the production process), they demonstrate that merger activities in contrast aim at the most critical side of exchange dependency. In a nutshell, vertical mergers, in terms of the related balancing operation, take effect as follows: the absorbed organization is disjoined from its alternative exchange partners completely (through integration); devoid of emerging countervailing power within the relevant network, the acquiring firm thus controls a source of symbiotic dependence, and its own social discretion increases.

In a similar vein, competitive interdependence within the same industry is to be reduced by horizontal mergers. According to Pfeffer and Salancik (1978: 124), the discovered lower correlations between the percentage of intra-industry mergers and resource exchange variables have partly been due to differences in industry concentration levels; the latter have served as an indicator of competitive uncertainty within industry. The impetus for horizontal mergers was by the authors supposed to be low when firms are confronted with a huge number of competitors, thus acting within the meaning of the price-taker concept. Mergers should not reduce much critical interdependence in these settings. Things change with increasing concentration as outcome interdependence intensifies and the ability to control it through mergers rises. However, if a certain level of concentration is surpassed, merger activity should drop again. A silent cartel mode of cooperation starts to become more attractive, not least because of looming state interventions (Pfeffer, 1972: 390). It is shown that the proportion of intra-industry mergers is negatively related to the deviation from a (graphically determined) medium level of concentration. Additionally, the explanatory power of the resource exchange variables (sales and purchase magnitude) regarding merger activity is increased when medium concentration level deviation is accounted for (*Ibid.*). These results recommend that the motivation to form a new collective actor through a horizontal merger stems from the opportunity to reduce uncertainties rooted in competition offered by such a merger.

Conglomerate mergers, the third merger type, considered against the background of power-dependence theory do follow the balancing logic of extending or lengthening an existing power network (see Emerson, 1962: 36). Whereas vertical and horizontal mergers focus on the incorporation of organizations that directly or indirectly influence the operations of the focal organization, a conglomerate merger involves parties that had not previously been part of the same power network. It serves as a change strategy to avoid excessive dependence concentration (Pfeffer & Salancik, 1978:

109). Conglomerate or diversification mergers should likely occur when absorption is unattainable due to situational constraints (Pfeffer, 1972: 390). The argument is fleshed out by an analysis of firms that are highly dependent on governmental agencies. An empirical association between the level of diversification and the percentage of government transactions (based on Gort, 1962) is found. For his own empirical data, Pfeffer (1972: 391) demonstrates the percentage of government transactions to be correlated with the initially detected correlation coefficients between transaction interdependence and merger behavior. In the face of strict governmental regulations, a diversification merger provides a way of reducing restrictive domination by creating exchange alternatives.

Parallel to the common notational proximity of organizational integration to the concept of organizing, mergers in RDT are considered a special case of organizational growth. Merger analysis, from that point of view, instead of developing into a specialized subdiscipline, should be at the heart of any true organization theory. Growth of organizations is thereby for the most part not—as stated by internal perspectives—motivated by organizational commitment, executive compensation / prestige, and economies of scale and / or profitability. It rather represents a survival value in itself: the sheer size of many organizations creates dependencies that can ensure survival and stability even beyond meeting societal demands.

In addition to such unconventional reasoning on the lacking direct necessity of post-merger financial performance, Pfeffer and Salancik (1978: 131ff.) provide two reasons for the performance paradox. First, in the case of vertical and horizontal mergers, the set of possible partner organizations is limited as the latter have to be part of the same power network. The characteristics of the pre-merger dependence relationship therefore narrow aspirations to account for the criterion of profitability. Since mergers are conceptually to be subsumed under the label of organizational growth, the second argument refers to the interorganizational effects of growth. The extension of a focal organization's boundaries means increasing power; other social actors will respond with balancing operations. Countervailing concentration activities of diverse relevant organizations or additional demands and governmental regulations are likely to ensue (*Ibid.*: 135).

In summary, many core propositions (Pfeffer, 2003: xii) of RDT are condensed in the chapter on mergers:

- Environment as a source of constraints and uncertainties drives and regulates organizational activities and structuring;

- Organizations are active political actors (instead of passive "price-takers"): measures to work against constraints and give the organization more discretion are undertaken;
- Individual administrator motives play a minor role (Pfeffer & Salancik, 1978: 132); social structures and especially power networks are decisive;
- Reciprocal power-balancing dynamics characterize the corporate world; interventions in power networks lead to countervailing reactions and yield concentration tendencies.

2.1.3 Opening the black box: RDT as a multilevel approach

Besides the fact that associated empirical analyses of mergers and other IOR-related activities have largely operated on the (macro) industry level (Davis & Cobb, 2009), RDT generally provides a multilevel explanation of the behavior of organizations (Campling & Michelson, 1998). The argument in this regard mainly rests on the *strategic contingencies' theory of intraorganizational power* (SCT hereafter) provided by David Hickson and colleagues (1971; 1974). Since for this and other reasons the SCT is of paramount importance for RDT as well as for the study at hand, it is succinctly outlined in the following.

Hickson et al. (1971), also drawing on Emerson (1962) and Thompson (1967), sought to explain power differentials between organizational subunits. Power, being conceptualized as a property of resource exchange relationships, depends on the relative extent of departmental control over environmental contingencies. This extent is in turn determined by four basic variables (Hickson et al., 1971: 218ff.):

(1) *Effectiveness of coping*—the ability of a subunit to successfully handle environmental uncertainty by means of prevention, information and absorption and
(2) *Uncertainty of inputs* in terms of variability and directness of environmental feedback;
(3) *Substitutability*: the availability of alternatives to the activities provided by the unit;
(4) *Subunit centrality*, which breaks down into a) a unit's internal *pervasiveness* and b) the *immediacy* of its workflows, which refers to the resource-related weight of the subunit.

The first, the effectiveness of coping is analytically distinguished from the degree of input uncertainty that a focal organization faces, as it is not uncertainty in itself but coping that gives power (Hickson et al., 1971: 219). They together capture Emerson's (1962: 32) *motivational investment* in goals mediated by the coping subunit. The third one, the substitutability of activities, accordingly refers to the availability of alternatives to the activities of the subunit. While the effectiveness of coping is supposed to increase the dependence of other subunits, substitutability has the reverse effect. Finally, subunit centrality, also being positively related to dependence / power, refers to the task inter-connectedness between subunits as a defining element of organizations. Its two sub-dimensions *pervasiveness* and *immediacy* relate to the degree of interconnectedness of the subunit on the one hand as well as the "speed and severity with which the workflows of a subunit affect the final outputs of the organization" (Hickson et al., 1971: 222) on the other. The interplay of these four variables together with their quality to be influenced gives environmental uncertainties their strategic character. Increasing imbalances in the ability to control contingencies, differences in interconnectedness and diverging substitutability further subunit-related intraorganizational power and, consequently, discretionary differentials.

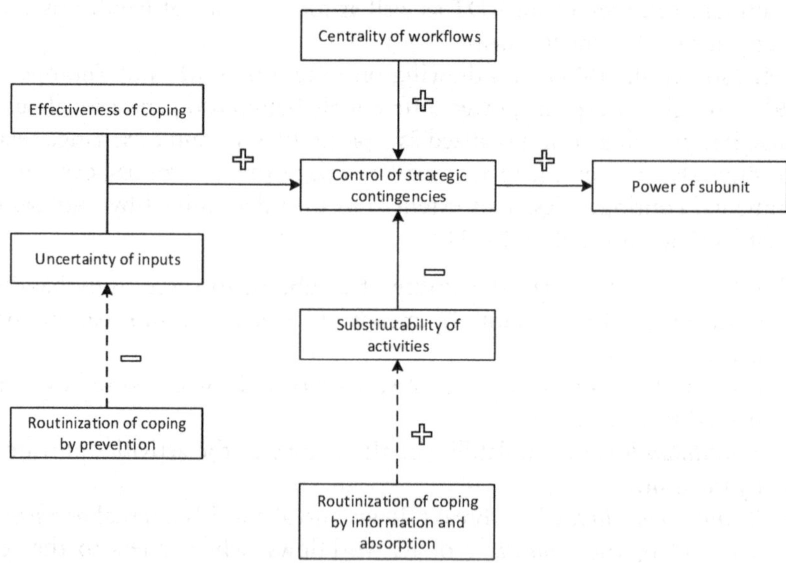

Figure 2.1: Strategic contingencies' theory of intraorganizational power (adopted from Hickson et. al (1971: 223))

Intraorganizational power gains encourage countervailing power: the two forms of routinization (indirectly related to subunit power) mark typical balancing operations against a focal subunit. Routinization of coping through information and absorption enhances the substitutability of its activities, thus equaling power relation balancing operation 2 (Emerson, 1962: 35). In line with Crozier (1964), it has been claimed that organizational rules and standard procedures take effect against non-routinized expert power (Hickson et al., 1971: 224). The second form of routinization is associated with similar tactics, but by means of preventing uncertainty aims at the effectiveness of coping. Organizational programs and appropriate contracting have been stated as examples (*Ibid.*). Such preventive routinization thus refers to Emerson's (1962) first balancing operation, the reduction of motivational investment in resources mediated by a subunit.

The SCT has been fundamental to RDT in two respects. Firstly, it seems to have partly served as a conceptual template for the analysis of interorganizational power exchange dynamics within RDT. As mentioned earlier (2.1.1), Pfeffer and Salancik (1978: 43ff.) have singled out three factors which influence the probability of successful external influence on organizations: *resource importance* (in terms of relative exchange magnitude and functional criticality), *extent of discretion over resources* and *concentration of resource control*. Those three factors largely correspond to the above-stated basic intraorganizational power variables:

(1) *Resource importance* is paralleled by *subunit centrality*, especially in the former's sub-dimension of *criticality* (*Ibid.*: 231);
(2) The extent of *discretion over resources* resembles the *effectiveness of coping* as both refer to the capabilities of social actors to reduce uncertainty[10];
(3) As regards the *level of concentration*, Pfeffer and Salancik (1978: 50) state: "Rather, the important thing is whether the focal organization has access to the resource from additional sources"—this obviously finds its counterpart in the *substitutability* of subunit activities.

Hence, Pfeffer and Salancik in part translated the SCT by changing the level of analysis from subunit level to industry level.

Secondly, RDT embraces SCT as a whole, building on it as the central mediating mechanism between external environment and intraorganizational decision-making (Pfeffer & Salancik, 1974; 1978: 230ff.).

10 Pfeffer (2005) considers this the main (even though small) difference: coping with uncertainties (SCT) vs. coping by ensuring resources (RDT).

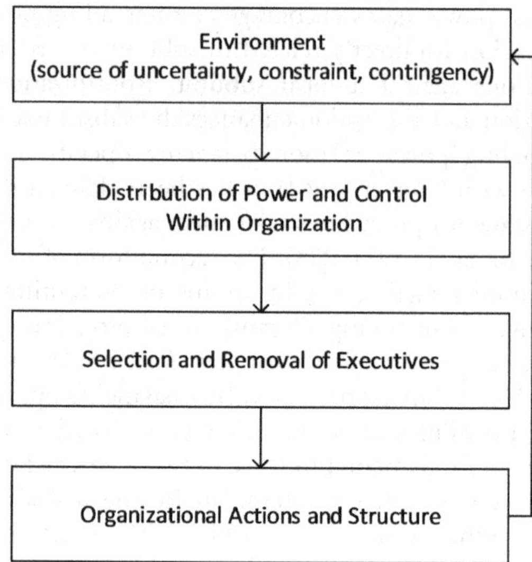

Figure 2.2: Model of environmental effects in RDT (Pfeffer & Salancik, 1978: 229)

RDT, by way of incorporating SCT, relates characteristics of the organizational environment (macro-level) and the subunit (meso-)level to each other. To put it bluntly, the two levels of analysis can be considered as two interconnected sides of the same mirror-inverted power struggle. On the one hand, there is the inward perspective of the external actors onto the focal organization: those of the many environmental actors who most exclusively control the most and most critical resources of the focal organization attain the largest relative share of external control over organizational activities and structures. On the other hand, from the outward subunit level perspective, those subunits / internal coalitions who most effectively and exclusively cope with the external demands and constraints in turn gain the largest relative internal discretion.

The small group and individual (micro-)level of organizational analysis is also involved, but has not been RDT's focal point of interest. This is partly due to its basic orientation within the larger narrative of organization theory: from the outset, Pfeffer and Salancik (1978: 7ff.) attempted to formulate a counterpoint to approaches that reduce their explanations of organizations to individual attitudes, motives and leadership. They do not provide an explicit micro-foundation of the coalitional model of organization—the concept was adopted from the Simon-Cyert-March strand of behavioral theory (see Pfeffer & Salancik, 1977; Astley & Zajac, 1993: 402). RDT claims that individual interest formation within a formal subunit or coalition basically follows the same power exchange principles as on the aggregate level, on which the organization has to maintain a contributive coalition of parties (Pfeffer & Salancik, 1978: 232). The terms *participants* and *coalition* are thereby partly used interchangeably: "The power of the participant is a function of the dependence of others in the organization on his contributions, activities, capabilities" (*Ibid*.: 27).

As a result, it has been shown that RDT embraces all analytical levels relevant to complete explanations of organizational behavior and structures; it is neither to be designated a mere "macro theory" (Drees & Heugens, 2013: 22) nor any other kind of reductionist approach. However, the three levels of analysis, in the course of RDT's empirical application regarding the different uncertainty management activities, have certainly not been addressed evenly. Specifically, the examination of IORs and M&As has almost entirely been focused on the analytical macro-level (Davis & Cobb, 2009). As far as the internal micro- / meso-perspectives are concerned, board composition issues have clearly come to dominate empirical research (Pfeffer, 2005). This vast stream of studies has, for instance, addressed selection, tenure, administrator characteristics and related resources (see Hillman, Withers & Collins, 2009). Decidedly fewer studies, most of which have HEIs as a research subject, have attended to intraorganizational resource flows or aspects of formal structure. We will turn to them in the following.

2.1.4 RDT and institutions of higher education

From its early outset, organizations of higher education have provided an important object of investigation for RDT (Pfeffer, 2005: 439). Against the background of the power-political coalition model of organizations, which in the field of higher education sociology is commonly traced back to a study by Viktor Baldridge (1971), Pfeffer and Salancik (1974; Salancik & Pfeffer, 1974) examined allocation decisions within the University of Illinois at Urbana-Champaign. Proportional general budget allocation was hypothesized to be a consequence of subunit power rather than of bureaucratic (rational) departmental workload. Power itself was measured via interview ratings of department heads and relative representation of the 29 departments on 13 committees. The results show "a separate and significant effect of subunit power on resource allocation outcomes" (Pfeffer &

Salancik, 1974: 144). In the second of the two closely related studies, measurement of power and its use were refined in the same research setting. Subsequent to a basic concept validation, it was demonstrated that power, especially when based on acquired external grants, predicts internal allocation patterns of several types of scarce funds and fellowships. Salancik and Pfeffer (1974: 470) pointed to the Matthew Effect entailed in this: "power derived from acquiring resources is used to obtain more resources, which in turn can be employed to produce more power—the rich get richer". Furthermore, the results underline the weight of external funding for organizational decision-making as against unit positions in national rankings (another bureaucratic / universalistic criterion).

Hills and Mahoney (1978) connected themselves to these studies by likewise contrasting the effect of power variables on resource allocation with universalistic budgeting criteria. Operationalization of the latter was, for example, found in the previous period's budget and the subunit workload efficiency. In the behavioral theory of the firm, to which Hills and Mahoney adhere, such "arbitrary allocative rules" (Cyert & March, 1963: 270) serve as decision guidelines to reduce complexity and conflict. Hills and Mahoney hypothesized that power exertion was limited to periods of resource scarcity. Using archival data from the 30 departments of the University of Minnesota, they compared the effects of the two groups of criteria over cycles of resource scarcity and abundance. Hills and Mahoney (1978: 464) reported the considerable influence of universalistic decision criteria over all periods, and therefore recommended shifting interpretation of university budgeting processes toward a more harmony-oriented coalitional model.

Pfeffer and Moore (1980) replicated the original Illinois study and criticized Hills and Mahoney for failing to reproduce the important connections between representation on committees, grants, and budget allocation. Simultaneously, the original study (Salancik & Pfeffer, 1974) was extended by employing indicators of the discipline level of paradigm development (Salancik, Staw & Pondy, 1980) as a power factor in universities. A cross-sectional and longitudinal comparison of two campuses that had faced different faculty-cutback situations yielded additional support for the promoted connection between scarcity and power exertion.

Saunders and Scamell (1982) chose HEIs as research subjects to replicate the original SCT validation study by Hinings et al. (1974), which had been conducted in a context of industrial organizations (mainly breweries). A combination of interviews and a questionnaire survey was employed on a sample of 74 top administrators from six small and medium-size US universities. The authors (1982: 198) reported evidence supportive of SCT, but based on their own results saw limited relevance of the coping with uncertainty variable. The rather moderate correlations in this respect were suggested to be due to informal workflows in universities on the one hand as well as to supposedly more stable organizational environments in higher education on the other.

Blending a grounded theory approach (Glaser & Strauss, 1967) with a quantitative survey, Judith Hackman (1985) similarly examined the connection between subunit power and internal resource allocations. Her research subjects were six HEIs that differed considerably in terms of general type and size. One central aim of her study was to compare university subunits according to their intraorganizational *centrality*. Deviating from the SCT, Hackman (1985: 61) conceptualized centrality as a dichotomous category comprising *core units* (academic departments) on the one hand and *peripheral units* (i.e. administrative / supportive units) on the other. Power was not directly treated as a dependent variable, but instead captured by its influence on critical decisions about internal resource allocations. Furthermore, by separating environmental from institutional power, she attempted to draw a sharper distinction between internal and external environment. Hackman (1985: 72) found unit centrality to interact with environmental power, and negotiation strategies to influence internal resource allocations in situations of increasing financial scarcity. The gross results of the study are in line with central RDT concepts and propositions.

In order to reduce subjectivity and ambiguity in Hackman's centrality measurement, Ashar and Shapiro (1988) suggested a more fine-grained analysis of subunit centrality. Focusing on actual workflow interdependencies, they introduced *research and teaching collaboration counts* as well as *non-major student numbers* and *broad-class proposition* to distinguish between central and peripheral units. In a multiple regression, the resulting centrality index was combined with measurements of productivity, paradigm development and external support to explain differences in faculty size reduction under financial pressure (Ashar, 1987; Ashar & Shapiro, 1988). The data was attained from 40 subunit reports (1980 / 1984) from a large US arts and sciences college (about 23,000 students). In line with Pfeffer and Salancik (1974), Ashar and Shapiro (1988: 281) considered their convincing results to confirm the value of nonobtrusive archival data in power measurement.

By handling the control of strategic contingencies as a moderator variable and disclaiming the effectiveness of coping, Saunders (1990) tested a modified version of the SCT on a sample of 74 departments from six small and medium-size HEIs. The study is based on questionnaires and structured interviews. With *participation* and *positional power*, two dimensions of the dependent variable were extracted from the data (and suggested to be specific for universities). Saunders (1990: 13) reported partial support for her own assumption (moderator effect of control of contingencies), and for Hackman's (1985) analytical distinction between core and peripheral units.

In a quantitative study on organizational differentiation in higher education, Tolbert (1985) fused RDT and new explanations of institutional theory. She analyzed differences regarding the adoption of dependence-managing administrative positions between public and private HEIs; her sample comprised 167 public and 114 private US institutions. While publicly funded organizations with an increasing dependence on private funds showed a rising tendency to install private-funding offices, they didn't react the same way to increasing dependence on public funding. The results yielded a similar relationship for the adoption of offices that manage public and private funds in private HEIs. Tolbert established those differences in differentiation with the effect of institutionalized expectations: traditional (i.e. socially accepted) patterns of interorganizational relationships relieved organizations from the pressure of aligning their internal structure according to changes in environmental dependencies.

Covalevski and Dirsmith (1988a; 1988b), in combining interviews and archival data, applied a grounded theory approach to analyze budgeting practices between the University and the State of Wisconsin. Conceiving of RDT more as a part of the new institutional program (1988a: 2ff.), the case study examined the university's refusal of student enrollment as a (highly institutionalized) formula-category to assign state funds. Covaleski and Dirsmith (1988b: 585) "found that the processes of institutionalization as expressed through the budget appear to be infused with power and self-interest within the organization and in extraorganizational relations". Institutional expectations and attempts to modify them were shown to be linked to economic pressures—the study hence addresses central criticism aimed at new institutional theory (*Ibid.*: 563).

Overall, studies on budgeting (as a structural element) have dominated empirical examinations of HEIs from an RDT perspective; the theory has had considerable influence on research concerning managerial accounting in general (Covalevski, Dirsmith & Samuel, 1996) and HEI budgeting specifically (Schick, 1985; Harold, 2010).

Beyond questions of internal resource allocation, board cooptation, as probably the most prominent field in RDT research (Hillman et al., 2009), has also been explicitly addressed in the context of higher education. Nienhüser and Jacob (2008) reported evidence of university council composition in German universities being a function of organizational finance structure, and therefore of resource dependencies. Using website information and telephone interviews, they gathered data on council member backgrounds for 55 out of 89 relevant public HEIs. The results show a noticeable connection between the proportion of third-party funding and the share of business representatives within the faction of external university council members. In addition, minor representation of other interests outside academia (e.g. culture, unions, and media) and a higher relative chance for top managers to chair the council was reported. The suchlike influence of business representatives conflicts with a common political rhetoric that justifies non-university members having active governance responsibilities by claiming it creates a pluralistic representation of society (*Ibid*.: 2).

In its empirical applications on HEIs, RDT has not been confined entirely to the analytical meso-level of subunits and organizational coalitions. In two studies, Pfeffer and Davis-Blake (1987; 1992), to take a case in point, developed and tested typical propositions on the (micro-)level of individual coalition members. The first study (1987) analyzed the connection between the relative importance of positions at HEIs and relative individual salaries accrued in those positions. Differences in the importance of particular positions between public and private institutions were found to be associated with according compensation patterns. Instead of the individual attributes of incumbents, earnings were, according to the external perspective, found to be a consequence of organizational resources (political support vs. tuition / donations). Connections between wage dispersion and individual behavior (turnover) were put forward in the second study (1992). The overall level of salary dispersion in combination with an administrator's location within the overall salary structure turned out to increase individual willingness to leave the organizational coalition (Pfeffer & Davis-Blake, 1992: 762). Both studies used administration compensation survey data referring to a large number (600–800) of US HEIs.

Taken as a whole, genuine empirical applications of the resource dependence framework in the context of HEIs, however, have remained limited. Since the late 1990s, institutionalist perspectives on organizations in higher education have been sharply on the rise (Krücken & Röbken, 2009)—materialist and resource-related explanations seem to have been crowded out at some point. Comprehensively considering higher education in all its facets *an institution* (Meyer, Ramirez, Frank & Schofer, 2007) today has clearly become the dominant paradigm in higher education organization research.

2.2 *RDT in the field of organization theory*

Up to this point, we have delineated the basics of RDT and some of its relevant empirical applications. The outline has been geared to the subject-specific adequacy criteria derived from Chapter 1: RDT's analysis of mergers, its multilevel character, and its record in the context of organizations in higher education have been traced. To prepare the concluding discussion in Section 2.3, a more abstract perspective will be added in the following. To begin with, some relations of RDT to approaches in its direct theoretical environment, like contingency and power-exchange theory are broached. Subsequently, the Burrell–Morgan (1979) frame of reference will be used to briefly point to prospects and challenges regarding RDT's metatheoretical classification.

2.2.1 RDT precursors and related approaches

As should be apparent from the foregoing discussion, two main approaches have played a pivotal role within RDT. Firstly, the *behavioral approach* to organization theory (Barnard, 1938; March & Simon, 1958; Cyert & March, 1963; March & Olsen, 1976), as the main fundament of all open systems theories, has been central to both SCT and RDT. This stream of research, amongst other things besides the coalitional model of organizations (see Stevenson et al., 1985), has introduced a critical perspective on rational choice, and numerous sub-theories on organizational decision-making, information processing and information systems.

The second crucial paradigm has been *contingency theory*. With the *strategic contingencies' theory of intraorganizational power* (Hickson et al., 1971; Hinings et al., 1974) an important representative has already been introduced. In addition, the importance of James Thompson's (1967) landmark volume *organizations in action* on RDT (as well as for SCT) can hardly be exaggerated. Thompson himself is somewhat inconsistently referred to, sometimes cited as a founding father of contingency theory (Schoonhoven, 1981; Zald, 2003; Astley & van de Ven, 1983; Bourgeois, 1980; Donaldson, 2001) and sometimes in terms of a hard-to-classify integrationist approach (Scott, 2003; Tosi, 2009; Hargadon, 2003). His work has elaborated basic theoretical elements of RDT: organizations as resource dependent open systems, power relations with the environment, the management of contingencies and the coalitional nature of organizations, to just name a few. Although *Organizations in Action* and *The External Control of Organizations* therefore always have to be named in the same breath, some differences shall be revealed superficially here:

- Pfeffer and Salancik put stronger emphasis on active uncertainty management and the scope of activities they discuss is far larger: political action, cooptation, advertising and many more;
- Thompson focused on organizational structures—RDT centers on organizational action;
- Thompson implied a much stronger assumption of rationality, while Pfeffer and Salancik adopted Emerson's (1962; 1976) rationality interpretation;
- Thompson, in his "conceptual inventory", aimed exclusively at theoretically generating "potentially significant propositions" (1967: 2) and preferred casual illustrations. *The External Control of Organizations*, despite being more essayistic in style, comprises vast empirical evidence and systematic inference.

RDT's reference to contingency theory is twofold. On the one hand, models that focus on functionalist adaption have contributed important theoretical concepts. On the other hand, as a paradigm, contingency theory has been RDT's main subject of critique. This critique has been targeted at the core characteristics of the contingency approach, namely deterministic and unidirectional causation in combination with a black box conception of organizations. Assenting to John Child's (1972) strategic choice perspective, Pfeffer and Salancik (1978: 227; Pfeffer, 1978: 81) rejected determinism and conceptually left more room for managerial discretion instead (see next section). They discard restrictive unidirectionality in causation, which implies organizations exclusively *re*act to environmental stimuli, in favor of proactive management of constraints and contingencies. Pfeffer and Salancik (*Ibid.*: 226) challenged contingency theory for its inherent neglect of specifying causal mechanisms that mediate between organization and environment. Instead of explicating such mechanisms, the contingency approach has tended to fill the black box with strict and often implicit premises on actor rationality and the general functionality of social systems.

Emerson's (1962) power theory, as RDT's central instrument of critique, provides core assumptions and mechanisms. Power-dependence relationships, which are fundamental to the system-environment relationship, are rooted in mutual dependencies and are generally conceptually opposed to unidirectionality. Balancing asymmetric relations comprises *passive* adaption toward demands as well as *actively* working the power bases of the demanding party. Furthermore, power-dependence theory entails significantly less rigid assumptions on rationality. Emerson (*Ibid*.: 41) has emphasized alterable actor perceptions of exchange conditions and has employed a very broad concept of goals, referring "to gratifications consciously sought as well as rewards unconsciously obtained through the relationship" (*Ibid*.: 32).

A second means of critique is the interpretive approach of Karl Weick. He draws on the concept of *enactment* (Weick, 1979) within RDT to substantiate the theoretical relevance of attention processes and information systems. Processing information from and about the organizational environment(s) is *active* and *retrospective* in character; environmental stimuli *in themselves* are not the basis of planning and action; it is their socially constructed representations that are. Organizations can solely deal with those *past* contingencies and constraints that are "successfully" enacted by their subunits. This suggestion stands in opposition to the notion of organizations passively perceiving neutral and objective information, which is favored in the contingency approach. With the idea of *loose coupling*, a further concept introduced by Weick (1976) has served Pfeffer and Salancik (1978: 13, 227) to defy environmental determinism.

For the sake of completeness, the relationship between RDT and sociological neo-institutionalism needs to be addressed. The passage on socially attributed organizational legitimacy especially (Chapter 8 in the 1978 volume), as part of the discussion of the wider societal context, reveals considerable parallels. It is admitted that a general public acceptance of goals and operations may occasionally be of greater relevance for organizational survival than economic viability (Pfeffer & Salancik, 1978: 194). A further prominent theoretical concept that both theoretical approaches have in common is the *decoupling* of structures and activities. In their examination of ways to control external demands, Pfeffer and Salancik (*Ibid*.: 98) referred to the example of psychiatric hospitals signaling therapeutic efforts to the environment while actually mainly drugging patients—the same analogy was used by Meyer and Rowan (1977: 351). Resource dependence and neo-institutionalist explanations have been found difficult to disentangle regarding the conducting of empirical analyses (Zucker, 1987: 457; DiMaggio, 1988).

Though there have been attempts to integrate both schools of thought (Tolbert, 1985; Covaleski & Dirsmith, 1988a, b; Oliver, 1991; Sherer & Lee, 2002), some substantial conceptual cleavages remain. The most frequently discussed difference, besides RDT's stronger focus on material resources, lies in varying foci on organizational responses. While institutionalist approaches have underlined conformity and societal invisibility, RDT has pointed out *active* interference with the environment (Oliver, 1991). Compliance with external demands has been considered a general threat to long-term survival (Pfeffer & Salancik, 1978: 94); organizations choose strategic options with a lower discretionary potential only if inevitable. As a further aspect, the active management of constraints and contingencies goes along with a much higher level of consciousness and deliberateness regarding environmental demands and their handling (Leblebici, Salancik, Copay & King, 1991). Mizruchi and Fein (1999) have persuasively explicated that proponents of institutional theory have, to the contrary, further shifted their conceptual focus toward *mimetic* isomorphism, which favors passive "nonchoice behavior" and the strategy of "acquiesce" (Oliver, 1991: 152). Last, but not least, Pfeffer and Salancik in their consideration of legitimation as a process have not committed themselves to any specific theoretical foundation: except for Weick (whose role within RDT is clearly circumscribed), basic approaches pertaining to *phenomenology* (e.g. Schütz, 1971) or *social constructivism* (Berger & Luckmann, 1967) are not referred to anywhere. After all, the respective passage seems rather foggy on the whole and somewhat distant—the process of legitimation, as well as the proportion of society being necessary to attribute legitimacy, is labeled "unclear" (Pfeffer & Salancik, 1978: 194). The overall conceptual weight of wider (socially constructed) norms and values within RDT might thus have been inflated and its focus on sociomateriality been underestimated.

The role of trade associations and professional organizations in defining, promoting, and dispersing best practice rules is addressed in all four streams of research. Hence, it may serve to conclude this section with a glance at the differences in explanatory topoi on the one hand, and illustrate the positioning of RDT within the field of organization theory on the other. According to...

- Cyert and March (1963: 119–120), good business practices are part of a negotiated and devised environment to reduce complexity. They help to avoid individual predictions and thus relieve the organizational coalition from conflict-prone and error-prone planning requirements in the face of bounded rationality;

- Thompson (1967: 93ff.), in the case of impossible internal assessment of the "fitness of organizational components" due to incomplete cause / effect relationships, technical rationality gives way to organizational rationality. The extrinsic standards of the task environment ("confidence of assessors") hence serve as a surrogate for measurement (yet only, if absolutely necessary);
- Pfeffer and Salancik (1978: 178ff.), trade associations do more for their members: they exert political influence and, somewhat akin to mergers, enhance organizational power by reducing competitive uncertainty. They do so by enforcing pricing systems, by utilizing norms and quality standards to reduce product diversity, and / or by preventing innovations (e.g. Dunford, 1987);
- DiMaggio and Powell (1983: 147; 153ff.), the phenomenon is due to the process of normative isomorphism: trade associations are arenas for the diffusion of norms and standards. They further the visibility of center organizations. Isomorphism is deemed to emerge out of structuration (Giddens, 1979); thus, best practices are an organizational field-level consequence of general uncertainty reduction and homogenization tendencies inherent in human societies.

2.2.2 Paradigmatic assumptions and positioning

The hitherto course of positioning RDT within the field of organization studies has shown that it has brought together quite different models and strands of debate. To complete the argument and further systematize some of RDT's premises, we will now employ the well-established paradigm classification scheme provided by Gibson Burrell and Gareth Morgan (1979). Theoretical approaches are categorized within the scheme according to their implicit or explicit meta-theoretical assumptions. Burrell and Morgan (1979) differentiate between two major independent bipolar dimensions:

1) The *subjective vs. objective* dimension, which, as sub-dimensions, encapsulates ontological, epistemological, human nature-related and methodological basic assumptions and
2) The *regulation vs. radical change* dimension, which contrasts basic assumptions regarding the nature of society.

The combination of both dimensions yields four basic meta-theoretical paradigms:

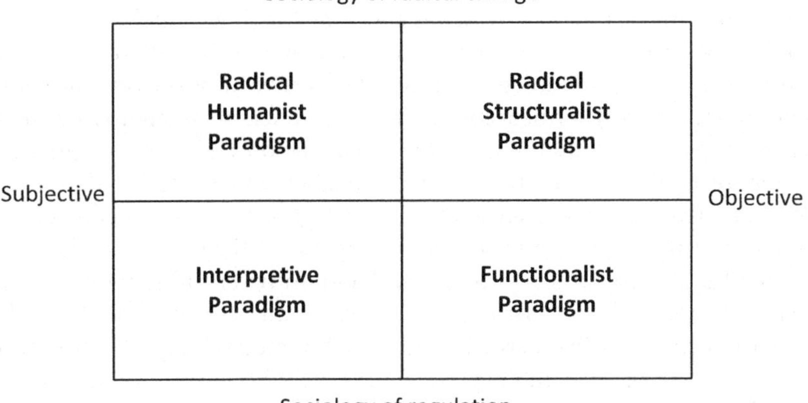

Figure 2.3: Meta-theoretical classification scheme (based on Morgan, 1980: 608)

Morgan (1980) localized RDT within the functionalist section of the scheme, together with contingency theory, population ecology, scientific management and others. Since the rationale given for this is rather brief, we will examine the assignment in more detail. If we begin with the *subjective–objective dimension*, the positioning toward the objectivist pole is substantiated with the quality of political activities "as occurring within a contextually defined and hence ontologically real setting" (*Ibid.*: 616). Morgan thus referred to only one of the four sub-dimensions, which the subjective–objective dimension consists of according to Burrell and Morgan (1979). It is yet worthwhile to concisely scan RDT's positioning on each of them.

The *ontological* sub-dimension contrasts realist and nominalist positions: is there an observer-independent world that produces objective facts or does it consist solely of labels and nominal conventions? Although ontological assumptions are not explicitly discussed by Pfeffer and Salancik, RDT belongs on the realist side of the continuum. This, for example, becomes apparent in its distinction between organizational behavior and outcomes: "the environment of an organization can affect an organization's outcome without affecting its behavior" (Pfeffer & Salancik, 1978: 62). Another instance is provided in the final chapter on organizational design, where the discussion focuses on role-related and other perception errors.

The above-mentioned lacking reference to any "anti-positivist" basic literature may also underpin the strong realist tendency inherent in RDT's argument.

Sub-dimension 2 pertains to *epistemological* foundations. As it is closely related to sub-dimension 4, which is concerned with *methodology*, both are conjointly dealt with here. Not without inclination, Burrell and Morgan have, as regards epistemology, distinguished between positivism and *anti*-positivism. The first term, according to them, refers to all approaches that focus on patterns, causal relationships, explanation and prognosis in analyzing social phenomena. The second term labels all perspectives that stress the subjective qualities of social reality and highlight the social embeddedness of researchers; it comprises the proponents of the continuing linguistic / cultural turn hinted at in 1.3.4. Anti-positivists (subjectivists / relativists) therefore favor *Verstehen* over explanations and methodologically endorse techniques like hermeneutics or ethnomethodology. With regard to its underlying epistemology, RDT can safely be located on the "positivist" pole in this respect. Although in drawing on the phenomenologist approach of Karl Weick it initially seems to include a good portion of subjectivism—a steady commitment to empirical evidence and causal inference does yet portend underlying objectivism and a nomothetic methodology.

The debate on core assumptions regarding *human nature* is the basis of sub-dimension 3, which ranges between *voluntarism* and *determinism*. In this regard, Pfeffer and Salancik have advocated an intermediate position. This is, for instance, to be felt in their remarks on administrator discretion in general:

> A more realistic perspective on organizational action would recognize that organizational actors mold organizational activities, but do so within constraints which limit their discretion to take action (1978: 245).

Although a slight argumentative bias in support of behavior constraint can be recognized, one can nonetheless find contentions against both extremes, against the overestimation of individual action and against a complete denial of human agency. The classification of RDT as an objectivist approach hence turns out to be largely consistent across all four sub-dimensions.

With regard to the *second main dimension* of the scheme, Morgan's (1980: 616) overall subsumption of RDT under the functionalist paradigm is justified by the adaptive nature of political activities. As far as this matter is concerned, Morgan contrasted the upper with the lower half of the scheme:

> From the perspective of these paradigms, both functionalist and interpretive theory fail to understand that the apparent order in social life is not so much the result of an adaptive process or a free act of social construction, as the consequence of a process of social domination (Morgan, 1980: 619).

Even though acknowledging the fact that some accuracy has to be relinquished in the wake of any abstract classification of organization theories, that assignment can be denoted as a misinterpretation of RDT for good reasons. The main fallacy relates to the conceptual nature of stability and the use of power. In the context of a sociology of regulation, adaption has to be understood in terms of serving the somehow superordinate goals of society, such as providing stability and cohesion (Burrell & Morgan, 1979). However, this is not the kind of stability that Pfeffer and Salancik mostly refer to. In contrast, they describe a form of stability that is *sclerotic* in nature, stability that is a consequence of the actor-driven and self-reinforcing institutionalization of power. The concept of strategic fit implied by RDT rests on the self-interests of single corporations and organizational networks (Venkatraman & Camillus, 1984: 519). It encompasses a kind of social stability that is beneficial mainly to those who control critical and hard-to-substitute resources, but by no means to society as a whole. It may account for the short-term retaining status quo, but rather jeopardizes adaptive capacities of social systems in the long run.

Mergers and trade associations can be used to illustrate the sclerotic stability that is produced by organizational activities on the industry level of analysis. Vertical and horizontal mergers certainly produce stability: they reduce resource-related uncertainties for the absorbing company or for a set of companies situated in a competitive relationship. Yet they do so to the detriment of other members of the power network. Pfeffer and Salancik have shown that this is not a random anomaly but a *systematic* tendency —concentration breeds balancing counter-concentration. If left unregulated, organizations thus tend to eliminate competition. Such implications might raise sympathies for state intervention and are really bad news, especially for those who adhere to the idea of the general supremacy of decentralized societal coordination. If trade associations use production standards to limit product variation or even prevent innovations[11] "that would disrupt competitive equilibria" (Pfeffer & Salancik, 1978: 179) in an organizational network, in whose interest is this? Such "adaptive behavior" curtails overall societal adaption capacities, though it may stabilize a certain coalition of interests on an industry level. Therefore, it can hardly be regarded to serve any kind of superordinate system stability requirement. Skepticism as to the corporate power-reinforcing effects of interorganizational relations becomes evident throughout the volume.

The same argument equally holds for the intraorganizational (meso-)level of analysis. Power accrues to those subunits that effectively and efficiently cope with the environmental uncertainties of the organization. However, in contrast to Hickson et al. (1971: 224), power is not "self-defeating". It is cemented through institutionalization, either by biased problemistic search (Cyert & March, 1963: 121) or by the intentional actions of the dominant coalition: "Whatever the source or form of institutionalization, the effect is to extend a subunit's power *beyond* its utility to the organization for its survival" (Pfeffer & Salancik, 1978: 235, emphasis added, mk). Amongst the intentional actions, the configuration of information systems especially is a point that is further elaborated on (*Ibid.*: 77f., 269ff.). As information on the environment is related to sub-coalition power and enhancement, it is bias-prone; its collection, preparation and reporting are sensitive strategic issues. The consequence of selective information processing may be strategic inertia. Power relations thus endanger intraorganizational adaptivity as well.

2.3 Is RDT an appropriate framework for post-merger integration analysis?

Jeffrey Pfeffer himself, not in an excessively enthusiastic manner, sums up RDT's achievements as follows:

> If RDT made a contribution to organization theory, it was primarily by bringing a lot of theoretical ideas together in a comprehensive framework, by forcefully arguing for understanding the effect of the environment as means for understanding organizations, and by arguing for the importance of the material conditions of organizational transactions with the environment (Pfeffer, 2005: 444).

---

11 Dunford (1987) reported evidence for innovation prevention as a dependency-reducing strategy.

That statement points to the highly integrative character of RDT, a commonly neglected feature that should have also become apparent in the course of this chapter. It is integrative in that some of the theoretical ideas it has brought together have been in deep meta-theoretical opposition to each other. In this respect, RDT differs from its three main (coeval) rival theories—population ecology, institutional economics, and sociological neo-institutionalism—all of which have been built on more self-consistent theoretical fundaments.

In RDT, conflicting approaches have however partly been brought together upon the avoidance of engaging too much in the many disagreements—(meta)theoretical debates are not the focus of the 1978 volume. Pfeffer and Salancik sometimes seem to implicitly suggest to bridge existing chasms by just keeping a satisfying compromise between extreme positions as to determinism vs. voluntarism; internal adaption vs. natural selection (Astley & van de Ven, 1983); or emancipation vs. system performance. Their own theoretical premises have not been clarified sufficiently (Davis & Cobb, 2010; McKinley & Mone, 2003).

The ambiguity of some of its concepts is reflected by the rather inconsistent reception of RDT. As discussed in the context of Burrell and Morgan's (1979) classification scheme, the theory has often been discarded as a functionalist–managerialist approach by both critical (e.g. Reed, 2006: 22; Levy, Alvesson & Willmott, 2003; Morgan & Spicer, 2009) and constructivist scholars (e.g. Morgan, 1980; Weick, Sutcliffe & Obstfeld, 2005: 15). And, indeed, if one considers the criteria that a theory needs to fulfill to qualify as a part of critical management studies (as suggested by Fournier and Grey, 2000), Pfeffer and Salancik's dedication to an anti-performative stance, denaturalization and reflexivity is not as distinct as it could be.

However, the true advocates of functionalism have likewise rejected RDT. In referring to Pfeffer (1978), Oliver Williamson, to whom "The crucial issue is whether there is an efficiency justification of hierarchy" (1980: 7), labeled power theory a "pied piper" (Williamson, 1981: 573). In a similar vein, Lex Donaldson (1995: 135) initially designated RDT an "anti-management theory" with a "New Left counter-culture of the sixties" background; a few years later (2001: 53ff.), he tried to reduce it to its contingency theory heritage and subsumed it under the latter. On the whole, deep-seated distrust in large companies, their control through market forces, and lacking faith in managerial sagacity in combination with its sympathy for democratic control of the corporate world have left RDT far too poisonous to become a leading paradigm within business studies in the long run.

The integrative character of the approach and the associated drive toward classification contingency should have, together with a number of further factors—like a current broad promotion of a more conservative social science (Pfeffer, 2005: 454)—contributed to its shift toward a "metaphorical statement" (Pfeffer, 2003: xvi). A large proportion of the SSCI citations reported by Davis and Cobb (2010) should be due to superficial hit-and-run references instead of indicating RDT's current vitality.[12]. On the whole, a recent tendency to implicitly typify RDT in terms of a "strategic branch of institutionalism" (Suchman, 1995: 572) instead of treating it as a distinct theory can be observed (e.g. Tosi, 2009).

What is important for the assessment of RDT's objective-specific applicability in terms of the criteria determined in Subsection 1.3.3? Let us take the obvious things first. Mergers have been an important focus of inquiry within RDT literature. The results of a recent meta-analysis of 157 empirical studies (Drees & Heugens, 2013) support the theory's basic propositions regarding the connection between exchange interdependence and different forms of IORs and mergers. Within RDT, the latter are viewed from a broader angle, that is, as one of many means of reducing organizational uncertainty, like the decoupling of factual and formal processes, political influence, or board cooptation. The isolation problem of the prevailing literature on mergers is therefore potentially counteracted twice: merger analysis can be intra-paradigmatically conceptually developed and its respective empirical results can be checked relative to and in connection with other organizational phenomena. Secondly, through being connected to meta-theoretical considerations, the basic premises of merger analysis may be unveiled, criticized and refined across different theories.

Furthermore, RDT's qualities of allowing for complete explanations of organizational phenomena across all analytical levels should have become evident. This general advantage in comparison with all holist and black box approaches is due to the integration of the SCT; it is of particular importance regarding the study of the intraorganizational consequences of mergers. However, empirical resource dependence merger research has almost exclusively been focused on the analytical macro-level (Davis &

12 A merely symbolic or even defacing reference to original writings is by no means an exclusive problem of RDT. Especially in Continental European research on higher education, Cohen, March and Olson's Garbage Can Model of Organizational Choice (1972) represents the ultimate example in this regard. Another case in point is the ambiguous use of Weick's concept of "loose coupling" (see Orton & Weick, 1990). Non-contextual citation counts generally say little about how a theory is interpreted or applied (if at all).

Cobb, 2010); a rare exception in this regard is provided by Campling and Michelson's (1998) analysis of union mergers. Drawing conclusions from industry-level relations as to firm-level merger motives (the association between industry-level exchange patterns and merger activity) is characteristic of Pfeffer's (1972) original merger studies as well as of the replications and extensions that followed (e.g. Burt, 1980; Finkelstein, 1997; Casciaro & Piskorski, 2005). The empirical analysis of the organizational subunit level has, on the whole, become somewhat one-sidedly dominated by board composition issues:

> [...] but there is little research that attempts to explore the complete connection between environmental constraint and internal organizational dynamics, including outcomes other than who occupies critical organizational positions and their backgrounds (Pfeffer, 2003: xix).

One important and sometimes forgotten reason to this effect lies in the largely deficient availability of relevant corporate data. Scientific transparency standards do regularly collide with organizational interests of information control. RDT itself provides the corresponding rationale: visibility of behavior and outcomes, for instance, makes it easier to formulate demands and tends to limit organizational discretion (Pfeffer & Salancik, 1978: 104ff.). Access, especially to intraorganizational data, is usually heavily restricted in business firms, and released data is, for the most part, nonessential in terms of power-dependence theory. Board cooptation research can, by contrast, rely on minimum information access, at least regarding top-level administrators.

The third criterion concerns RDT's appropriateness in approaching the idea of organizational integration. As discussed earlier, a striking proximity to the concept of "organizing" has ensued from integration literature, often with a notion of physical structures. The question of when we rightly consider two organizations to be *integrated* instead of *separated* is close to the distinction between organized and non-organized parts of society.

In contrast to contingency theory, capturing organizational structures has so far been neither a theoretical nor an empirical focus within RDT. The shaping of organizational structures has just been broadly subsumed under behavior that reduces uncertainty (Nienhüser, 2008). Initially, the approach sought to prove organizational behavior regarding its motives to be a response to resource-exchange-related environmental uncertainties (Pfeffer, 2005: 440)—and not, for instance, a rational pursuit of efficiency, or a mere handling of bounded rationality. Some affinity to capturing internal structural differences can be found in the studies explaining subunit budget allocation or organizational differentiation which are described above. Analyzing internal structures is not a weak point exclusive to RDT; Hinings and Tolbert (2008: 483) even state there has been a general "lack of success by sociologists in coming up with agreed-upon conceptualizations and operationalizations of such broad dimensions". However, as a broad dimension of organizational structure, the post-merger level of integration is not easily adopted from RDT literature: the associated conceptual triad of integration, internal differentiation, and external distinctiveness of formal organizations is indicated, yet not sufficiently explicated.

Finally, yet importantly, applicability as a theory regarding HEIs is clearly given. As laid out in Subsection 2.1.4, higher education has provided an important organizational context for RDT development from the beginning (Pfeffer, 2005: 439)—easy access to internal budgeting data was recognized as a huge advantage of this organization type early on (Hills & Mahoney, 1978: 456). On a more abstract level, the enhanced relevance in considering non-profits is mostly due to softening goal criteria. Organizational survival as a goal concept is employable to a far broader range of organizations than economic goals like profit maximization or cost efficiency.

3 Resource interdependence and organizational integration: concepts, mechanism and hypotheses

3.1 Bridging the gap: meta-theory matters

In the course of outlining the literature on mergers in Chapter 1, we stated some general theoretical and conceptual deficits concerning the role and definition of organizational post-merger integration. A lack of communication between M&A research and broader theorizing on organizations was queried. However, as mergers are commonplace phenomena and the integration concept bears a notion of *getting organized*, a definite two-way liability regarding the subject becomes evident. To what extent are theories of organization capable of furnishing empirical research with adequate basic concepts, definitions and causal mechanisms? Couldn't we even consider an explicit and analytically sound reference to the merger phenomenon to be a hallmark of true organization theory?

As it has an explicit focus on mergers, in Chapter 2 we examined RDT in terms of its analytical potential regarding post-merger integration. We discussed its contributions to the merger debate along with its omissions. The latter were identified in *a)* the underdevelopment of the structural perspective inherent in RDT (its one-sided focus on activities), as well as *b)* regarding the elaboration of the intraorganizational perspective on merger dynamics. In order to conclusively analyze post-merger integration on this basis, we have to deal with these omissions. The theoretical proximity of organizational integration to the concept of organization itself brings the discussion back to the respective definitional basis of RDT. In Section 2.1, we briefly outlined some of these deliberations, which can be found in Chapter 2 of *The External Control of Organizations*. Pfeffer and Salancik (1978: 24f.) have basically characterized organizations as *markets for influence and control*. Their terminology features concepts like *coalition*, *processes of organizing support* and *exchange settings*. However, their argument in this regard proceeds in a somewhat casual and essayistic manner; it seems to avoid an explicit definition and is neither particularly systematic nor extensive. As RDT has empirically been applied with a primary focus on organizational activities, this has largely remained without (negative) consequences regarding the choice of variables or operationalization.

As far as the puzzling challenge of defining organizations and distinguishing them from their environment / the larger society on the one hand and individuals on the other is concerned, a reticent and axiomatic approach is common to many organization theories. Therefore, the field has seen a wide-ranging spectrum of terminologies. This may be illustrated by means of the following small selection of definitions or defining statements, partly belonging to different paradigms:

1. An organization is a body of thoughts thought by thinking thinkers (Weick, 1979: 42).
2. [...] we act on the assumption that all social systems, and thus also organizations, consist of communications and *solely of communications* [own translation, original emphasis, mk] (Luhmann, 2000: 62). Original: [...] gehen wir davon aus, dass alle sozialen Systeme, also auch Organisationen, aus Kommunikationen *und nur aus Kommunikationen* bestehen.
3. [...] a system of consciously coordinated activities or forces of two or more persons (Barnard, 1938: 81).
4. Organizations are assemblages of interacting human beings and they are the largest assemblages in our society that have anything resembling a central coordinative system (March & Simon, 1958: 4).
5. An organization is the nexus of contracts, written and unwritten among owners of factors of production and customers (Fama & Jensen, 1983: 302—based on Jensen & Meckling, 1976).
6. Organizations are institutions—indeed, the central defining institution of modern cultural systems (Zucker, 1983: 37).
7. The organization is the total set of interstructured activities in which it is engaged at any one time and over which it has the discretion to initiate, maintain, or end behaviors (Pfeffer & Salancik, 1978: 32).
8. This definition is similar to that of Pfeffer and Salancik (1978) and March and Simon (1958) and identifies organizations as a set of parties whose actions are interstructured (Salancik, 1984: 618).

Variance in terminology becomes evident even between closely related theories and schools of thought. Chester Barnard, for instance, claimed organizations to consist of "activities or forces", while March and Simon (1958) highlighted human beings as basic components. In a similar vein, Pfeffer and Salancik (1978) oriented their definition toward activities as elements, while Salancik (1984) preferred to prioritize "sets of parties" as the carriers of activities.

This refers to a certain facet of the problem of *incommensurability*, which describes a situation in which at least two competing and radically different systems of orientation (i.e. theories or paradigms) presumably cannot be evaluated against an accepted frame of reference (Lueken, 1992; Scherer & Dowling, 1995; Scherer, 1998). With regard to the striking differences in definitional terminology, the theories touched on above partly seem to be incommensurable in terms of their *ontological* assumptions. Though Burrell and Morgan (1979) have reduced this aspect to the "nominalism vs. realism" sub-dimension in their classification scheme, the term *ontology* encompasses more than conceding the world's very existence apart from its nominal representations. An elaborated ontology provides a taxonomy of general conceptual terms, categories and relations between them—Pooley (2013: 544) compactly defines the ontology of a theory as "the objects to whose existence a theory is committed". If we draw on our choice of definitions of organizations, possible questions regarding the underlying ontology might, for instance, be: *What is a thought and what is its status compared to the thinking thinker? Do we need different categories to classify thoughts, communications and discourses as research subjects, and if so, based on what criteria? Are activities and the individuals performing them equitable or interchangeable for definitional purposes, or is there a logical rank order?* In many organization theories, ontological assumptions remain implicit, are treated axiomatically, or are ceded to their respective parent disciplines.

Though it may appear a mere intellectual pastime to some, the elaboration of ontological basics of theories is a highly significant condition of the possibility of scientific progress. If differences in definitional terminology are seriously accounted for, comparability regarding potential conceptualizations of organizational integration and other relevant concepts must necessarily be impaired. Adhering to Karl Weick, post-merger organizational integration is about somehow forming one "body of thoughts" out of at least two. According to Niklas Luhmann, communications between two systems might become related to each other, while Lynne Zucker would probably urge us to conceptually focus on (de)institutionalization processes and outcomes. Even if a consensus regarding epistemological and methodological aspects, let's say, *sensu* Popper, was reached, theories could, for the most part, still be evaluated only against the background of their own (implicit) ontological frame of reference.

The comparability of basic constructs and empirical results attained is highly relevant, not only to organization theories and the social sciences they mostly belong to, but to all factual sciences. For instance, the question of *what information is* and how the concept may be used to construct theories in a reasonable manner is, in the end, pertinent to psychology, computer science, engineering, and organization theory as well. The ontology and epistemology of theories are meta-theoretical characteristics; they are aspects of a logically prior philosophy of science that a particular theory addresses (Bunge, 1996: 6). The various factual science disciplines should be in contact with each other via meta-theory and can be assessed in terms of the criteria derived from it. In turn, different philosophies of science are in competition themselves: they may, amongst other criteria, be evaluated and discarded regarding their general potential to guide the improvement of hands-on factual science, their *fertility*, *exactifiability* and their *originality* (*Ibid*.: 11). From this perspective, specific fields of study should be in permanent dialogue with the philosophy of sciences; seeking scientific quality should be based on reciprocity.

To unfold the explanatory potential of RDT regarding post-merger integration, its definitional basis is thus of particular importance. In order to develop organizational integration as our dependent variable and clarify a plausible multilevel causal mechanism, in the following we will supplement RDT with a *materialist ontology* that was established by the physicist and science philosopher Mario Bunge (1979a; b; 1981; 1996; 1998; 2004). His delineation of *emergentist (or scientific) materialism* will provide us with what is desperately missing in many organization theories, let alone the field of M&A research: a comprehensive and consistent terminology for describing and examining complex (social) systems. Besides referring to numerous meta-theoretical controversies concerning several disciplines, Bunge (1996; 1998) has been pronouncedly devoted to the dominant philosophical cleavages in the social sciences and economics in his work. However, though typical research subjects like schools or supermarket chains are often directly addressed, Bunge's ontology by itself is not an organization theory and shouldn't be mistaken as such. It has little to say about specific variables, causal mechanisms, or how certain types of organizations are actually to be classified. Emergentist materialism is the ontological doctrine of a broader philosophy of science that is able to guide the development and refinement of specific theories. The basic terminology and categories of emergentist materialism are introduced in 3.1.1; its application on HEIs is demonstrated in 3.1.2. The overriding philosophy (*systemism*) is touched upon in 3.1.3 and contrasted with the main opposing basic meta-theoretical approaches.

3.1.1 Emergentist materialism: basic terminology and categories

The main postulate of *scientific (or emergentist) materialism* says: "An object is real (or exists really) if, and only if, it is material" (Bunge, 1981: 23). To be real thus equals being material and "Reality is the set of real objects" (*Ibid.*). Concrete material things may, but don't have to, be perceptible, locatable or have to display a physical shape to be qualified as "material". Perceptibility may, for instance, be given regarding a group of seminar participants or a copier in a library. A university, like many social systems, can neither be observed as a whole, nor is its boundary to be identified easily. Real things have to be distinguished from *immaterial* or *abstract* objects. These are, for example, constructs, myths, numbers, or ideas (Bunge & Mahner, 2004: 21). The main categorizing criterion is their *changeability*. Real things are in a permanent state of flux: the seminar group dissolves at the end of the term; new professors join the university; institutes are founded and closed; the copy machine is used up physically. Immaterial things, in contrast, are generally *unchangeable*: "only the brains that think them are subject to change" (Bunge, 1996: 17). Objects are either change able or unchangeable; being material or immaterial are mutually exclusive categories.

Real things can never be devoid of *properties*; Bunge discerns various kinds of them:

- *Intrinsic vs. relational*: the first are properties "that a thing possesses regardless of other things, even if acquired under the action of other things" (*Ibid.*)—for instance, the number of seats in a lecture hall or the skills of a laboratory assistant. Relational properties can only be possessed in relation to another thing: being a student or a chair-holder is only defined in relation to a specified HEI;
- *Essential vs. accidental*: Essential properties determine the *quiddity* (essence) of a thing (Bunge & Mahner, 2004: 24)—e.g. that a HEI provides advanced learning opportunities to the population is central to its quiddity. If a university started to produce car tires instead of providing education and research, it would change its essential character. Accidental properties, in contrast, do not influence what a thing is. Examples might be the average age of lecturers or the arrangement of buildings on the campus;
- *General vs. individual*: All HEIs have a student population and provide study programs—these are therefore general properties. Accordingly, any individual HEI has an overall individual student count and an individual study program profile (Bunge, 1996: 19).

In the factual sciences, real properties have to be distinguished from their conceptual representations, called *predicates*. The latter neither have to be congruent with real properties, nor do all real properties have to be represented conceptually (*Ibid*.: 18).

A property type of special salience are *laws*: "A law is a stable pattern that holds independently of human knowledge or will: it inheres things" (Bunge, 1996: 27). The behavior of things becomes lawful, in that some of their properties are systematically related to each other; laws are relational properties of properties, and hence indirect (essential) properties of things. The postulate that *there are no unlawful essential properties* is central to scientific materialism. According to Bunge and Mahner (2004: 42), as an ontological principle it is the fundament of all factual sciences, technology and knowledge generation.

The collectivity of all the properties of a thing at a certain point in time defines its *state* (Bunge & Mahner, 2004: 57). The state of a concrete thing cannot be arbitrary; it depends on its past and has to be in accordance with the lawful relations between its essential properties. The ordered set of all its states constitutes the *history* of a thing. A change in state is an *event*; a sequence of events is a *process*. Concrete things are defined by their changeability; changes in material things constitute time. In social systems (complex things, see next section), components are mainly connected through *activities* that affect them (Bunge, 1981: 120), like communicating, exchanging or competing. Relevant processes in social systems are typically series of state-changing activities. The definition of a process as a sequence of states can also refer to *classes of processes*, which most factual sciences refer to (Bunge & Mahner, 2004: 57). The term *organizational merger*, for instance, refers to a subclass of organizational change processes that embrace at least two complex things (organizations).

The benefit of an explicit and systematic ontology as a fundament of theorizing thus becomes apparent. As regards the ontological assumptions of theories, we do not have to resign ourselves to a *relativist* solution to the incommensurability debate, which is, for instance, reflected in the following statement by organization sociologist Richard Scott:

> Definitions are neither true nor false but are more or less helpful in calling attention to certain aspects of the phenomena under study (Scott, 2003: 30).

The scientific–philosophical position represented in this assertion gently seeks to abandon the search for truth as the superior lodestar of factual science in favor of some helpfulness criteria. The corresponding rationale, which has become a silent and all too convenient consensus in vast parts of the field, may be sketched like this: organizations as a research subject are so amazingly complex, colorful and multifaceted that any search for a unified paradigm has to end up in an inadequate oversimplification. Since ultimate decision criteria are deemed inaccessible *on principle* (e.g. Scherer, 1998: 156), the choice and definition of relevant aspects is in the eye of the beholder (*anything goes*) or of the beholding scientific community (*isolationism*; Burrell & Morgan, 1979; Morgan, 1980; 2006). According to a strict postmodern interpretation of this "solution", there are so many perspectives or even "alternative realities" (Morgan, 1980: 607), one should take leave of the very idea of science: "Through language, science, art, and myth, for example, humans structure their world in meaningful ways" (*Ibid.*: 610). As mentioned above, all definition attempts are, corresponding to the relativist perspective, equally justified, as long as they are considered conducive to completeness and plurality by some.

An explicit ontology can, by contrast, serve as a guiding framework to overcome such a dissatisfactory mode of theorizing. If one considers again some of the definitions stated above, it becomes clear that they are not equally consistent with Bunge's ontology:

- Definitions one and two are at variance with scientific materialism. According to the phenomenological approach of Weick (1979), definitional priority is on "thoughts": the existence of organizations as concrete (material) social systems is thus either denied, or thoughts are identified with reality—either of which is false. Luhmann (2000) maintains organizations consist exclusively of communicative acts. However, the latter represent one type of relation in social systems; being related is a property of things and properties have no existence on their own (Bunge, 1996: 59);
- Just like definition two, number three (Barnard, 1938) and seven (Pfeffer & Salancik, 1978) imply *process metaphysics* that claims the logical priority of processes over things (Bunge & Mahner, 2004: 61). Activities in organizations relate (interstructure) their components and cannot themselves be related. Approaches that consider organizations to *be* processes are frequent in organization theory (Emirbayer, 1997; van de Ven & Poole, 2005);
- Definition 4, from March and Simon (1958) is thoroughly consistent with Bunge's materialist ontology;
- Definition 8 is close to March and Simon (1958), yet imprecise, for Salancik (1984), in line with general systems theory, identifies organiza-

tion as a "set of parties". Sets are, however, abstract objects and cannot constitute concrete systems (Bunge, 1996: 21).

Even though Scott is right in that a definition is not a falsifiable statement, it can prove to be consistent or inconsistent with the ontology of a certain philosophy of science. Consequently, the discretion in selecting and combining definitional concepts is fairly limited. This is exactly the guiding function for developing and refining specific theories—we will make use of it in deriving a concept of organizational integration from RDT. Following Bunge, there are no insuperable problems of paradigm incommensurability: proponents of approaches being at variance with scientific materialism should make their meta-theoretical frame of reference transparent, and join the philosophical debate.

3.1.2 Higher education institutions as systems

We have hitherto more or less implicitly treated HEIs as composed entities. To organization studies, as to most factual sciences, the focus of inquiry is on such complex things—(social) systems. They are constituted by relations between their components, and are distinguished from internally and externally unrelated entities, the so-called aggregates (Bunge & Mahner, 2004: 70).

For instance, a university as a system consists of and is interconnected with a multitude of other systems on different analytical levels. There are diverse departments, institutes, and professorship chairs. We will find administration units, laboratories, and cafeterias. The campus library may be divided into different sections, each being equipped with service teams, storage magazines, and interconnected workstations. One could add a number of more temporary systems, like student learning groups or conference meetings. Any university is itself a subsystem of a number of superordinate systems: research associations, institutional federations, or the system of higher education of the regional municipality it belongs to.

The analysis of systems, that is: objects (*relata*), the relations between them and the properties / effects emerging therefrom, is at the heart of *systemism* as a fundamental research approach (see 3.1.3). Accordingly, a vital assumption of scientific (or emergentist) materialism, its corresponding ontology, is that there are no isolated objects: every object is a system itself or a component of a system. With the exception of the universe itself, every system is a subsystem of another system (Bunge & Mahner, 2004: 71).

Systems are distinguished from aggregates by the way they come into being. System components are precisely not aggregated, but cohesively combined. The members of a faculty council, to take a case in point, are bindingly related during a meeting through communication and voting procedures. In contrast, a student crowd at a campus bus stop is not bindingly related; it grows through aggregation and tends to dissolve spontaneously.

Of outstanding significance, since they are defining ones, are those properties that develop in systems exclusively because they are systems:

> A system is a complex object every part or component of which is connected with other parts of the same object in such a manner that the whole possesses some features that its components lack (Bunge, 1996: 20).

Such features are designated *emergent*; a materialist ontology that emphasizes emergent features is labeled *emergentist materialism*[13] (Bunge, 1996: 303). The formation process (i.e. sequence of events) of emergent properties is called *emergence*. Those features that an entity gains because it already belongs to one of its parts are, in contrast, labeled *resultant* properties (Bunge & Mahner, 2004: 79). Emergence refers to the development of *qualitative* as opposed to *quantitative* newness:

> P is an emergent property of a thing b if b and only if either b is a system no component of which possesses P, or b is an individual that possesses P by virtue of being a component of a system (Bunge, 1996: 20).

Organizations' emerging ability to produce certain sorts of goods and services or to solve some specific societal problem is typical of them as complex social systems. A department of chemistry in a university, for example, has the ability to provide a versatile and complete master's program in chemistry. None of its numerous subsystems (components), like research teams or professorships could do this alone. If the department intensified its cooperation with, let's say, the biology and engineering departments, the three could form a new subsystem within the university. As a qualitative new property, the ability to launch research projects in bioengineering could emerge. In the wake of becoming part of such a new project, a professor of biology within the university would hence gain the emergent property of being a bioengineering scholar. If the cooperation collapsed for whatever reason, that property would submerge (Bunge & Mahner, 2004: 80).

---

13 Bunge uses the labels *scientific* and *emergentist* synonymously.

At this point, the conceptual proximity to the term *synergies* in the M&A context becomes clear. Synergies are properties that are sought to emerge from integrating at least two organizations (social systems) into one. They relate to enhanced value creation or, more generally, problem-solving by integrating at least two social systems into one. To speak of a new organization in the long run, these properties per definition have to be qualitatively new, rather than just result from the sum of parts.

To comprehend their fundamental aspects, Bunge introduces the (C)omposition (E)nvironment (S)tructure (M)echanism (CESM) model of concrete systems (Bunge, 1996: 270ff.; Bunge & Mahner, 2004: 72ff.):

- The *composition* of a system *C(s)* is the set of all things (along with their properties) it consists of. A university is a social system composed of individuals, artifacts and numerous subsystems that comprise both. For instance, the members of its senate (things) and their professional or political background (subsets of properties) are part of the composition of an organization;
- A system's *environment E(s)* consists of all things that may interact with a focal system or may be acted upon by the latter, but are themselves not components of the focal system. We will examine the system environment and boundary conception in the context of HEIs more closely in Subsection 3.2.3;
- The overall system *structure S(s)* comprises all relations concerning a focal system (and its components). Bunge differentiates between two mutually disjointed subsets, (scientifically relevant) *binding* (i.e. affecting, and therefore system-constituting) and *nonbinding* relations. Furthermore, the internal relations in their entirety, which form the system's *endostructure*, are distinguished from its *exostructure*;
- *Mechanisms M(s)* as a further dynamic aspect of systems are greater processes that characterize certain (sub)classes of systems. HEIs as organizations display three partially intertwined mechanisms: *education*, *research / transfer* and, as a supplementary mechanism, *administration*.

As systems are complex material things and as such are permanently in flux, the resulting general model

$$m(s) = \langle C(s), E(s), S(s), M(s) \rangle$$

has to be specified in relation to a certain point in time. In addition, any specific CESM model refers to a distinct system level; Bunge and Mahner (2004: 85) distinguish between the physical, chemical, biological and social levels. HEIs, as complex systems on the social level, can again be divided into several sublevels (see Subsection 3.2.2).

3.1.3 Systemism as a worldview, scientific orientation and research strategy

Up to this point, we have discussed emergentist (or scientific) materialism as an aid to orientation regarding the ontological assumptions of theories. Inasmuch as it helps to clarify the general status and relations of concepts, it can guide the development of system-specific theories as well as their layout regarding particular research problems. Emergentist materialism is the *ontological doctrine* of *systemism* as a fundamental scientific approach (philosophy of science). The corresponding *epistemology*, which (like its moral aspects) for the sake of brevity is not explicated here, is labeled *ratio-empiricism* or *scientific realism*. Bunge (2000: 149) describes the systemic philosophy as a comprehensive worldview, a way to approach reality. Blending facets of its epistemological (3–5) and ontological doctrine (1, 2), Bunge derives five central postulates of systemism (*Ibid.*):

1. Everything, whether concrete or abstract, is a system or an actual or potential component of a system;
2. systems have systemic (emergent) features that their components lack, whence
3. all problems should be approached in a systemic rather than in a sectoral fashion;
4. all ideas should be put together into systems (theories); and
5. the testing of anything, whether idea or artifact, assumes the validity of other items, which are taken as benchmarks, at least for the time being.

As a socio-scientific research approach, systemism is thus in explicit opposition to two competing extreme (reductionist) positions, which are widespread in the social sciences as well as in economics. They are both focused on different parts of the CESM model and therefore, each in its own way, are incompatible with the world's systemic nature:

According to *individualism* (micro-reductionism), the individual is deemed the one and only nucleus of social phenomena and their inquiry. It focuses on the micro-level components of social systems, neglects the internal and external relations between them, and therefore misconceives of social phenomena as mere aggregates of individual action. Bunge (1996: 244ff.) explicates the *ontological* and *epistemological / methodological* doctrine of individualism. Ontologically, societies are handled as collections of isolated individuals (*atomism*). Social systems appear as mere fictions (i.e. immaterial objects), they cannot change, interact with each other or (re)act as units toward (to) individuals. Epistemologically, the study of individual actions, which is frequently accompanied by rigid assumptions, is the only legitimate aim of and background to testing hypotheses (*Ibid.*). Max Weber, James Coleman (e.g. 1986), Karl Popper and Jon Elster have been important philosophical proponents. Since methodological (and often ontological) individualism is predominant in economics, it is mainly represented by descending *rational-choice institutionalism* in organization theory. Scherer (2003: 332) has convincingly shown that agency theory (Jensen & Meckling, 1976), property rights (Demsetz, 1967; Furobotn & Pejovich, 1974) and transaction cost theory (Williamson, 1975; 1985; 1991) all boil down to a rational choice argument. As laid out by Reed (2003: 292ff.), influential parts of decision-making theory, especially the work of March and Simon (1958), likewise represent a definite case of individualism.

Holism (macro-reductionism), as the scientific–philosophical counterpart of individualism concentrates exclusively on the structure of systems, while largely denying its components (Bunge, 2000). It thoroughly disregards the role of agency in explaining social phenomena, which accordingly can only be analyzed as wholes: "structure is regarded as an independent, *sui generis* entity" (Reed, 2003: 294, emphasis in original). The ontological doctrine associated with holism understands society as a total whole that displays global emergent properties, and as a whole largely determines individual behavior (Bunge, 1996: 260). With regard to the corresponding epistemology / methodology, social inquiry therefore has to consider social wholes, supra-individual units have to be the center of explanations, and macro-level data is to be preferred. In organization studies, theoretical developments adhering to the holistic approach have been manifold. Chester Barnard (1938: 77) left no doubt regarding his devotion to holism. Proponents of the 1950s / 1960s general systems theory[14] (Hall & Fagen, 1956; Boulding, 1956; Katz & Kahn, 1966), which played a central role in the development of the open systems perspective in organization

---

14 Proponents of the "Bertalanffy-program" (general systems theory) were holist in orientation: systems were conceptualized as differential equations, a change in any variable was deemed to change the whole system; see Müller (1996: 205ff.) for a detailed discussion.

theory, were also holist in orientation. The same holds for functionalist system theory *sensu* Luhmann (2000), as well as for the black box rationalist contingency theory (see Scherer, 2003: 327) and population ecology (Hannan & Freeman, 1977; McKelvey, 1978). Neo-institutionalism, since it has largely been built on *social constructivism* (Berger & Luckmann, 1967) and *phenomenology* (Alfred Schütz / Edmund Husserl) is prone to being identified with providing a holist version of subjectivism (Bunge, 1998: 228). As we will discuss in Chapter 6, theories of organizational culture and identity may be deemed macro-reductionist for the same reason.

Within the meta-theoretical discourse particularly concerned with organization theories, systemism has rarely been directly referred to but is close to *critical realism* (Ackroyd & Fleetwood, 2000; Reed, 2005; 2009). Specific theories that are consistent with the systemic approach, as laid out by Bunge, are further to be found amongst the voluntarist critics of structural determinism, who are subsumed under the strategic choice perspective by Astley and van de Ven (1983) (e.g. Child, 1972; Crozier & Friedberg, 1980). Because of its coalitional multilevel perspective and its rejection of causal unidirectionality / determinism, RDT can equally be considered to be largely consistent with systemism.

3.2 *A systemist perspective on higher education institutions as integrated and distinct social systems*

Describing organizations as complex social systems against the background of Bunge's materialist ontology immediately calls for complementing such a description with an appropriate specific theory. In 3.1.2, we approached HEIs in a general way and hinted at their composition, structure and mechanisms. Since meta-theory, however, "does not dispute the turf of the social scientist" (Bunge, 1996: 6), it is our task to point out these ontological categories in terms of the particular social facts under consideration. As they are of notable significance for the integration variable, our priority will be on the specific relations between the system-constituting components of HEIs. Being *integrated* as a system implies being *discernable* from other things: a system that cannot be distinguished from the environment it interacts with is not a system (except for the universe). In the following, the character of these specific relations, together with the criterion for being integrated / distinct, will be clarified against the background of RDT as our specific organization theory.

3.2.1 HEIs as open allocation systems: from transformation to power

Systems are generally constituted by binding relations (links) or connections between their components (-to-be):

> A link between two things relates them in a way that affects them. Attractive and repulsive bonds, cooperative and competitive relationships, and relationships of social exchange, whether cohesive or disruptive are all links or binding relations (Bunge, 1992: 216).

As regards organizations as social systems, in 3.1.1 we asserted that these links are activities that *affect* the system components (Bunge, 1981: 120), where *to affect* means: altering the state (collectivity of properties) of the related objects. Processes in organizations are consequently series of state-changing activities. To resolve what these activities are about, it is helpful to consider the superordinate mechanism that characterizes system class. Pursuant to the open systems perspective in organization theory, the only one that conforms to systemism, that mechanism is *resource transformation*. Organizations absorb input resources from their environment and internally transform them into output resources. HEIs represent a subclass of organizations; their typical transformation mechanisms are *education*, *research*, and (supportive) *administration*. From a legal perspective (Chapter 1), a further main transformational aim of state-funded HEIs in Germany is the provision of a material basis to enable the protection of basic civil rights. Numerous subprocesses over several levels could be descended from the mechanisms of education, research, and administration: study program planning, lecture preparation, proposal writing, book ordering and many more.

Transforming resources, and this is true for all organizations, means permanently assigning scarce resources to alternative use possibilities—*allotting* them. In universities, laboratory facilities are assigned to research teams, study programs to steering commissions and examinees to chairs. The dean's office may assign a third student assistant to the faculty manager; staff and cleaning agents are needed to prepare a filter system. Input resources of HEIs run through complex series of allocations that are transformative in character, i.e. the things involved change their properties. Typical output resources of HEIs are advisory opinions, certificates, publications, and patents. Being a *resource* ontologically is a relational property of a thing, a property that it possesses relative to other things. A resource has an exchange value within an exchange relation.

To take a case in point, one might look at a list of exam grades. The list contains information that exists as a configuration of some memory medium (sheets of paper or a data file). It is the result of a sub-allocation process called "exam correction". Many different system components have been involved in its production process; staff and office materials have been deployed. As it has an exchange value in the relation between the subsystems that carry the correction process and the administration unit, the list is a resource. By receiving it, the administration unit changes its status—it gains the property of controlling (or being an owner) of the grade list. HEIs can thus be described as allocation systems. The fact that some of their components are sometimes functionally related to each other in transformation is the *first system-constituting moment*.

The system-specific links or binding relations between organizational components are hence activities, specifically: allocative acts to sustain resource transformation. As resources are allotted, patterns of interaction and dependence develop between the functionally related exchange parties. To stick to our example: the administration unit needs the grade list and cannot generate it autonomously. It is an input to further transformation processes like issuing certificates and documents, or student admission procedures. Functional relations between participants in organizations occur as *exchange relations*: if the list is not transmitted in due time, the respective administration unit will start exerting pressure to avoid being pressed itself. Functional relatedness leads to exchange dependencies, which, due to process-related asymmetries, are just one important source of power relations (Astley & Zajac, 1991: 399; Pfeffer & Salancik, 1978: 27; Hickson et al., 1971).

The power concept comprehended by RDT can thus serve to specify the general system model in more detail. Components of HEIs do not behave randomly; they are systematically—lawfully—related to each other. Laws are essential properties of things and lead to analyzable (may they be manifest or imperceptible) activity patterns (Bunge, 1996: 27). Since the binding relations in organizations have been identified as exchange relations, and HEIs are a subclass of organizations, the relevant laws needed to conceptualize the essence of these patterns are basically represented by the nomological hypotheses regarding power-dependence relations, as laid out by Richard Emerson (1962). They accordingly complement the materialist ontology depicted, as famously put by Bertrand Russell ([1938] 2004: 4): "the fundamental concept in social science is Power, in the same sense in which Energy is the fundamental concept in physics".

3.2.2 HEIs as integrated social systems: from power to control (and back)

To identify a proper integration / distinction criterion, it is not enough to focus solely on functional relatedness / resource transformation and the corresponding systemic power relations between potential components of organizations. Consider a research project assistant who negotiates the properties of a software package with an IT supplier. Since shaping and selecting an adequate software solution is necessary for the project, it is a form of allocation to sustain resource transformation. Why are we right to consider the software supplier to be located in the environment of the research project and of the university, of which the project is a temporal subsystem? What criterion distinguishes the software supplier from the research assistant and allows us to classify the latter as a component of the university?

The answer lies in the organizational *regulation* of resource transforming allocations and their inherent power relations. Most relevant activities in organizations are regulated by *allocation rules*; individual and collective discretion regarding the allocation of resources is thereby constrained and enabled respectively. There are, for instance, rules that concern the exam correction process: sample solution templates have to be used; the proceeding has to be conducted comprehensibly for students; deadlines and storage standards have to be met. Employment procedures are another case in point: job advertisement channels and information requirements are specified; there are rules for assessment procedures and model contracts. One will find distribution keys for institute budgets, sabbatical term intervals for professors, senate majority rules, opening hours for buildings, and library access guidelines for visiting scholars. Many of these allocation rules are codified, many are not. An off-the-record institute-level allocation rule might, for instance, say that project-assistant employment contracts should not exceed a 75% part-time level, while an officially codified rule may direct the regular extension of employment contracts due to parental leave periods.

Allocation, together with the rules that regulate it, determines what will be labeled in the following as the *configuration* of the HEI: those elements (subsets) of the CESM model which can be influenced by the *political system* of the focal organization explicated below. This refers to the system's components, its binding endostructure, the influenceable parts of the binding exostructure as well as its processes and mechanisms. A focal HEI can, for example, control the qualification profile of professors, the number of facility managers, the location of supportive workshops on the campus, study program characterization / interconnectedness, or the extent of student services to a certain degree. Considerable parts of the CESM model are not at its discretion, since they are under the direct control of external actors (e.g. state law). In public HEIs in Germany, this would, for example, apply to the permission to smoke in buildings, the complete substitution of on-campus lectures through e-learning, the replacement of deans through faculty managers with extensive veto-rights, or the introduction of student exam fees to relieve the budget.

The production of allocation rules, ergo the right to regulate (constrain and / or enable) transformative allocation (allocation responsibilities) and shape the configuration, is not far-flung or randomly dispersed all over the system. Neither power nor the rights to constrain it are free-floating in organizations. There are system components, some of them individuals (professors), most of them subsystems, which play an important role in this respect; their collectivity is the *political system* of a focal HEI. This is the *second and decisive system-constituting moment*: organizations are constituted by a discretion-reducing shift of allocation responsibilities. System levels in HEIs are established by the transfer of resource control to the relevant political subsystem: we speak of the chair because of the professor; of an institute instead of an aggregate of chairs because of the respective directorship and board; of a department because of its council and the corresponding deanery. In German HEIs, the central level is constituted by the rectorship (*Rektorat / Präsidium*), the academic senate, and a university council (*Hochschulrat*). The formal, codified political system commonly comprises a large number of further subsystems on all levels, like steering committees, chambers, or study program heads. Besides the formal ones, a number of informal political subsystems usually develop: consider regular meetings of department deans or of professors (German: *Professorium*) within the same department. Herein lies the conceptual basis of our dependent variable: organizations as resource transforming allocation systems are *integrated* by discretion-reducing shifts of allocation responsibilities.

The subsystems of the political system are the stages where coalition formation takes place. According to Cyert and March (1963: 27), coalitions are negotiated orders of individuals or subgroups, based on resource exchanges between them. These orders partly arise out of the system reproducing transformative allocation patterns and their inherent power relations. Consequentially, the source of those allocation rules that are within the discretion of a focal organization is not the political system *in itself* but the *dominant coalition*[15] that forms within the latter. It thereby becomes clear that the status of being a component of a political subsystem is not necessarily accompanied with being in control. Consistent with the SCT / RDT framework, those components that create the most asymmetric resource dependencies theoretically gain the ability to influence the allocation rules that regulate their own activities (and the activities of the powerless components).

Consider for illustration purposes the regulation of a (bothersome) routine activity at the end of each term: written student exam supervision. In most German universities, this is commonly the sole obligation of non-professorial staff; professors are not involved and are therefore relieved of this duty as a group. However, that allocation rule could well be subject to organizational shaping within the relevant political subsystem; there is no legal restriction—exam supervision should (in most cases) just be conducted by teaching staff, which includes professors. Still, a change of the rules could never be implemented. Professors as a group are, in this respect, the dominant coalition within every (faculty) council; they are thus able to maintain an allocation rule that relieves (enables) professors and constrains the non-professorial teaching staff.

Building on RDT as the system-specific explanation, we have hence arrived at the theoretical fundament of one of the central hypotheses promoted here (see 3.4.). Organizational integration is generally oriented toward the (most) powerful coalition(s). The term *orientation* comprises two aspects: firstly, and this should be particularly apparent in merger situations, the discretion-reducing shift should move away from the units who have few resources at their disposal and toward those who control important and hard-to substitute resources. Bluntly put, weak system components tend to be (or to come) under the control of strong system components. Secondly, the allocation rules regarding their content, and thus the configuration of the system, mainly follow the interests of the powerful coalitions: "By power, we mean the ability of a subunit to influence organizational decisions in ways that produce outcomes favored by the subunit" (Pfeffer & Salancik, 1978: 230). Resource control is thus closely connected to political control, and political control, as laid out in 2.2.2, can in turn be a means to enhance resource control.

15 For a discussion of the coalition concept see Stevenson et al. (1985). The concept as used here is largely in line with Thompson (1967).

3.2.3 HEIs as distinct social systems (interior, exterior, boundaries)

At this point, our conceptual notion of organizational integration has become considerably more specific. HEIs have been introduced as allocation systems, which transform resources through education, research, and administration. It is justifiable to regard them as integrated, since their components are linked through *functional and power-exchange relationships* on the one hand, and *shifts of allocation responsibilities into a political system* on the other. Following RDT and its inherent coalitional perspective as the system-specific theory, the control of the system's configuration rests with the powerful coalitions. To add some precision and further elaborate the integration criterion, we will now turn to the other side of the coin: differentiating a focal HEI from its environment. As system *integration* implies system *distinctness*—the very idea of merging refers to the integration of two or more formerly distinct and therefore separate organizations into a single one—both necessarily have to apply to the same criterion. A theory that in principle cannot provide such a criterion can hardly be regarded as a truc organization thcory.

Pfeffer and Salancik (1978: 37) conceptualized the interior, exterior, and boundaries of a focal organization as follows:

> The organization's boundary, then, can be defined in terms of its influence over activities compared to the influence of other social actors over the same activities of the same participants. When the focal organization's influence is greatest, we can say that those activities are included within its boundaries.

Relevant activities in HEIs relate to the allocation of resources to sustain transformation. Hence, the actual binding of an object to a focal system (or its detachment), besides the necessary functional relatedness, depends on the magnitude of control that is accrued by the system-(level)-constituting political system. Every time, a person performs a transformation-relevant activity (implying functional relatedness) and the relevant discretion is regulated for the most part through the focal organization`s political system, that person is a system component; she is integrated and therefore an element of $C(s)$. Accordingly, any person who is functionally related to the focal organization and the lion's share of discretion regulation rests with another (external) actor or allocation system, then she is outside the system, an element of the organization's environment $E(s)$.

Consider the example of an exchange relation between a university professor and a research-funding agency. The scholar transforms the funds into research results, publications, or patents. Obviously, the smaller the magnitude of allocation rules set by the external actor, the more her control over the funds rises. If the agency's position was: "We just like you and your research. Please do some for us. What do you think might interest us in particular?", the scholar's discretion would be high. In fact, the right to control the funds would come with a huge number of allocation rules, which would be negotiated in a power-dependence relation. The agency wants a detailed and meaningful proposal, hypothesis, project milestones, a list of equipment / staff needed, expected results, regular reports and much more. If the larger part of potential resource discretion is regulated through the funding agency board, e.g. through content-related specifications, the professor (maybe illegally) becomes a component *C(s)* of the allocation system *funding agency*.

As already pointed out at the outset of Section 3.3, it is important in this regard to recognize that the character of HEIs as material (real), integrated and distinctive objects does not hinge on them being locatable or possessing a physical shape. The aforementioned project assistant who negotiates the software solution, irrespective of his spatial position, is a system component as he is functionally related to his research project, and the allocation rules (budget level, software requirements, what have you) will have been set by the political subsystem responsible (e.g. project board). A second relevant question that has puzzled students of organizations refers to the issue of the diachronic identity of organizations (e.g. Barnard, 1938: 71f.; Scott, 2003: 146f.). Organizations rather "flicker" instead of displaying spatiotemporal stability: the CESM model always has to be specified in terms of a certain point in time (Bunge & Mahner, 2004: 77). At the very moment our assistant works for the project and his activities are regulated by the relevant political subsystem, he is a component of the system. During his leisure time, he ceases to be a component, until he (soon after) takes up work again.

With explicit reference to organizations, yet without a system-specific theory, Bunge (1992: 216ff.) has suggested a general definition of system boundaries (based on general topology) which is worth looking at.

It starts with the basic set union of all system components and environmental elements,

(1) $X = C(s) \cup E(s)$

which initially comprises all binding and nonbinding relations between a focal system and its environment. Subsequently, the neighborhood of a thing p in X is defined as a subset of things q in X

(2) $N_p = \{q \in X | (\exists q)Lpq\}$

where L designates relations that are a) *binding*, in case of organizations: functional and power-exchange-related and b) *direct*, i.e. not mediated by any other object. The system boundary between focal system and corresponding environment at a *certain point in time* is defined as follows:

(3)

Definition (Bunge, 1992: 217)	Specification / Comment
i. p is exterior to s *iff* p is not in $C(s)$	This is to say that, during the performance of an allocative act, *p's* discretion is for the most part *not* regulated through the focal political allocation-subsystem, that is, set by its dominant coalition.
ii. p is a boundary component of s *iff*; every neighborhood of p in X contains at least one component of s and at least one component of $E(s)$	Less stringent formulation: the boundary of a system is the subset of its components that are included in its exostructure (Bunge & Mahner, 2004: 77).
iii. the boundary is the set of $\partial C(s)$ of all the boundary components of s	Being an element of $C(s)$ is a necessary condition for being a boundary component.

Complex systems like organizations exhibit different kinds of environmental links L; the analytical focus according to RDT is on transformative resource allocation and exchange links. In line with Bunge (1992: 218), different neighborhoods and boundaries exist for every kind of link. For a department in a university, one could, for instance, distinguish between a *student neighborhood* and accordingly a *student boundary*, a *funding-agency neighborhood* and *funding-agency boundary*, and many more.

The overall boundary of a system (for a certain kind of link, resource-exchange links in our case) is thus captured as the set union of all boundary components:

$$(4)\ \partial C(s) = \bigcup_{i=1}^{n} \partial_i C(s)$$

with the subscript indicating the different neighborhoods and boundaries. From this, Bunge defined the *interior* of a system:

$$(5)\ Int[C(s)] = C(s) - \partial C(s).$$

An example of typical interior components of a university can be found in the many student assistants who are not directly linked to any element of *E(s)*. The criterion according to (2) is that any allocative act they perform is mediated by another system component (professor or staff)—there is commonly no direct (functional) contact with students, equipment suppliers or visitors. Accordingly, the overall environment *E(s)* of a system is captured as the sum of the neighborhoods of its components (Bunge, 1992: 218).

Empirically determining the status of things relative to a focal system nonetheless always remains a difficult task. Consider, for example, students attending a university lecture. They can decide on their own when to enter the room and when to leave it. Some loosely binding exchange relation exists: without student participation and cooperation the success of the lecture may be at stake. Students can decide to what extent they partake in a group discussion (allocate themselves). They may also check their emails or take a nap instead. Lecturers have to offer resources to raise the audience's interest and make it contribute. In a lecture situation, students occur pretty much as external actors.

Student status changes in a written exam situation. As with the group discussion during lectures, they are bindingly linked with the allocation system, contributing their resources to a transformative allocation subprocess of *education*, labeled *examination*. However, for the time being, they have to surrender almost any control over their activities. No more loose coupling. Candidates are told when to be at what location, from which side they have to enter the hall, how to leave it and where to sit in the meantime. During the examination, they are not allowed to speak or go to the lavatory without special permission. Supervisory staff may search personal belongings like books or pencil cases. In brief, students find themselves in a situation of tight control, which in open societies is normally associated with other types of organizations, like prisons or hospitals. Allocation activities during examinations are regulated through at least two of the university's political allocation subsystems. The chair / professor responsible has decided on the exam's properties as regards the content of tasks and difficulty. The examination's ancillary regulations have been agreed on by the respective faculty council. As granting certificates in Germany is a sovereign state responsibility, the council itself is comprehensively constrained by state ministry guidelines on the shape of such regulations. Control over student activities is hence shared between a university and the state ministry. Presuming that the most part is regulated through the political system of the university, the student is an element of its composition *C(s)* during examinations.

3.3 *General (dis)integration dynamics in the context of interdependence pattern management*

Organizational integration as our dependent variable (together with some basic propositions on its character) has been derived by fleshing out RDT with Bunge's emergentist materialism. Consequently, we will build on this fruitful synthesis to set up our analysis of organizational integration following mergers. On our way to a merger-specific explanation (3.4.1) and some hypotheses (3.4.2), we will proceed by explicating the concept of (post-merger) organizational (dis)integration (3.3.1) before elucidating its general connection to organizational resource interdependencies (3.3.2).

3.3.1 The dependent variable: organizational integration defined

We have characterized HEIs as integrated and distinct social transformation and allocation systems. Two system-constituting moments have been identified. Firstly, some components of HEIs are sometimes functionally related in transforming organizational input-resources into output-resources. As transforming scarce resources in series of activities permanently means allotting resources to alternative uses, organizations (HEIs) are resource transforming allocation systems. Secondly, they are distinct and integrated systems: the allocative discretion of its many components is reduced by a concentrating (integrating) shift of allocation responsibilities toward the appertaining political subsystem. This is due to resource control related asymmetries following from exchange dynamics, their system-stabilizing control, as well as to the self-perpetuating institutionalization of power. In conclusion, the external environment, boundaries, and interior of HEIs as distinct systems have been specified by us drawing on the relative magnitude of discretionary control of a focal organization's political system over transformative allocative activities.

Organizational integration refers to the act of shifting control to other system components and thereby mostly concentrating it within the (emerging) organization. Political allocation subsystems are therefore reduced, either in absolute numbers and / or as regards the scope of control responsibilities (the relative magnitude of controlled resources). Accordingly, *disintegration* by contrast means increasing the allocation discretion of subunits by reducing the responsibilities of the superordinate political allocation subsystems; control is dispersed over the system.

Two basic types of integration have to be distinguished:

First-order integration (*across-direct*), as against *second-order* (*within-indirect*) integration, refers to directly relating the constituting political (sub)systems of two allocation systems to each other. *Allocation responsibilities* of at least one unit—the potential to execute, enable or restrict allocative behavior—are completely or partially shifted away from the existing (sub)systems toward other existing or newly installed political allocation (sub)systems. This usually portends across-system (merging party) concentration of control. Shifting may thereby occur

- either *horizontally* on the same subsystem level: e.g. from one faculty council to another;
- or *vertically*, toward a higher system level, equaling organizational *centralization*: e.g. from chair-level toward the directorate of the research institute.

Organizational integration can thereby occur in the guise of homogenizing allocation rules across at least two political allocation-subsystems. Examples could be unified rules and procedures for professor sabbatical terms, or a common fixed minimum budget share for gender equality activities over all departments. The rules of one unit may be adjusted to the rules that are exercised within another unit, or the rules of a number of units may be adjusted to a new set of rules. Homogenization has the same effect as shifting control, since the capability to set subsystem-specific allocation rules and shape their content is reduced.

Second-order integration (*within-indirect*) is different in that the political systems of at least two units are not directly but, in a coordinating manner, indirectly related to each other. Shifting allocation responsibilities or homogenizing rules appears *within*, not across the units: it is commonly executed against the background of an attempted overall unified resource transformation process. Exam schedules of a number of institutes within a department, to take a case in point, may be homogenized to avoid potential time conflicts with a second department. In merger situations, second-order integration refers to integration measures that are restricted to subsystems within the respective merging parties. It is integration since it aims at reducing and concentrating control. However, the responsibilities of the system-level political subsystems of the merging parties are not directly related to each other.

Accordingly, organizational *disintegration* has to be logically explicated as the opposite of integration. Instead of horizontally or vertically shifting and concentrating allocation responsibilities, the latter are dispersed, thereby increasing the number of political allocation subsystems, rather absolutely in numbers or relatively regarding the relative magnitude of controlled resources. Internal resource control may be dispersed on the same system level or downwards (*decentralization*). Departments may, for instance, split up and form separate councils and deaneries; budgeting responsibilities may be partly transferred from faculty level to one or more institutes; sabbatical term procedures may become locally disarranged.

Hence, disintegration can serve as a starting point to clarify the *level of organizational integration* as a general aspect of HEIs as well as a specific merger outcome. The zero-point of the integration level, as for example in the wake of fully dissolving an institution, would be the completely *disintegrated organization*—a straightforward contradiction in terms. As integration is system-constituting, the organization would then cease to exist, turning its status into that of an aggregate of individuals. All systemic properties would be lost: no functional relatedness, no power relations arising from it, no need to control power and no basis to institutionalize it. There would be no emergent effects, no coalitional side payments, and no force. Everybody would individually regulate their own resources. The other (holistic) extreme would be found in a totally integrated organization, which is as equally bizarre to imagine. Any relevant form of allocation would be completely regulated (enabled, restricted) by a single governing body[16]. Both extremes of integration would either collapse the system into a congregation of unrelated individuals or conflate it into something akin to a collective individual downwards or upwards. However, beginning with a certain status quo and for a defined period of time, the overall level of integration would rise, with the *relative magnitude of resources being involved in first-order and / or second-order integration measures*.

Ultimately, the problem of generally identifying mergers with a high level of organizational integration has to be readdressed at this point. As discussed in Chapter 1, it is prevalent (at least implicitly) to use the level of post-merger integration in distinguishing mergers from both other types of IORs as well as different merger cases from each other. From the perspective of the theoretical framework provided, it is essential to strictly differentiate between *formally induced (by law)* and (consequently) *actually realized* integration levels. Mergers and incorporations are themselves integration measures: allocation responsibilities of extant central level political subsystems are shifted; a new organization is formally founded in case of the former. Indeed, the formally induced level of integration is higher, for example, than in a federation of universities, where only a cutout of the disciplines represented is involved in the new organization, and the formation of corporate resources remains voluntary. Resources are pooled to a larger extent and "automatically" in full mergers / incorporations. Conceptually, however, this needs to be rigorously detached from the level of "post-integration integration", which is of a far greater analytical and practical interest. In the extant M&A literature, both are commonly interfused, yet with a focus on the latter. Categorizing mergers and incorporations a priori as an extreme type of IOR on a basis of the level of integration that develops *subsequent* to their technical execution is inadequate.

3.3.2 Interdependence patterns and their general relation to organizational (dis)integration

Since there should not be an isolated ("specific") merger theory, our explanation of organizational integration in merger contexts has to move on with a more general analysis of (dis)integration dynamics and its antecedents. In line with RDT, internal structures and activities are influ-

16 A close approximation to this would be the regulation of the resource transformation process of rowing on a type of 16th century war galley. Every stroke by any member would have to be regulated by a single supervisor.

enced by items of the organizational environment. In order for us to comprehend the entirety of external demands a focal system has to handle, the concept of *interdependence patterns* will be introduced in the following.

The term is repeatedly alluded to within *The External Control of Organizations* (Pfeffer & Salancik, 1978: e.g. 123ff., 126, 138ff.), as for example in considering the general adaptiveness of organizations: "changes or disruptions in the patterns of influence and / or interdependence require new organizational adaptions to the context" (*Ibid*.: 138). Against the background of analyzing industrial mergers, these adaptions are deemed to "follow patterns of resource interdependence" (*Ibid*.: 139). However, the concept is not explicitly defined anywhere. With regard to mergers, as discussed above, it has solely been employed on the analytical macro-level: Pfeffer and Salancik thus had to infer from inter-industry and intra-industry exchange patterns to the exchange patterns of individual companies (*Ibid*.: 116; Davis & Cobb, 2010). In doing so, they confined the interdependence pattern to the character of the direct relationship(s), with exclusively those organization(s) a focal corporation might strategically merge with. Symbiotic interdependence with a supplier suggests an across-industry vertical merger; a solution to competitive interdependence may be provided by horizontally acquiring the rival, etc. In terms of examining the field-level / population-level consequences of mergers, the *multitude* of demands an organization confronts has been neglected.

An implicit definition that acknowledges all environmental resource-exchange links nevertheless unfolds in the method for assessing organizational effectiveness provided in Chapter 4. Pfeffer and Salancik (1978: 84ff.) developed three basic steps to practically derive criteria to evaluate the effects of a focal organization's activities on the environment:

1) *Determining external interest groups*: starting with the identification of critical input resources, the controllers of these resources have to be singled out;
2) *Weighting external interest groups*: a multidirectional rating procedure of all relevant interest groups or actors is suggested to determine their relative importance;
3) *Assessing group criteria*: values and standards of environmental actors have to be appraised, as do actual and / or potential conflicts between them.

The environmental interdependence pattern of a focal organization can thus be defined in terms of a *rank-order of the resource-related external demands it confronts* (similar: Jacobs, 1974). The concept encompasses information on the entirety of environmental actors, the criteria by which organizational actions and structures are evaluated (demands) as well as the relative importance of the resources involved. It thus displays two dimensions. First is (a) the *qualitative dimension* that relates to effectiveness[17] as an external criterion. *What* needs to be done, to transform resources in a manner that satisfies demand? According to the very nature of the demand: how has the system to be configured and resources to be specified? Second is the (b) *power dimension*, which prioritizes external actors and their conflicting demands. It relates to resource importance: the relative magnitude and criticality of the input resources being associated with the identified external demands.

RDT postulates a non-determinist and bi-directional relationship between the environmental interdependence pattern on the one hand and the configuration of the focal system on the other. Let us supplement this argument with an illustration of qualitative and quantitative pattern dimensions, considering the case of a small university of applied sciences (UAS / German: *Fachhochschule*) for social work and a specific part of its environment.

An important and obligatory part of study programs in social work are practical study periods that have to be completed within the later occupational field. One relevant neighborhood comprises organizations that provide such traineeships and permanently search for qualified students. It is *highly fragmented*, consisting of a large number of medium-sized to very small welfare institutions within a radius of 50 km: sheltered workshops, children's homes, drug counseling agencies, or community work offices. In terms of the systemist terminology introduced here: the traineeship-related exchange link L is qualitatively characterized by a need for permanently informing students, by providing intermediation and coordination. To ensure the permanent flow of the associated resources, the university has to handle the demand somehow. Without respective efforts, internship placement would become more time-consuming, intermittent, and arbitrary. Study programs in turn could lose their attractiveness and variety, and providers of internships could start looking for more stable alternatives. Organizational uncertainty would rise and social discretion be diminished. The specification of resources into a certain configuration

17 The problem of identifying criteria of organizational effectiveness (recall 1.2.2) is therefore not solved, but turned into the difficulty of validly identifying external actors, their demands, as well as the relative weight of demands on the level of individual (focal) organizations.

should thus *echo* (not: "reflect") the qualitative aspect of the pattern. The focal institution may thereby strategically choose from a limited range of appropriate solutions, like for instance a Web database, a traineeship advice office, regularly organized contact fairs, or some other kind of service.

What about the power dimension? According to the political / coalitional perspective underlying RDT, qualitatively different environmental demands within the same interdependence pattern are regularly in conflict (Pfeffer & Salancik, 1978: 28; Cyert & March, 1963). These conflicts are either consensually solved by productivity gains allowing for side payments, by the exertion of power, which means issue-related interest domination within the political system, or, as a further option, by organizational subsystem *decoupling*:

> The structural solution to conflicting demands is a differentiated organization of loosely coupled subsystems, each of which deals with special environmental interests and each of which is only slightly interdependent with other subunits within the organization (Pfeffer & Salancik, 1978: 275).

Inasmuch as they all depend on resource control, these options are closely connected to intraorganizational power differentials between coalitions. This is the power dimension of the pattern: external demands are linked to input resources that stabilize existing coalitions or make way for the formation of new ones. In the light of our example: a coalition will form within the political allocation subsystem, which is supportive of system configurations that allow for extended traineeship service. Given the fact that it is a university of applied sciences, (without knowing the complete pattern) it is quite clear that research plays a minor role and professional student training a major role in acquiring resources. We may therefore reasonably assume that the coalition will be sufficiently strong to realize an appropriate configuration. The set of allocation rules follows the interests of the powerful / dominant coalition. Its strength would be consequence of the relative resource weight of the traineeship exchange relation and hence of the interdependence pattern's power dimension. The realization of system configurations and the handling of resource-related conflicts depend on and vary with the intraorganizational power distribution, or, as Hickson et al. (1971) put it, the *discretionary differentials* between subunits.

We can hence tentatively comprehend the general argument regarding (dis)integration dynamics in the context of interdependence pattern management. In any organization, two antipodal forces, *integrative* and *disintegrative*, are permanently at work. (1) The *integrative* force on the one hand originates in functional relatedness (qualitative pattern dimension), which can be a source of collectively enhanced reduction of environmental uncertainties. Asymmetries in cooperation, in giving rise to power relations and their counteractive control, lead to organizational integration. Such integration may be rooted in consensus and coalitional side-payments. On the other hand, power differentials may be used to "resolve" conflicts without consensus, by enforcing certain integration measures, impropriating pooled resources and / or impeding balancing operations. Intraorganizational conflicts are also the source of (2) *disintegrative* forces. Disagreements regarding organizational activities and structures can be settled by dispersing resource control (Pfeffer, 1978: 240; Pfeffer & Salancik, 1978: 275; Astley & Zajac, 1991: 402). Dispersing allocation responsibilities among differentiated political subsystems therefore calls for an appropriate resource base (pattern power dimension) to uphold the coalition beneath. Such resources may be provided by changing environmental demands (new external actors and resources) or already exist as *organizational slack* (Pfeffer & Salancik, 1978: 274f.). Both forces, integrative and disintegrative, thus attain their directionality from the qualitative pattern dimension, and their magnitude from the power dimension of the overall interdependence pattern.

3.4 *Organizational (dis)integration and mergers in higher education: mechanism and hypotheses*

3.4.1 The explanatory variables: qualitative (in)consistency and the power relation of interdependence patterns

Mergers in HEIs are by definition realized with the execution of an integration measure: the system-constituting political allocation subsystems of the central level are amalgamated. In Germany, the allocation responsibilities of at least two "old" senates, university councils and presidencies (rectorships) are concentrated into new governing organs. This marks the beginning of the post-merger stage, in which the parties are deemed to grow together; additional integration measures across the new system are supposed to follow.

Mergers therefore create a situation in which at least two formerly separated interdependence patterns have to be abruptly managed within one and the same political subsystem (although they are negotiated successively). A part of the merging parties' resources are in fact pooled "automatically" and, from that point on, have to be allotted jointly. As there is a general connection between the environmental interdependence pattern and organizational (dis)integration dynamics, which is mediated by a political process, it is the central suggestion of this study that *level and orientation of organizational integration following a merger (or incorporation) systematically vary with the relationship of the respective interdependence patterns to each other*. This requires further elaboration.

The relationship of interdependence patterns to each other can again be characterized in terms of their qualitative and power dimensions. As regards the qualitative dimension, their relationship is captured in terms of pattern (in)consistency. This refers to the combined effectiveness of the merging parties—their ability to continue to cope with environmental demands in a unified resource allocation and transformation system. It can be circumscribed as the *extent of overlapping between the respective ranges of system configurations that ensure the resource-related status quo or even increase social discretion for both (all) parties*[18]. The consistency aspect thus parallels the definition of the set of viable coalitions provided by Cyert and March (1963: 39):

> That is, we will identify a class of combinations of members such that any of these combinations meet the minimal standards imposed by the external environment of the organization. Patently, therefore, the composition of the viable set of coalitions will depend on environmental conditions.

A coalition is considered viable when it is able to generate the resources to satisfy its members (March, 1962: 672). The smaller the extent of feasible common configurations between the parties, which at least preserve transformation, the harder it gets to form viable coalitions that back them. The possible number of viable coalitions between merging parties thus gets smaller with rising qualitative inconsistencies.

For illustrative purposes, we, in this respect, will compare the aforementioned UAS for social work with the technical UAS it was incorporated by in 2005[19]. We will again look at the management of practical study peri-

18 In line with Emerson (1962), defending or improving their own resource-related status quo is implied as the fundamental goal of all merging parties on all system levels.

19 The incorporation of the *Hochschule für Sozialwesen Mannheim* by the *Hochschule für Technik und Gestaltung Mannheim* (this case was examined in the course of pre-study explorations).

ods. The two organizations differ considerably with regard to the set of providers of student traineeships. While the social work institution is confronted with a highly fragmented field of rather small providers, the vast majority of the engineering students complete their practical period within one of a few large multinational enterprises situated in the surrounding area. These enterprises, as opposed to the social welfare institutions, have huge and differentiated HR departments at their command; they dedicate considerable resources to actively searching for and recruiting student trainees. Consequently, the technical university has "traditionally" left all traineeship-placement activities to their students.

Qualitatively different demands (i.e. evaluation criteria of environmental actors) regarding the same exchange relation are inconsistent between the merging parties in that no common configuration exists to handle the demands without one party exacerbating its resource situation. Although the social work UAS has a strategic choice on how to handle the demand, in a material world it somehow needs to be done and the number of alternatives is limited. Its engineering counterpart does not need to allot resources to the same task *at all*. If one homogenized allocation rules accordingly, either the social work institution would lose its student service, or the technical university would suffer from a misallocation of resources. Concentrating operative control in a common political subsystem also increases uncertainty for both sides, especially under a condition of decreasing state funds. The fewer possible common system configurations exist, the larger the qualitative pattern inconsistencies, and the harder it becomes to identify and negotiate the former.

On the other hand, with an increasing overlapping between the spectrums of possible (at least resource-neutral) configurations, the scope of consensual bargaining solutions should rise. Albeit we refrain from a detailed example at this point, some instances that resemble organizational founding conditions may be hinted at. The merging parties could pool their resources to establish a new study program or to set up a common research project by means of shifting allocation responsibilities en bloc or in part to existing or newly founded political subsystems. This would be integration based on functional relatedness, creating emergent effects, which in the merger context are labeled synergies (recall 3.1.2). Coping capabilities could collectively be enhanced by expanding resource transformation toward new environmental domains. This has a notion of James Thompson's concept of *domain consensus*, which "defines a set of expectations both *for members of the organization* and for others with whom they interact, about what the organization will do and will not do" (Thompson,

1967: 29; emphasis added, mk). The resources to be derived from entering new domains, or improving the ability to cope with requirements from existing domains, would enhance the merging parties' power position vis à vis a common environment.

Possible post-merger integration measures, may they be planned by the state ministry responsible or initiated from within the merging system(s), will always be evaluated in terms of their potential impact on resource discretion on the level of coalitions. Anticipated losses in discretion due to a rising distance from the range of adequate system configurations might thereby be compensated for by future enhancements in coping with uncertainty. Needless to say, integration consequences regarding qualitative pattern (in) consistencies, positive and negative, are always *prospective* in character. Unified study programs have to be set up and run through accreditation procedures; cooperation between individual scientists has to develop; joint research proposals have to be formulated and passed. New allocation rules need time to take effect as regards resource transformation.

However, organizational coalitions are not so much kept together by ideas, plans and prospects, but *by a continuous influx of (present) material resources* from the environment. Teaching assistant capacity has to be provided, project contracts extended, and commitments met. This leads us to the relation of interdependence pattern power dimensions to each other. While the effects of qualitative (in)consistency in a unified allocation and transformation system are prospective and often quite speculative in nature, the power(-dependence) relation of subunits is affected definitely and immediately by the execution of the merger. In contrast to potential future activities, power is *retrospective* in nature, as it is the result of preceding resource transformation and power-institutionalizing processes (Lachman, 1989). Coalitions gain and maintain their stability from the ongoing distribution of these resources down to the individual level. As the decisions about system configurations and the management of conflicts generally depend on subunit power, we therefore have to consider changing post-merger power distribution.

Whether disintegrative or integrative forces will actually entail observable manifestations is thus largely due to the intraorganizational power of force-exerting subunits and therefore the political coalitions beneath. This brings our analytical focus back to the organizational environment: according to RDT / SCT, power mostly accrues in those subunits that play a pivotal role in external demand satisfaction. If system configurations serve to provide resources for powerful external interests, it will be hard to form a coalition to change these configurations. The level of organizational integration following a merger will therefore vary with the degree of organizational dependence on those external interests that may be offended by integration measures. Large qualitative pattern inconsistencies, which are at the same time associated with important and hard-to-substitute environmental resources, will impede both decision-making and attempts at implementing post-merger integration effectively.

3.4.2 Interdependence pattern relationship and post-merger (dis)integration: hypotheses

The mechanism offered to explain post-merger integration is by no means different from more general (dis)integration dynamics in terms of its fundamentals. Just like in a single organization, the entirety of external dependencies of the parties post-merger forms a rank order displaying a qualitative and a quantitative dimension. The environmental demands involved may or may not imply overlapping between the respective ranges of configuration requirements; intraorganizational power differentials are decisive in the realization of (dis)integration. The main distinguishing characteristics of organizational mergers from this perspective lie in the suddenness and extent of demand confrontation.

Our main proposition is that the level and orientation of post-merger organizational integration systematically vary with the relationship of the parties' resource interdependence patterns to each other. To allow for a closer empirical examination, three major hypotheses are subsequently advanced. The first Hypothesis concerns the *political positioning* of existing organizational subunits and coalitions as regards attempted integration measures. Hypotheses two and three deal with the *potency* behind the resulting forces and its consequences for the level and orientation of observable post-merger integration.

To begin with, the qualitative dimension of the relationship of merging parties' interdependence patterns is reflected in Hypothesis 1:

H1 (Directionality Hypothesis): The degree of qualitative (in)consistency between the merging parties' interdependence patterns affects the subunits' political positioning toward the realization of integration measures.

a. Qualitative inconsistencies between the merging parties' interdependence patterns should further disintegrative forces within the political system of the merged organization.

As the range of possible system configurations to encounter environmental demands adequately is limited, a deviation from that range curtails resource acquisition and transformation. Inconsistent environmental demands should make it difficult to find and negotiate common structural configurations between the parties and therefore suggest the persistence of separate organizations. Disintegrative forces should express themselves multifariously in the political system (and its various subsystems) of the merging parties. Through the underlying coalitions the units affected should work towards retaining their status quo. They should reject integration attempts and seek to impede their effective post-merger implementation.

b. Qualitative consistencies between the merging parties' interdependence patterns should further integrative forces within the political subsystem.

The complementary second sub-Hypothesis accordingly refers to the case of larger overlaps in system configuration ranges between the merging parties. In that these allow for stabilizing or enhancing the control of resource uncertainties, they should heighten the probability of positioning of the units concerned that supports integration. There is some allusion to Thompson's (1967: 28) concept of domain consensus: acquiring surplus resources from existing domains or making new ones accessible through common system configurations should permit and sustain the formation of pro-integration coalitions across the merging parties.

Besides its association with the coalitional perspective, as explicated by March (1962) and Cyert and March (1963), Hypothesis one emanates from the design principles included in RDT:

> The larger and more diverse the coalition that constitutes the organization, the more differentiated the organization is likely to be, permitting each of the diverse interests to operate with a minimum amount of interdependence and thus conflicts with others in the organization (Pfeffer, 1978: 240).

The connection between disparities in environmental demands and structural differentiation can be regarded a widely accepted supposition across open systems theories of organization. Similar hypotheses have, for instance, been provided by Thompson (1967: 70), Lawrence & Lorsch (1967: 11), Meyer & Rowan (1977: 377), and, likewise with a pronounced drive toward neo-institutionalism, by Christine Oliver (1991: 162).

The subunits' positioning toward integration attempts based on their evaluation of resource-related consequences is one important jigsaw piece in explaining post-merger integration. However, as we are interested in real-world material manifestations of merger processes, it is not enough to account for these content-related preferences and attitudes toward attempted integration measures. As James Thompson hypothesized:

> The more sources of uncertainty or contingency for the organization, the more bases there are for power and the larger the number of political positions in the organization (Thompson, 1967: 129).

To come to a valid analysis of integration actually realized, we always have to consider the direction of merger dynamics in combination with the newly created intraorganizational power distribution. We formulate:

H 2 (Level Hypothesis): The actual realization of attempted integration measures depends on the degree of resource dependence on the potentially impaired external demands.

Hypothesis two concerns the actual potency behind the respective political positioning of coalitions toward post-merger integration endeavors. While the relation of interdependence patterns regarding their qualitative dimensions may be subject to bargaining pre- and post-merger, a unified internal power distribution (which follows external control) is definitely realized with the execution of the merger. As organizations are resource transformation systems, they depend on and strive for the stable flow of resources for their own survival. Their dependence on external groups / actors grows with an increasing relative magnitude of externally controlled resources, their criticality, and non-substitutability (Pfeffer & Salancik, 1978: 45ff.). Integration measures following mergers, as is true of any organizational change measure, will be evaluated regarding their influence on the subunit's capabilities to satisfy external demands—to be potentially impaired in this context means that restrictions of demand fulfillment as a consequence of integration cannot be precluded. Since it is defined as the relative magnitude of resources being involved in first-order and / or second-order integration measures, the overall level of integration should decrease with rising dependence on those external groups / actors whose interests are potentially offended. We therefore specify:

a. The higher the resource dependence on those external demands that are potentially impaired by the overall qualitative pattern inconsistencies of the merging parties, the lower the overall level of integration following a merger.

Since interdependence pattern (in)consistencies regularly unfold successively as many (dis)integration measures are negotiated step-by-step during the post-merger stage, a second sub-Hypothesis is added:

b. The higher the resource dependence on those external demands that are potentially impaired by qualitative pattern inconsistencies, the lower the probability of the associated integration measures being realized.

The conceptual focus on qualitative interdependence-inconsistencies (instead of consistencies) thereby follows from the retrospective nature of the power dimension. Coalitions and whole organizations obtain their internal stability and external discretion from current resource control, which is a consequence of past resource transformation. Future coalition members-to-be usually do not take part in negotiating the overall rank-order of external demands. The first coalitional priority should thus be the post-merger protection of existing external demands and the system configurations that are needed to constantly meet them. As regards resource control, it is hence implied that actuality tends to beat potentiality.

As they bring about extensive demand confrontation within the political allocation subsystem of the newly merged organization, mergers unveil external dependencies, structural requirements and yet the new power distribution on a departmental level. In Subsection 2.1.3 we described the SCT-based multilevel connection between external dependencies, departmental power distribution and the associated intraorganizational discretionary differentials. It was suggested that the subunits during the post-merger stage continue to use their power to protect and further their own resource-related interests. This should manifest itself in the orientation of observable integration:

H3 (Orientation Hypothesis): The overall orientation of post-integration measures actually realized should be toward the powerful subunits.

It's a central RDT / SCT tenet that organizational behavior and structures tend to be shaped by those subunits which successfully cope with organizational resource-related uncertainties (Pfeffer & Salancik, 1978: 230). Consequently, post-merger integration can only be realized with, but hardly against, the interests of powerful internal coalitions, and therefore of potent external resource holders. Mergers are hence conceptualized as conservative change measures. Integration measures that are actually realized are expected to follow the interests of those subunits that have been able to create the largest asymmetries in resource control.

As regards shifting allocation responsibilities as the second system-constituting moment, we asserted in 3.2 that this shift is generally oriented toward the powerful internal coalition(s). Hence, the post-merger shifting of responsibilities actually realized should tend away from those subunits that have controlled few resources toward the powerful ones; therefore:

a. Intraorganizational power increases the probability of the status quo being retained or other subunits being absorbed.

Likewise, a second aspect of the orientation of integration relates to the contents of homogenized post-merger allocation rules:

b. Intraorganizational power increases the capacity to shape the content of homogenized post-merger allocation rules.

In conclusion, the three hypotheses reflect the central aspects of the explanation provided for organizational post-merger (dis)integration. Firstly, Hypothesis one concerns the directionality of intraorganizational forces as a consequence of qualitative pattern (in) consistencies. Secondly, Hypothesis two relates to the potency behind the resulting (dis)integrative forces. To explain the resulting level of organizational integration, it focuses on the impairment of external demands according to the retrospective nature of power. Thirdly and finally, the complementary but more general third Hypothesis deals with the theoretically expected orientation of integration measures that are actually realized.

4 Case study I: the merger of the Universities of Duisburg and Essen

To investigate the proposed mechanism and hypotheses in a particular empirical setting, a number of challenges have to be met:

1) The qualitative pattern aspect has to be made tangible: how do the interdependence patterns of the merging parties relate to each other qualitatively? (Hypothesis 1);
2) The quantitative pattern aspect has to be disclosed: post-merger power relations have to be captured and quantified;
3) The connection between qualitative inconsistencies and integration realization, as mediated by intraorganizational power, has to be laid out (Hypothesis 2) together with
4) The resulting orientation of observable post-merger integration measures (Hypothesis 3).

The following empirical inquiry rests on two merger case studies that have been conducted with different analytical emphases. Case study number one (Chapter 4) concerns the merger of the Universities of Duisburg and Essen in 2003. With both parties exceeding 15,000 students, in the context of the latest merger wave in Germany it represents by far the largest case. It thus provides an interesting extreme case and, because of its size, fulfills some technical criteria for a quantitative case study and the application of potent tools of analysis. In order to provide evidence for H2 and H3, the scaling and measurement of intraorganizational subunit power is at the center of interest. Though voluminous qualitative data was analyzed, the overall focus is placed on quantitative methods; the research design is explicated in Subsection 4.1.2.

The second case study (Chapter 5) examines the incorporation of the former Hamburg Universität für Wirtschaft und Politik (HWP) into the University of Hamburg. The social science and economics departments of the University of Hamburg were merged with the HWP in 2005 to form a large new faculty within the first. Chapter 5 focuses on Hypothesis one and in particular centers on the qualitative aspect of interdependence patterns: the multiplicity of subunit interests, integration attempts, and intraorganizational coping strategies are examined.

4 *Case study I: the merger of the Universities of Duisburg and Essen*

4.1 *Merging the Universities of Duisburg and Essen: case introduction and research design*

4.1.1 Background information and time frame

The former University of Duisburg was founded in 1972 as the result of the merger of an engineering school and the local settlement of a larger regional college of education. Like its counterpart in Essen, it had been established back then as a prototype of a new model of organization in German higher education, the *Gesamthochschule*, which aimed at the integration of the traditional two-tier UAS / university system: student access criteria were unified, traditional university-oriented and the more application-oriented UAS programs were combined, and a broader range of academic staff[20] was brought together. Student numbers in Duisburg had been growing from 3,400 in 1972 to 16,000 in 2003, the merger year; 93 study programs were offered. The university comprised five departments (German: Fakultäten), five central level and nine associated research institutes. Besides its traditional engineering orientation, it displayed a focus on social sciences and economics (see Table 4.2).

As the second and larger merging party (distance 25 km), the former University of Essen was likewise brought into being in 1972, during the first German merger wave, through a series of mergers: a mechanical engineering school, a college of education, an art academy, and the local subsidiary of the University of Bochum's teaching hospital had been successively combined. Its 21,000 students were registered in about 100 different study programs in 2003. Within the institution, a broad range of disciplines was represented in teaching and research; distinct emphases were on the natural sciences, economics (with a special information systems orientation), teacher training, and humanities. As regards internal organization, three central level and two associated research institutes complemented the 13 regular departments.

Merger plans were, which was typical of the second wave, initiated by a para-constitutional parliamentary expert commission, which had been set up to evaluate the overall system of higher education in North Rhine-Westphalia and to propose concrete means of reorganization. In its review of all 27 HEIs within the state ministry domain, the commission attested the University of Duisburg particularly to be in a substandard condition. An

20 Professorships with extensive teaching obligations and no assistant support are typical of UAS.

inferior degree of program capacity utilization in the engineering disciplines, natural sciences, and humanities was indicated (CD1|1: 318). As regards research activities, low dissertation output and below state-average third-party funds were queried. For the University of Essen, mixed assessment results were reported. Capacity utilization was found to be very high in some humanities and pedagogics, but too low in physics and chemistry. Substandard research indicator values were stated as regards economics, engineering and the natural sciences (*Ibid.*: 335). Both universities had already had to face substantial state budget cutbacks (Essen: 128 faculty positions until 2009; Duisburg: 116). To achieve a rise in performance indicators while simultaneously dealing with cutbacks and the unfavorable status composition of the faculty, the commission suggested resource pooling and coordination through a merger (*Ibid.*); the amalgamation thus seems to have served as a politically feasible alternative to the closure of the University of Duisburg (1–II: 588ff.). A number of integration measures and attempted implementation consequences are roughly sketched in the report. Teacher training was to be mostly ceased in Duisburg, and further strengthened in Essen (CD1|1: 342). The humanities were recommended to be focused on in Essen (*Ibid.*: 327), whereas the engineering disciplines were to completely move to Duisburg. Some teaching-related coordination as regards chemistry and physics was advised (*Ibid.*: 328).

The pre-merger period started in late 2000 with sporadic department level consultations about cooperation possibilities (e.g. economics: ID1|1: 10). A first informal meeting on the central executive level took place in January 2001; the first officially mandated talks were to follow two months later. Both parties in the early negotiation stage had been supportive of the merger; the state ministry attended the meetings and offered to back the process by absorbing relocation expenses and eventually suspending cutbacks (ID1|2: 4). In July 2001, the two rectorates agreed to allow in-camera moderation of negotiations to dispel remaining discrepancies. The moderated talks ended in November 2001; the two rectorates, in a scanty press release, presented an attempted basic post-merger campus profile:

- Duisburg: engineering, social sciences, and economics;
- Essen: medicine, humanities, and economics.

Dissent remained as to the allocation of teacher training, mathematics and physics, as well as regarding a large research center for humanities, which the University of Duisburg wanted to install. Additionally, both parties claimed several natural science units to be located on their respective campuses in order to support the core profiles they were pursuing.

After the press release, the rectorate of the University of Duisburg shot forward by unilaterally supplementing the results with its own strategic draft of the Duisburg campus profile (ID1|4: 3). The mood started tipping in Essen afterwards; central level executives came under pressure for negotiating against the interests of their own organization. The whole consultation process was henceforth challenged for being undemocratic and, despite the remaining controversy, for a full merger having been prematurely and publicly decided on (ID1|5: 3). Bilateral negotiations between the merging parties came to a halt while the state ministry had already signaled its willingness to enforce the merger per law (ID1|6: 5; ID1|7: 4)—a first draft was transmitted in May 2002. After it had turned out that ministry commitment in terms of absorbing merger costs would, against original agreement, be restricted, the rector of the University of Essen was replaced in a vote of no confidence in June 2002; the senates of both universities officially rejected the merger (SP1 13|2002 (Essen); ID1|9). Accompanied by public protests, some muckraking, and several lawsuits initiated by the two parties, the parliament of North Rhine-Westphalia finally sealed the merger by law, which technically came into being on January 1st 2003.

We hitherto have identified a full merger as the discrete act of shifting the allocation responsibilities of at least two separate central level political subsystems toward a "new" and unified single one (1.1.1). If we take this definition as a starting point, it is relatively easy to empirically delimit the pre-merger stage—it starts with the first interorganizational merger-related negotiations. Though a process-oriented and long-term perspective on mergers and integration has become established within the literature on this subject (Teerikangas & Joseph, 2012), little consensus as to the far more difficult and precise specification of the following post-merger stage has emerged. The question remains, and an (at least tentative) answer needs to be found for the study at hand: at what point in time can such processes be considered complete in a sense that reasonably allows for empirical evaluation of integration outcomes?

From the perspective of Bunge's materialist ontology, processes are series of states (Bunge & Mahner, 2004: 57). In social systems like organizations, this mostly refers to series of state-changing activities (Bunge, 1981: 120). Organizations are material systems and permanently changing—being in flux is a constitutive meta-property of material things. Implying "static" periods as a contrast, the issue of "organizational change" may thus even raise suspicions of conceptual artificiality. The "normal" course of life in large organizations is always accompanied by the foundation and closure of subunits, by seeking interorganizational cooperation / integration as well as by many other system-changing events. An organizational change process can thus solely refer to a temporary widening of the usual corridor of actual or potential changes of the system configuration. Hence, we are still left with the puzzling task of empirically discerning workaday state changes from extraordinary changes.

An unequivocal solution to this problem is, in my opinion, given only in cases where another comparable process begins to unfold post-merger. Since organizations are resource transforming allocation systems, and the bare act of merging relates the central level political subsystems of at least two of them to each other, a comparable process or event must be effective on the same level.

On this note, full mergers of two large organizations can be "completed" by

- a further merger or another reform affecting the central level (of the political system);
- comprehensive organizational breakup: insolvency / closure;
- a demerger: substantial or full retrogression of the initial change measure.

In cases without such a concluding or replacing process, an exact determination of merger completion is impossible. It is nonetheless plausible to assume a time-limited core post-merger negotiation and implementation stage will follow the technical execution of a merger (law / deal closure). During that stage, fundamental sets of allocation rules are negotiated and implemented for the merged organization. In German HEIs, one should think of the 'Grundordnung' (basic statute / constitution); the number, structure, and location of subsystems; basic responsibilities as well as strategic research and education foci. Pragmatic considerations thereby suggest a general time limitation of those core post-merger negotiations: permanent far-reaching change options relating to the overall system configuration would require leaving the latter in a constant state of enormous contingency. Due to the resulting broadly based resource uncertainties and huge administrative costs, in large organizations it is neither desirable nor feasible for administrators to maintain such a situation for several years. Following the core negotiation and implementation stage, the number and substance of integration attempts should drop significantly—the merged organization converges toward a ("new") regular corridor of changes. Still, that doesn't imply the merger / integration process has concluded—integration measures that wouldn't have been possible without a unified central level political allocation system may continue to occur.

The time frame adopted for this case study corresponds to the described pragmatic approach. After the technical execution of the merger, a state commissioner was installed as the new universities' transient head executive. He was to administratively prepare the post-merger integration stage and work out several possible integration suggestions. Regular central level political allocation subsystems were elected and installed in July (*founding senate*) and October (*founding rectorate*) 2003. The following 14 months marked the core post-merger negotiation and implementation stage. The lion's share of integration measures realized was decided on in May 2004 and came into force in late 2004—the resulting structure has for the most part been retained to date. The end of 2004 saw a second intensive, but shorter negotiation stage. The beginning of 2010 was chosen as the date of the empirical integration outcome assessment. Seven years after the technical execution and five years after the core negotiation stage, most (though not all) of the announced integration and removal measures had been accomplished.

4.1.2 Research design

We have argued that level and orientation of post-merger organizational integration systematically vary with the relationship of the parties' interdependence patterns to each other. Integration measures, whoever may have initiated them, will be evaluated on the level of subunits in terms of their resource-related effects: the way in which they are anticipated to change system configuration (qualitative interdependence pattern dimension) and the related ability to continuously manage external demands. Anticipated consequences for actual resource transformation are deemed to influence the political position of subunits toward integration measures (H1).

To come to a valid analysis of post-merger integration realization, it is of utmost importance to determine post-merger intraorganizational power distribution, which refers to the quantitative relation of the merging parties' resource interdependence patterns to each other. The new power distribution is induced by merger execution, the units become related in a common political "arena" via their central level political subsystem. Since two environments have henceforth to be handled in a unified central level political system, there is a new collectivity of external interests and external resources, and hence a new form of intraorganizational power distribution arises.

As laid out in Subsection 2.1.3, RDT embraces the SCT model of subunit power as a link between organizational environment and structure (Pfeffer & Salancik, 1978: 230ff.). We will consequently draw on the SCT to scale and measure intraorganizational power, and therefore estimate the post-merger power distribution within the newly founded University of Duisburg–Essen. In a similar vein to Lachman (1989), we conceive of intraorganizational power as a latent variable. The influencing factors of power as stated by Hickson et al. (1971), *centrality of workflows*; *effectiveness of coping; input uncertainty* and *substitutability of activities*, can thus be approximately considered as the equally latent dimensions of what Lazarsfeld (1937) and Barton (1955) have termed a *property space*. According to its power characteristics, any subunit within the merged university should be locatable within such a power space. To technically determine the latter, principal axis factoring was applied as a scaling instrument. Factor analysis is an appropriate method, since it seeks to reproduce correlations between variables in a lower-dimensional space (Überla, 1971: 44, 93ff.). Therefore, the central intent of this first part of the theory-driven dimensional analysis (4.2.1) is to prove a larger number of power related indicator variables to be reducible to a set of power factors (dimensions) that conforms to the theoretical considerations of the SCT.

The processed quantitative data refers to 38 teaching and research units (TRU hereafter) within the merged university. It was mainly derived from internal reports having been gathered on behalf of the state commissioner responsible to prepare post-merger decision-making of the founding organs. Tables 4.1 and 4.2 report on both parties' merger year TRUs, the formal departments (German: Fachbereiche) they were associated with, as well as some basic quantitative properties. The TRUs listed do not always refer to the same level of the formal political system (and do not have to); they were used in the reports to make both universities comparable. Some of the units had to be omitted due to missing data or irrelevance. This applied to literature, communication, and Turkish language studies, as well as the music unit in Essen. For landscaping and surveying, two UAS level units, no meaningful comparison data could be found. Due to its local hospital responsibilities, the medical unit in Essen had never been subject to integration considerations. As for the former university of Duisburg, no data could be obtained for the Japanese and Jewish studies departments, or for the material sciences unit. A second general data source, especially for the research-related variables, was the websites of both merging parties; they were assessed via an Internet archive (www.waybackmachine.org), using early 2003 as an access point.

Merger-year departments Univ. of Essen (2003)	TRU (No. in dataset)	Student count	Academic personnel count	Integration status (2010)
1. Philosophy, history, religious studies and social sciences	PHI (4)	349	12	Target
	H (2)	767	19	Target
	SOC (9)	1313	54	Target
	TE (5)	72	5	Target
	TC (6)	112	10	Target
2. Pedagogics, psychology, sports science	P (7)	1356	43	Bidder
	PSY (8)	Inc.in P	18	Status quo
	SP (21)	420	14	Status quo
3. Literature studies and linguistics	A (1)	643	21	Target
	LIT	42	3	(Target)
	G (3)	2059	34	Target
	COM	765	10	(Target)
	TURK	187	10	(Target)
4. Arts (design, arts, music)	D (19)	572	73	divested (SQ)
	ART (20)	385	17	Target
	MUS	34	4	divested
5. Economics	ECO (10)	4998	123	Bidder
6. Mathematics and computer sciences	MA (13)	708	63	Target
	I (18)	322	30	Target
7. Physics	PHY (14)	481	66	Target
8. Chemistry	C (12)	595	70	Bidder
9. Biology, geo sciences, landscaping	B (11)	939	39	Status quo
	GEO (17	115	21	Status quo
	LAND	379	24	divested
10. Construction engineering	CON (15)	982	76	Target
11. Surveying & mapping	SU	46	10	divested
12. Mechanical engineering	MEC (16	278	35	Target
	TEC	52	7	(Target)
14. Medicine	MED	1764	874	(Status quo)
$\sum$		**20735**	**1778**	

Table 4.1: University of Essen: basic quantitative properties of departments and TRUs in the merger year (ID1/10)

Merger-year departments Univ. of Duisburg (data: 2003)	TRU (No. in dataset)	Student count	Academic personnel count	Integration status (2010)
1. Humanities and social sciences	TED (27)	30	5	Target
	HD (23)	241	15	Target
	JEW			divested
	PHID (25	164	6	Target
	SOCD(30	3085	59	Bidder
2. Pedagogics	PD (28)	814	25	Target
	PSYD (29)	147	10	Target
3. Language studies	AD (22)	560	16	Target
	GD (24)	1190	23	Target
	R (26)	263	15	Target
	JAP			Status quo
5. Economics	ECOD (31	4376	82	Status quo
6. Chemistry & geo sciences	GEOD (37	77	10	Target
	CD (32)	471	42	Target
7. Mechanical engin.	MECD (36	1003	102	Bidder
8. Material sciences	MAT	154	20	Status quo
9. Electro engineering	ED (35)	1260	88	Status quo
10. Physics	PHYD (34)	364	52	Target
11. Mathematics & computer sciences	MAD (33)	599	50	Target
	ID (38)	993	50	Status quo
$\sum$		**15791**	**670**	

Table 4.2: University of Duisburg[21]: basic quantitative properties of departments and TRUs in the merger year (source: ID1/10)

Over the course of the *first part* of the data analysis procedure, the scaling and measurement of power through factor analysis, three different objectives were pursued:

21 It is important to note that in 2001 the University of Duisburg had shifted from a structure of 11 departments to a structure of five faculties. The 2001 department structure was drawn on during the dimensional analysis to generally allow for a more fine-grained analysis and subunit comparability (particularly as regards organizational pervasiveness). The actual merger-day faculty structure was, however, used to capture post-merger integration (shifting subunit assignments). A respective overview of the merger-day faculty structure can be found in Appendix C.

1) A falsification attempt of the SCT. Data reduction may fail to produce interpretable results: a meaningful correlation pattern between relevant variables may not ensue; power factors may not be selective in an SCT-sense;
2) Determining the post-merger intraorganizational power distribution as well as the power profiles of subunits as precisely as possible;
3) Attaining reduced data for the following steps of analysis.

Objectives two and three directly lead to the subsequent *second part* of the theory-driven dimensional analysis (4.2.2). Cluster analysis was employed to identify groups of subunits that display similarities in terms of their power profiles, while in this regard being different in comparison to other groups in the sample. This on the one hand completes the dimensional analysis on the subunit level and on the other allows us to link it with post-merger organizational integration, our dependent variable. To what extent groups with similar power profiles showed comparable integration characteristics was examined.

We will hence be provided with helpful background knowledge for the causal analysis (4.2.3). The level of post-merger integration as a function of the degree of the merged organization's dependence on eventually impaired external interests (Hypothesis 2) is delved into on grounds of cluster analysis results. Prior to this, Hypothesis 3a will be examined on the basis of logistic regression analysis: the supposed connection between the intraorganizational power of subunits and their chance to retain status quo or absorb other units.

The remainder of the chapter (Section 4.3) is concerned with the overall complex of the relation between interdependence patterns, but with a focus on the qualitative aspect (Hypothesis 1): the (attempted) integration processes of three large subunits-to-be are explicated as intra-case studies. The foundation of a common faculty of physics (4.3.1) provides an example of successful integration due to profile-related complementarities. Contrastingly, the failed establishment of unified economics (4.3.3) and social sciences departments (4.3.2) is used to demonstrate the integration-busting interplay between configuration-related inconsistencies and intraorganizational power.

Although it likewise makes use of findings from the dimensional and causal analysis, the emphasis in Section 4.3 is on the qualitative data. Six semi-structured expert interviews (60–90 min) were conducted; interview questions referred to subunit interests, dependencies, and integration-related negotiations in the political system (see Annex A). Respondents were ex-members of the founding senate, internal advising commission, and / or former or active organizational executives. Interview data was complemented by numerous documents:

- pre-merger and post-merger strategy papers and comments released by subunits;
- protocols of moderated post-merger bilateral integration talks between subunit representatives;
- senate protocols of the entire post-merger period;
- comprehensive documentation of a university-wide integration workshop;
- resolution drafts and central level planning documents.

Figure 4.1 provides a compact overview of the steps and aims of the following empirical analysis:

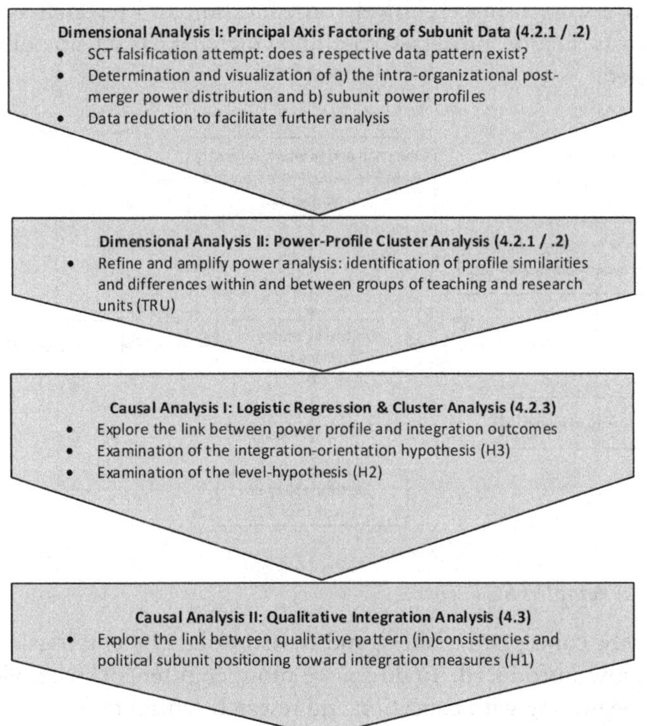

Figure 4.1: Steps and objectives of the empirical analysis (4.2.–4.3)

4.2 Data analysis and results

4.2.1 Scaling and measurement of post-merger intraorganizational power

To draw on the SCT as a basis to empirically determine post-merger intraorganizational subunit power, we have to substantiate its concepts with measures that are suitable in the context of higher education. HEIs have been identified as resource transforming allocation systems (3.2.1). Input resources run through series of allocations that are transformative in character, while output resources are emitted into the organizational environment. This transformation process, which within the SCT framework is termed "primary workflow" (Hickson et al. 1971: 221), again provides our starting point. Education and research / transfer[22] are its main subprocesses; they are complemented by administration as a third, but more peripheral subprocess. Focusing exclusively on education and research as separate main transformation processes, the following adapted scheme of the SCT is suggested:

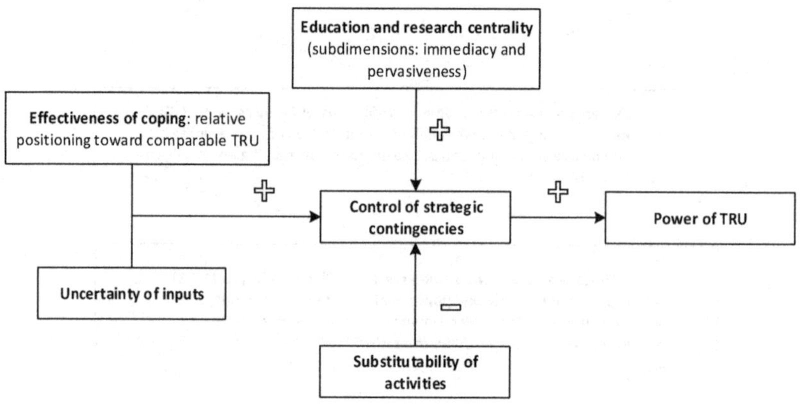

Figure 4.2: Adapted SCT scheme

Successively, concepts, variables, and measures for the empirical examination are now introduced. To do so, we move counterclockwise within the scheme, beginning with education and research centrality.

22 To enhance readability, in the following it is mostly referred to as "research" instead of "research and transfer".

Education and research centrality

Subunit workflow centrality with its two dimensions (immediacy / pervasiveness) is considered for education and research. *Workflow immediacy* refers to the "speed and severity with which the workflows of a subunit affect the final outputs of the organization" (Hickson et al., 1971: 222); it is captured in terms of the subunit share of organizational resources. A subunit's pervasiveness concerns the degree of interconnectedness of its processes.

The *education immediacy* of a TRU is captured by seven indicators; the input-throughput-output stages of the transformational allocation process are reflected in the variables (data reference periods in brackets):

1. total number of first year main subject students (summer term 2001 and winter term 2001 / 2002, KR);
2. total number of first year minor subject (combination) students (s. t. 2001 and w. t. 2001 / 2002, KR);
3. total number of enrolled main subject students (w. t. 2001 / 02, KR);
4. capacity-relevant total number of students (*Vollstudierende*) (w. t. 2001 / 02, KR);
5. total number of main subject graduates (w. t. 2001 / 2002 and s. t. 2002, KR);
6. total number of minor subject (combination) graduates (w. t. 2001 / 2002 and s. t. 2002, KR);
7. total teaching demand per term (i.e. the cumulated actual unit shares in all study programs it was connected to) (w. t. 2002 / 2003, KR).

The *pervasiveness of education* workflows is accounted for by

8. *supplier pervasiveness*: the total number of study programs which were not administratively associated with the focal subunit but were provided with teaching capacity by the latter (w. t. 2002 / 2003, KR);
9. *program pervasiveness*: the total number of *highly pervasive* study programs the unit was connected to (w. t. 2002 / 2003, KR).

A study program was coded as *highly pervasive* if it had been supplied by at least two non-home TRUs under the involvement of at least one external department (other than the one the home TRU was assigned to; w. t. 2002 / 2003). In terms of a threshold, the criterion was derived as follows: for both merging parties, a list of all relevant study programs with information on TRU program involvement was generated. For each program, the number of all TRUs involved (non-home, i.e. without the administratively responsive unit) was multiplied with the number of external political subsystems involved (departments other than the one the home unit was assigned to). A comparison of the dispersions of the resulting scores showed that, for both merging parties, between roughly 25% and one third of all programs displayed a minimum score of 2 (therefore, the chosen threshold). An example of a highly pervasive study program would be the diploma II program in chemistry provided by the former University of Essen. It was administratively associated with the chemistry unit (C), and supplied by the mathematics (MA), physics (PHY), and computer sciences units (I): three non-home TRUs under the involvement of two external departments (Depts. of Physics & Mathematics / Computer Sciences), yielding an education pervasiveness score of 6. Program pervasiveness was considerably higher in Duisburg, with 36 of 93 study programs (39%) having been central in comparison to 22% in Essen (100 programs). Study programs that in the pre-merger period had been decided to be shut down without replacement, or to be transferred to a third institution (divested) were generally not taken into account.

Research and transfer immediacy is indicated by two measures of effectiveness and two of efficiency:

10. total amount of third-party funding in monetary units (w. t. 2002 / 2003, KR);
11. total number of dissertations (a 5-year mean from 1997–2001 used here, KR);
12. third-party funding per professor in monetary units (w. t. 2002 / 2003, KR);
13. total number of dissertations per professor (5-year mean, KR).

The p*ervasiveness of research and transfe*r workflows is captured by:

14. the total number of research / transfer projects the unit was connected to (w. t. 2002 / 2003);
15. the total number of highly pervasive projects the unit was connected to (w. t. 2002 / 2003);
16. the total number of scientific staff engaged in projects associated with a focal TRU (w. t. 2002 / 2003);
17. the total number of TRU staff involved in highly pervasive projects (w. t. 2002 / 2003).

The criterion for a research or transfer project to be coded as highly pervasive is the involvement of at least three departments (5 such projects in

Duisburg and 7 in Essen). The term "project" comprises six types of research subsystems:

- DFG funded research groups / other third-party funded research groups;
- DFG funded collaborative research centers (*Sonderforschungsbereiche*);
- DFG or other third-party funded post-graduate groups;
- intra-university institutes that were exclusively dedicated to research and / or transfer (as indicated by their charter);
- extra-university but officially associated research institutions (German: *An-Institute*);
- participation in fairs.

Association with a project was determined either via a person's direct membership in the focal TRU, or, according to the theoretical considerations in Subsection 3.2.3, as proportional to the number of subsystem board positions held by TRU members. If, for example, the board of an institute had consisted of three directors, two of them university chair holders and one of them an external director, two thirds of that institute's scientific staff was assigned to the respective university TRU, while the remaining third was treated as part of the environment. The term *scientific staff* solely relates to professors and (post)doctoral candidates; administrative, technical, and undergraduate staff was not accounted for. The data for indicators 14–17 was obtained via self- and administrative portrayals of the units (internal written reports and an Internet archive http://waybackmachine.org). The former presence of the institutions and projects on the Web was analyzed, using April 2003 as a reference month—official organizational research profiles were checked, as were the department and / or chair websites. Participation in fairs (2002 / 2003) was globally factored in with one head per unit and fair; all kinds of fairs reported on were weighted equally.

Effectiveness of coping

The effectiveness of coping refers to the relative capacity of a TRU to deal with uncertainties that derive from the common post-merger organizational environment. It interacts with the level of uncertainty, which "might be indicated by the variability of those inputs to the organization which are taken by the subunit" (Hickson et al., 1971: 220). Since state universities in Germany depended (and still depend) by and large on state funding, I identified the political turn toward rising performance-based budget shares as the most important source of organizational uncertainties. Both of the universities involved had to deal with hefty budget cutbacks pre-merger, and an important (announced) strategic goal of the merger had been to somehow improve performance indicators. In an internal memorandum (ID1|11), the founding rector urged all professors to further work toward the enhancement of teaching-related and research-related indicators: annual budget losses threatened to surge from €900,000 in 2004 / 2005 to more than €3.5 million in 2006. This is the rising level of uncertainty (variability of inputs): performance-based budgeting increased from 14% in 2004 to 20% in 2006; a further upward tendency was looming (*Ibid.*).

The capacity of a unit to cope with environmental uncertainties was hence operationalized by its positioning regarding resource control *relative* to comparable TRUs from other universities located in the relevant federal state of North Rhine-Westphalia. The institutions of reference were the Universities[23] of *Bonn*, *Münster*, *Cologne*, *Aachen (RWTH)*, *Bochum*, *Dortmund*, *Düsseldorf*, and *Bielefeld*; the differences between a focal TRUs' indicators and the respective parameter means of all relevant comparison-TRUs were calculated. The higher the resulting score, the better the relative countrywide positioning of a focal TRU and the greater its relative capacity to reduce organizational uncertainties. Hence, only one of the three dimensions of coping with uncertainty suggested by Hickson et al. (1971: 219) was included: *coping by preventive activities* that reduce the probability of variations in inputs. Since education and research / transfer processes are conceived of as separate, coping-variables were calculated for the six input-throughput-output *education immediacy indicators* (1–6) as well as for *research and transfer immediacy* (10–13). The overall ten coping variables and their immediacy bases all refer to similar time periods (see above).

Before we attend to the results, three aspects of the database and research design have so far to be considered. Firstly, it is important to recognize that the concept of intraorganizational power is narrowed to objective measures of resource control. Many of the existing attempts to measure power in HEIs and other types of organization have included or largely been built on interview measures and rating procedures (e.g. Pfeffer & Salancik, 1974; Pfeffer & Moore, 1980; Hackman, 1985; Hinings et al., 1974). As for the study at hand, perceptual measures have not been included for data

23 Since the 'Gesamthochschule' model was abandoned during the second merger wave, only full universities were used for comparison.

quality concerns (level of measurement) on the one hand and validity issues on the other. About ten years after the merger, it would neither have been possible to reach all relevant unit heads, nor was a valid retrospective assessment over all subunits to be expected.

Secondly, and for similar reasons, measures for the substitutability of processes were not included in the dimensional analysis. Our suggested property space of intraorganizational power is thus just set up by indicators of *workflow immediacy*, *workflow pervasiveness*, and *effectiveness of coping*. However, substitutability was included in the regression analysis in Subsection 4.2.3 as a dummy variable. A unit was coded as zero (i.e. non-substitutable) if no comparable subunit had existed pre-merger on the part of the other merging party. Admittedly, this is quite a rough measure: determining substitutability is complex and would have called for further in-depth analysis (e.g. Cohen & Lachman, 1988). The restricted consideration of the important substitutability variable therefore represents a limitation of the study at hand.

Thirdly, the central level administrative subsystem of both merging parties is left aside completely. In line with Hackman (1985), administrative units, though they may to a certain degree control organizational resources on their own, are treated as peripheral—without sustained education and research processes, there is nothing to administrate on the central level. Moreover, the technical buffering of academic self-governance against state-derived administration (recall 1.3.2) may further substantiate treating the integration of administrative units as a partly independent subject of analysis.

4.2.2 Results of the dimensional analysis

The pattern matrix in Table 4.3 shows some results of the factor analysis. Principal axis factoring suggests a five-factor model to efficiently indicate the relations within our basic set of 27 supposed power indicators. The extracted factors account for 79% of total variance in the data; the initial correlation matrix was able to be reproduced quite well (16% non-redundant residuals[24]). The factors (1) EduIM, (3) EduCOP, and (5) EduPERV together stand for the intraorganizational *education power* of TRUs; the factors (2) ResCENT and (4) ResCOP respectively represent their *research and transfer power*. The results support the notion of education and research / transfer

24 Correlations that exceed a 5% deviation from the initial correlation matrix.

as being largely independent resource transformation processes (or workflows).

The empirically derived model thus slightly deviates from the theoretically implied 6 power dimensions—research immediacy and pervasiveness indicators do all load into one and the same factor (ResCENT). Being a heavyweight regarding third-party funding and having a high dissertation output is correlated with running large research projects, where *large* often means interdisciplinary and therefore highly pervasive. The same logic does not apply to education indicators: carrying pervasive study programs is quite possible without being associated with large student proportions: "The pervasiveness and immediacy of the workflows of a subunit are not necessarily closely related, and may empirically show a low correlation" (Hickson et al., 1971: 222).

Another striking feature of the pattern matrix is the high number of negative cross-loaders between the two research power dimensions (ResCENT and ResCOP), which is also reflected in the high correlation between the two factors. To understand this pattern, one has to remember that variables related to effectiveness of coping have been calculated as differences between TRU indicator values and the respective means of the (statewide) comparison units. Since comparison includes the *Rhine-Westphalia Institute of Technology Aachen (RWTH)*, Germany's largest engineering university by far, the coping values for all competing engineering and natural science TRUs are necessarily impaired. This leads to the seemingly absurd situation of high relative control of research-related resources being associated with low values in terms of coping with uncertainty.

Factors	EduIM	ResCENT	EduCOP	ResCOP	EduPERV
Rotated factor patterns					
Third-party funds total	.097	**.839**	-.162	-.754	-.092
Third-party funds per prof.	.009	**.693**	-.249	-.482	-.165
Dissertations total	.200	**.871**	.049	-.508	.037
Dissertations per professor	.085	**.796**	-.004	-.358	-.048
Research project count	.212	**.884**	-.077	-.465	.190
Perv. research project count	.172	**.839**	-.020	-.257	.201
Heads in research projects	.109	**.771**	-.008	-.475	.328
Heads in per. research projects	.097	**.793**	-.108	-.284	.248
Pos. third party funds	.096	-.445	.297	**.978**	.046
Pos. third party funds p. prof.	.136	-.363	.195	**.949**	-.024
Position dissertations	.054	-.614	.235	**.938**	.026
Position dissertations per prof.	.142	-.464	.072	**.812**	-.101
First year students main subject	**.937**	.063	.231	.163	.097
First year students combination	**.884**	-.011	.168	.259	-.044
Total student count main sub.	**.972**	.222	.225	.062	.046
Student count capacity corr.	**.941**	.115	.248	.104	.149
Graduate count main subject	**.889**	.335	.267	-.066	.-134
Graduate count combination	**.817**	.156	.194	.081	-.258
Teaching demand total	**.919**	.199	.313	.087	.113
Position first year stud. main	.368	-.139	**.827**	.392	-.170
Position first year stud. comb.	.102	.126	**.701**	-.036	-.141
Position total students main	.496	-.045	**.877**	.353	-.071
Position total stud. count cap.	.344	-.219	**.864**	.278	-.127
Position graduates main subject	.100	-.077	**.781**	.239	-.098
Position graduates combination	.008	-.035	**.815**	-.046	-.222
Study programs supplied	-.032	.143	-.215	-.069	**.933**
Perv. stud. Programs supplied	.010	.215	-.213	-.087	**.930**
Interfactor correlations					
Research Centrality (ResCENT)	.157				
Coping (education) (EduCOP)	.272	-.078			
Coping (research) (ResCOP)	.127	-.516	.231		
Pervasiveness (edu) EduPERV	.003	.101	-.132	.015	

Table 4.3: Rotated factor patterns and intercorrelations, Principal Axis Factoring (6 iterations; Rotation: Promax, $\kappa = 4$)

Figure 4.3 below shows a simple scatterplot of the subunits' factor scores (derived via multiple regression) of the first two power dimensions. We are thus provided with a first impression of the post-merger power relation of the subunits to each other. Two rough groups appear in the plot: the upper diagonal, led by the two economics units (as education-related outliers) is completed by the social science, electrical engineering and mechanical engineering units from Duisburg, as well as by German language studies, biology and chemistry from the former University of Essen. These units display relatively high scores on either one or on both power factors. A large bulk of medium to low scoring units below is headed by the social sciences and physics departments from Essen. Since it is reduced to two dimensions, the plot is, of course, an incomplete representation of power relations.

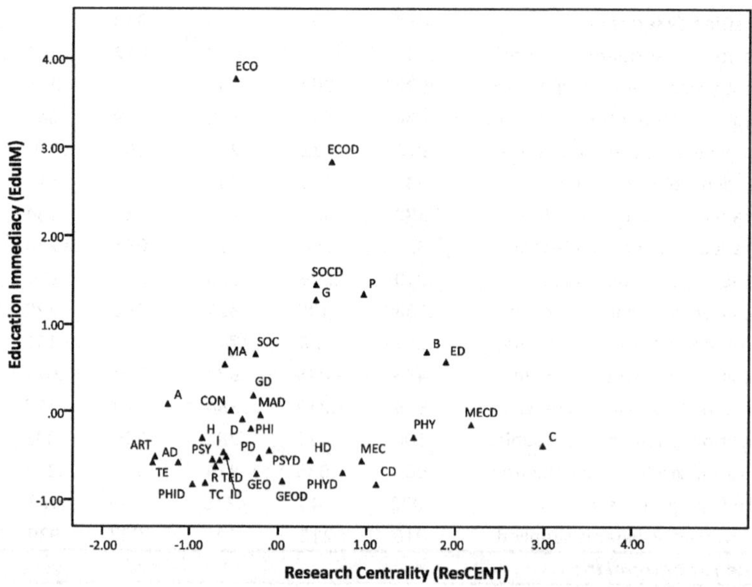

A(D) = Anglistics	**G(D)** = German language	**PHI(D)** = Philosophy
ART = Arts	**GEO(D)** = Geo sciences	**PHY(D)** = Physics
B = Biology	**H(D)** = History	**PSY(D)** = Psychology
C(D) = Chemistry	**I(D)** = Computer sciences	**R** = Romance studies (Duisburg)
CON = Construction eng.	**MA(D)** = Mathematics	**SOC(D)** = Social sciences
D = Design (Essen)	**MEC(D)** = Mechanical eng.	**SP** = Sports (Essen)
ECO(D) = Economics	**P(D)** = Pedagogics	**TE(D)** = Theology Protestant
ED = Elect. eng. (Duisburg)	[(D) stands for Duisburg]	**TC** = Theology Catholic (Essen)

Figure 4.3: Factor-score scatterplot for education immediacy and research centrality

Furthermore, principal components analysis was employed as a projection technique on the factor scores to "force" the five-dimensional power space into a more comprehensive two-dimensional plot, while taking a minimum loss of information (see Jolliffe, 1986: 66f.). Figure 4.4 shows the appendant components-score plot. Spatial proximity of TRUs in the plot hints at similar characteristics of their power profiles. Although some sketchy object grouping options already become apparent, overall the plot can do little more than complement the scatterplot in Figure 4.3.

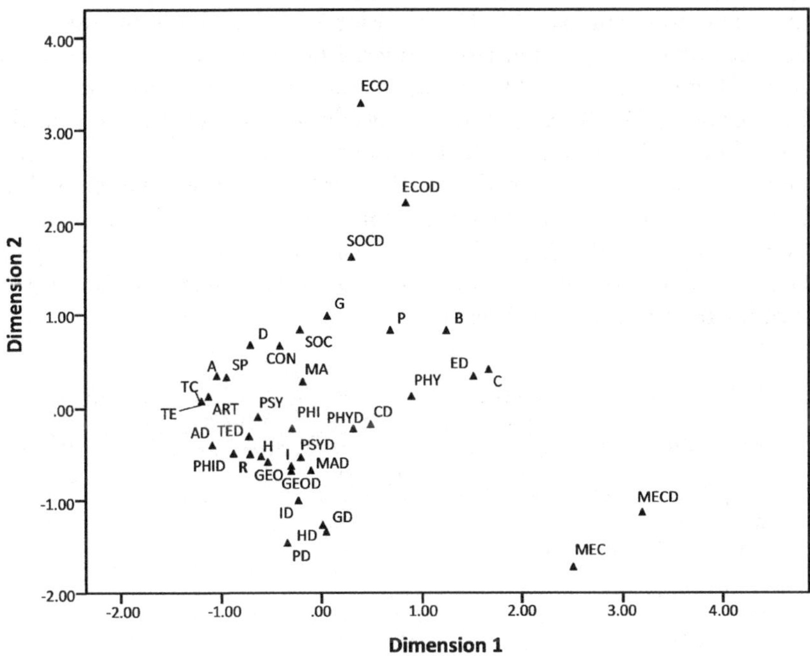

Figure 4.4: Components-score plot (PCA; Rotation: Varimax, 59% explained variance)

The analysis of post-merger power relations was further refined by processing the unit scores of all five power dimensions in a cluster analysis[25]. Preceding data reduction in this context generally serves three main purposes: firstly, and as a result of the scaling, all factor scores are standardized to ze-

25 Via R package "Cluster" (version 1.15.2; Maechler et al., 2013).

ro means and unity variance—the comparability of scales measured in different units (e.g. number of heads in projects, funding in monetary units) is assured. Secondly, the factors can be used as equally weighted variables in subsequent analysis, even though they are represented by differing numbers of variables within the raw data (Bacher, Pöge & Wenzig, 2010: 159). Thirdly, the stability of cluster solutions and comparability over different algorithms are increased.

A selection of hierarchical agglomerative and divisive cluster algorithms applying Euclidean and squared Euclidean distances was implemented and the results were compared[26]. The resulting partitions show themselves to be quite similar in general. Using squared Euclidean distances, the ward, centroid, median and McQuitty algorithms (all described in Kaufman & Rousseeuw, 2005) all reached their respective optimal fit measures for the nine-cluster solution (see Table 4.5). In the course of further argumentation, the partitioning attained from the *ward procedure* will be referred to, because it performed slightly better than its three alternatives and cut no single units out of the data. Table 4.4 displays the cluster means (i.e. typical factor scores of the units included) along with the standard deviations as a measure of intra-cluster homogeneity.

	Education Immediacy		Research Centrality		Coping (Education)		Coping (Research)		Education Pervasiveness	
C (n)	mean	SD	mean	SD	mean	SD	mean	SD	mean	SD
C1 (7)	-.356	.320	-.948	.382	.948	.263	.378	.297	-.940	.210
C2 (13)	-.384	.450	-.557	.337	-.012	.478	.225	.218	.133	.543
C3 (3)	2.685	.960	.167	.400	1.205	.368	.300	.095	.729	.763
C4 (2)	1.297	.041	.684	.265	-.573	.010	.797	.267	-1.070	.811
C5 (4)	.135	.478	2.014	.866	.221	.687	-.374	.085	-.523	.480
C6 (2)	-.356	.206	1.550	.618	-1.402	.284	-.393	.097	-.327	.709
C7 (3)	-.302	.337	-.054	.293	-2.451	.299	.573	.167	.179	.281
C8 (2)	-.767	.065	.909	.191	.810	.025	-.255	.016	1.464	.528
C9 (2)	-.275	.236	-.402	.192	-.776	.074	.046	.253	2.046	.225

Table 4.4: Cluster means and standard deviations

26 In general, the objectivity of data patterns was ensured by me employing, comparing, and combining a broad range of methods, algorithms, and distance measures. The results of principal axis factoring were successfully confirmed by further extraction methods (Maximum Likelihood, Unweighted Least Squares) and several rotation techniques—the differences were marginal. The factor structure was also replicated by applying cluster analysis of the 27 power indicators. Likewise, raw-data ULS-(Q-)factoring "over the cases" (see Bacher et al., 2010) supported the detected cluster solution as well.

Since any technical evaluation of model fit and model stability has to be necessarily complemented by a plausible content-related validation of the partitioning, this subsection closes with the description and labeling of the clusters:

Cluster 1 (C1; 7 units) → "*The isolated coping-winners*" includes *Catholic* and *Protestant religious studies*, *arts*, *design*, *construction engineering*, *sports science* and *English language studies* (all from Campus Essen). These units were characterized by coping well with education demands, low education immediacy and very low pervasiveness scores. Their coping with research demands was above the average and their research centrality extremely low. In short, they are isolated lightweight-units that were in a good comparison position.

Cluster 2 (C2; 13 units) → "*The powerless*" includes the *philosophy*, *geography* and *psychology* units from both merging partners, as well as *English studies*, *Romance language studies*, *religious studies (Protestant)* from Duisburg, and *computer sciences* and *history* (Essen). Those units largely display low scores on all five factors, with no distinct power base. The cluster comprises two exceptions: the *social sciences* and *mathematics* units from the University of Essen with scores that surpassed the cluster-mean; discordance between the different algorithms mainly concerned the assignment of these two units.

Cluster 3 (C3; 3 units) → "*The social sciences and economics pillar*" comprises the *economics* units from both universities and the *social sciences* unit from Duisburg, which all scored highly across almost all power dimensions. The Department of Economics from Essen displayed lower values in research centrality and education pervasiveness, but was an extreme outlier concerning education-related immediacy and coping. Some inconsistencies between the cluster procedures are paralleled by a relatively high intra-cluster variance and huge distances between the three units in the plots.

Cluster 4 (C4; 2 units) → "*The educational and German studies pillar*" is composed of *pedagogics* and *German language studies* from Essen. They displayed high values in education immediacy, research centrality and extremely high values in coping with research. Research pervasiveness was very low for German language studies and mediocre for pedagogics. The two units controlled the lion's share of the merged university's research potential beyond economics, and the social and natural science disciplines.

Cluster 5 (C5; 4 units) → "*The natural sciences engineering pillar*" contains biology, chemistry and physics from Essen as well as the electrical engineering unit from Duisburg. The main attributes of cluster 5 were mediocre coping / immediacy and low pervasiveness in terms of education. The units showed very high values in the research centrality factor. As with all units related to natural and engineering sciences, coping with research was sub-standard due to fierce competition.

Cluster 6 (C6; 2 units) → "*The outdistanced mechanics*" consists of the two mechanical engineering units. A cluster similar to C5, but with extremely low values in coping with research and education.

Cluster 7 (C7; 3 units) → "*The stronger* weak" includes history, pedagogics and German language studies from Duisburg. It may be described as the stronger complement of the relatively weak units in C2. The units in cluster 7 displayed contradictory coping-scores in terms of the two transformation processes: relatively high regarding research, and extremely low as regards education.

Cluster 8 (C8; 2 units) → "*The pervasive teaching-lightweights*" is composed of the chemistry and physics units from Duisburg. These two, in comparison to C5 and C6, showed lower education immediacy and research centrality values in combination with extremely high education pervasiveness.

The picture is completed by → "*The fundamentals-suppliers*" Cluster 9 (C9; 2 units), which is identical to the former mathematics and computer science department from Duisburg. Mediocre education immediacy and coping in union with extremely high pervasiveness scores marked it as an important supplier (of fundamental sciences).

Cluster	Ward	Centroid	Median	McQuitty
C1	1, 5, 6, 15, 19, 20, 21	1, 2, 4, 5, 6, 8, 13, 15, 17, 18, 19, 20, 21, 22, 25, 26, 27, 29, 37	1, 2, 4, 5, 6, 8, 13, 15, 17, 18, 19, 20, 21, 22, 25, 26, 27, 29, 37	1, 2, 4, 5, 6, 8, 13, 15, 17, 18, 19, 20, 21, 22, 25, 26, 27, 29, 37
C2	2, 4, 8, 9, 13, 17,18, 22, 25, 26, 27, 29, 37	3, 7	3, 7	3, 7
C3	10, 30, 31	9, 30, 31	9, 30, 31	10
C4	3, 7	10	10	11, 12, 14
C5	11, 12, 14, 35	11, 12, 14, 35	11, 12, 14, 35	16, 36
C6	16, 36	16, 36	16, 36	23, 24, 28
C7	23, 24, 28	23, 24, 28	23, 24, 28	30, 31
C8	32, 34	32, 34	32, 34	32, 34, 35
C9	33, 38	33, 38	33, 38	33, 38
Model fit measures				
Average silhoette width	.539	.533	.533	.521
Within-between variance ratio	.160	.192	.192	.195
Calinski & Harabasz index	104.43	88.134	88.134	86.959
Goodman & Kruskal γ	.938	.938	.938	.948
Cluster congruence measures: corrected rand index / Meilă's VI (Meilă, 2007)				
	Ward	**Centroid**	**Median**	**McQuitty**
Centroid	.585/.522			
Median	.585/.522	1/~0		
McQuitty	.611/500	.908/.026	.908/.026	

Table 4.5: Comparison of cluster assignments and validation statistics (see Bacher et al., 2010); via R cluster package "fpc" (Henning, 2013)

4.2.3 Post-merger integration: orientation and level analysis

At this point, we have come to a much more comprehensive and precise understanding of empirical post-merger intraorganizational power distribution. It has been shown that structural data on the merging parties' subunits can be reduced to education-related and research-related power factors as suggested by the SCT. Hence, the TRUs involved were able to be characterized and classified according to their position within the determined common property space. Besides the position of the units relative to each other, we have thus gained differentiated information regarding the respective transformation process-related bases of their power.

If we look again at the adapted SCT scheme (Fig. 4.2), the connection between intraorganizational power profiles and the external control of organizations becomes obvious. A high education immediacy score, for instance, is a consequence of fulfillment of study program-related demands. So both economics units, because of the high demand for economics-programs and degrees among students and corporations, together accounted for a large share of the students (about 25%). In a similar vein, the extensive involvement of units in research projects and high third-party funding partly[27] indicate the rewarding provision of research-related output resources to funding agencies. The demands of the state ministry as an important controller of funds are chiefly represented in the two effectiveness-of-coping factors: the better the relative comparison position of a TRU, the more substantial its relative contribution to granting favorable capital investment conditions.

This study claims the level and orientation of post-merger integration to be related to intraorganizational power distribution. We will open our specific empirical examination with Hypothesis three, which postulates that the orientation of post-merger integration will generally be toward the powerful subunits. The observable integrating shift of allocation responsibilities is expected to be oriented away from the weak and toward the strong units (H3a)—relatively weak units should fall under the control of the relatively strong units. Likewise, homogenized allocation rules should follow the resource interests of the latter regarding their context (H3b).

27 Still, it needs to be acknowledged that the connection is necessarily imperfect due to causal indeterminacy (Pfeffer & Salancik, 1978: 229). In this regard, the specific character of organizations in German higher education is of particular relevance: long-lasting attempts to structurally shield them against external control still take effect of course. Legal and resource dependence considerations are consistent in principle (recall Subsection 1.3.2): the larger the disposition of external actors over organizational resources, and the tighter the coupling to actual transformation-related demands, the more intraorganizational discretion of subunits can be explained by drawing on the environment—and academic liberties wane. Therefore, the explanatory potential of RDT / SCT in higher education contexts advances with ongoing neoliberal reorganization measures.

The rationale behind H3 has (in Section 3.4) been presented as one of the core arguments of RDT: the internal distribution of power and control is influenced by the environmental context. Successfully coping with external demands is the antecedent of intraorganizational resource control, which in turn is the basis of political power. Power breeds social discretion, and discretion will be used by the dominant coalitions to regulate organizational action, structure, and change in a way that maintains or enhances their power position (Pfeffer & Salancik, 1978: 228ff.).

With regard to observable merger outcomes, intraorganizational power should be positively associated with either the incorporation of other units (enhancing the power position of the absorbing unit) or the preservation of independence. Power should thus increase a unit's chance to become a *bidder* or a *status quo* unit. Units with relatively low power scores should in turn be prone to turning into targets. Keeping the status quo, i.e. remaining organizationally differentiated from other units in a merger situation, requires an appropriate resource basis. The new intraorganizational power distribution should become apparent as a general tendency in the observable post-merger integration outcome.

Let's begin with a brief description of basic structural merger outcomes. The integration process in the reference year 2010 had yielded 10 departments[28] structured as follows. A large Department of Humanities had been formed on campus Essen. It consisted of German language studies (G), history (H / HD), philosophy (PHI / PHID), and religious studies (TC / TE / TED) from both merging parties, as well as Turkish language and communication studies (TURK / COM) together with the Arts unit (ART) from Essen[29]. It was completed by the Romance studies unit from Duisburg (R). The attempted foundation of a unified department of social sciences had failed (see 4.3.2): vast parts of the social sciences unit from Essen (SOC) were integrated into a huge educational sciences department on the Essen campus instead. The latter had mainly been built around the former Department 2 of the University of Essen (pedagogics (P), psychology (PSY), sports sciences (SP)). By 2010, the new Department of Educational Sciences had also absorbed the pedagogics unit from Duisburg (PD). The De-

28 The Department of Medicine in Essen has been omitted.

29 Arts (ART) and design (D) formed their own department on campus Essen until 2007. Design was divested in 2007 (integrated into Essen's Folkwang University of Arts); the Arts unit was integrated into the Department of Humanities. Since it had not been subject to integration within the newly formed University of Duisburg–Essen, the design unit was coded as a status-quo unit, while the Arts unit was treated as a target.

partment of Social Sciences in Duisburg (SOCD) had thus maintained its status, and could absorb some smaller units below our TRU level of analysis.

The attempted integration of the two economics departments (ECO / ECOD) had likewise failed (see 4.3.3). Economics from Essen had incorporated the local information sciences unit (I) and had profiled towards wide-ranging fundamentals studies in micro-economics and macro-economics with a particular focus on business information systems. The department from Duisburg has since been transformed into a business school focused on business administration and micro-economics. To the present day, both have remained thoroughly separate units.

As regards the natural sciences, both physics units (PHY / PHYD) had been merged into a new Department of Physics on the Duisburg campus (see 4.3.1). The chemistry unit from Duisburg (CD) had likewise been integrated into the Department of Chemistry from Essen (C). The same had happened to the geography unit (GEOD), which had been incorporated by the Department of Biology and Geography (B / GEO / Land) on the Essen campus. The engineering disciplines from Essen (MEC / TEC / CON) had all been integrated into Duisburg's huge Department of Engineering (ED / MECD / ID / MAT); due to extensive relocation costs, the construction engineering unit (CON) has since remained localized on the campus in Essen. The mathematics units (MA / MAD) had become partly integrated through a common department council, but parts of the dean's office and department level administration had remained separate on both campuses[30].

The dendrogram of the ward-cluster solution (Fig. 4.6) may serve to complement the theoretical interpretation of post-merger integration provided. On the last but one agglomerative fusion-level, two large groups of units remain. The left-hand side group consists of the "outdistanced mechanics" (C6) and the three "pillars of power" (C3; C4; C5), which altogether roughly represent the relatively potent part of the merged university. The complementary right-hand side with clusters C1 / C2 and C7–C9 (see also the factor score-plot in Figure 4.4; think of a 3–3 diagonal) comprises the less powerful units. In line with the theoretical conceptualization of or-

30 Because of the post-merger common council, they were both coded as stationary targets. However, the binary coding in this case is attended by some loss of information.

ganizational integration, units were coded as *targets* if between 2004[31] and 2010 they had been integrated into another existing or a newly founded organizational unit post-merger; first-order integration and second-order integration were treated equally. Units were coded as *SQ / bidder* if they had retained their pre-merger integration status quo (SQ) or had absorbed other units respectively (bidder) (see again Tables 4.1 and 4.2 for unit assignments). If one considers post-merger TRU integration status in the year 2010, it turns out that 72% of the units from the powerful (left-hand side) clusters were able to retain their status quo or had acted as bidders in contrast to only 19% of units from the weaker clusters, a percentage difference of 53%.

31 An exception had been Essen's computer science unit (I), which in anticipation of the merger had already been integrated into the Department of Economics on the same campus in late 2002 (probably to prevent its possible removal to Duisburg).

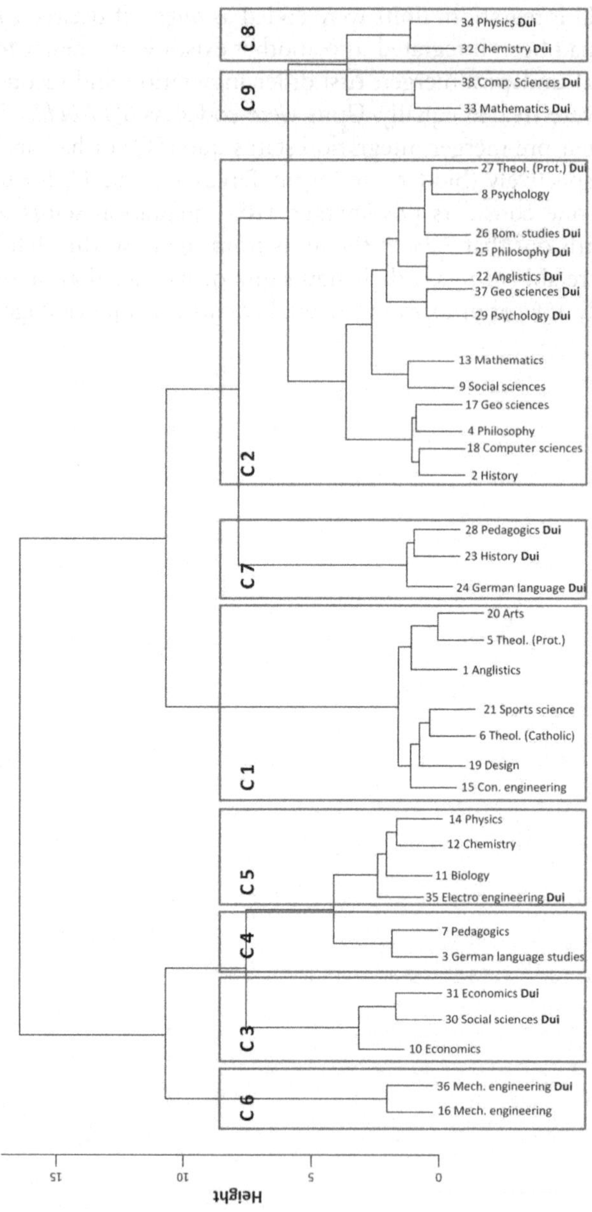

Figure 4.5: Dendrogram of the 9-cluster ward solution

To render the impressions from cluster analysis more precisely, binary logistic regression analysis was employed. Predictors of integration status are the five extracted power factors and, to complete the SCT model, process substitutability was introduced as a dummy variable. A unit was coded as 1 if a nominal match had existed on the part of the other merging party. The results in Table 4.6 show that subunit power can separate fairly well between integrated and status quo / bidder units overall. The power factors (except for ResCOP) all take effect in the hypothesized direction, with education immediacy and research centrality revealing the strongest impact. Substitutability of activities, in line with RDT / SCT, reduced intraorganizational power and decreased a unit's chance to defend its status quo or absorb other units.

	Status quo preserved or other units absorbed ("bidder")	
Covariates	Coefficient exp(b)	Standard Error
Intercept	1.479	1.110
Education Immediacy (EduIM)	2.742	.559
Research Centrality (ResCENT)	2.462	.512
Coping (Education) (EduCOP)	1.438	.533
Coping (Research and Transfer) (ResCOP)	.876	.469
Education Pervasiveness (EduPERV)	1.217	.478
Nominal Match (Substitutability)	.208	1.341
-2-log-likelihood	33.505	
Pseudo-R2 (Nagelkerke)	.459	
Pseudo-R2 (Cox & Snell)	.332	

Table 4.6: Results of logistic regression analysis (SQ / bidder); N = 38

In consideration of the merger case under study, a general connection between the distribution of intraorganizational power and the orientation of post-merger integration realized can thus be demonstrated. The observable integration had preserved or fostered social discretion among the potent TRUs. The internal power relations that had been created through the merger manifested themselves within organizational structures—they were reproduced and further accentuated. Merger implementation thereby patently became organized around intraorganizational power: integration appears to mostly have been conducted in line with the interests of the strong units.

What the analysis of general orientation of integration cannot reveal with sufficient rigor, however, is the content-related essence of the unit's interests. Intraorganizational power doesn't appear from nowhere; it emerges from and has to be maintained by a continued transformation of resources. Resource transformation calls for coping with external demands, and the essential interest of the subunits should be the protection of their ability to cope.

The connection between the specific character of an integration measure in terms of the qualitative and quantitative dimensions of the TRUs' interdependence patterns is the subject of our complementary second hypothesis. We expect the chances of integration measures being implemented to decrease with rising resource dependence on the potentially offended environmental demands (H2b). On the all-up system level, the overall post-merger integration level should sink accordingly the deeper the resource dependence on potentially impaired demands is (H2a).

To examine Hypothesis 2, we will exemplarily consider the spatial relocation of units as an integration measure. By 2010, 11 of the 38 TRUs examined had been removed from their respective campus and relocated during the merger process. As regards our theoretical conceptualization of integration, spatial relocation is homogenization of an allocation rule: the localization of one TRU is adjusted to the localization of the unit it is integrated into. What qualifies spatial relocation as a proper basis to inspect Hypothesis 2 is the fact that it definitely impairs one external demand that all the units considered have in common: that of students. Studying requires physical attendance regarding lectures, consultation, exams, and other activities. Relocation of a TRU 25 km away hence entails numerous problems for its students. It requires commuting and therefore complicates subject combination, working, and childcare. Student protests against unit removal are well documented in the reports (e.g. CD1|3). According to H2, the prevention of spatial relocation due to such conflicts with external demands should depend on the relative weight of a unit's power regarding education processes.

Thus, referring to the 2010 unit relocation status as the dependent variable, I calculated further logistical regression. Since process substitutability does not in itself represent an aspect of resource transformation, it was omitted in the second model; relevant predictors are solely the five extracted power factors. Probably due to a (small-n-related) completely separated data set, it unfortunately failed to yield interpretable coefficient estimates.

As an alternative, we therefore switch to a comparison of the corresponding unit power profiles (Figure 4.6). According to the dependent variable, all 25 target units are split into 14 stationary and 11 removed targets. The three resulting profiles (power factor means) of the groups are plotted against the profile of the 13 status quo / bidder units.

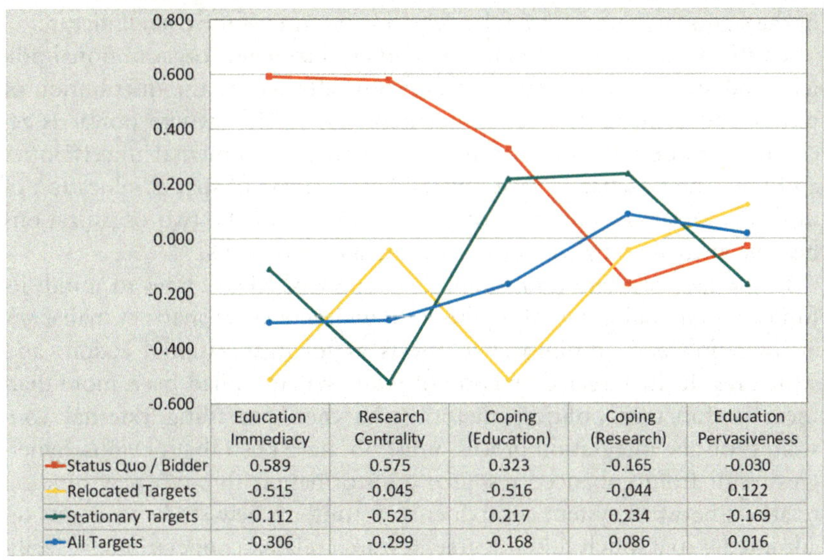

	Education Immediacy	Research Centrality	Coping (Education)	Coping (Research)	Education Pervasiveness
Status Quo / Bidder	0.589	0.575	0.323	-0.165	-0.030
Relocated Targets	-0.515	-0.045	-0.516	-0.044	0.122
Stationary Targets	-0.112	-0.525	0.217	0.234	-0.169
All Targets	-0.306	-0.299	-0.168	0.086	0.016

Figure 4.6: Education and Research / Transfer power profiles according to integration and relocation status

This visual representation suggests that the immediacy and coping factors of education strongly influenced a unit's chance to stay put. Small relative control over students and poor effectiveness of education-related coping were obviously necessary conditions to become a relocation candidate[32]. In contrast, research-related power factors hardly seem to have played a role in impeding unit removal—the mean research centrality score of the relocated targets is even higher in comparison to the overall targets. Differ-

32 This is the supposed "complete separation problem" in the context of logistic regression analysis (see Albert & Anderson, 1984; Santner & Duffy, 1986): education power in our case almost perfectly predicts unit relocation status, which leads to extremely high and uninterpretable odds ratios and standard errors.

ences considering research-related coping are limited; the small ResCOP scores of the more powerful (mostly SQ- / bidder units) have already been ascribed to the severe competition in the natural sciences and engineering disciplines. The likewise small discriminatory potential of education pervasiveness is rooted in the fact that 9 out of the 11 relocated units stem from the former University of Duisburg, where workflow pervasiveness had been generally higher. Furthermore, a unit's education pervasiveness may lose much of its power potential if education immediacy scores, as is true of the stationary targets, are relatively low in terms of the overall picture.

This is precisely the *external control of organizations*: "organizational policies and structures are results of decisions affected by the distribution of power and control" (Pfeffer & Salancik, 1978: 238), where power is accrued by those who successfully cope with environmental uncertainties and keep their exchange relations stable. The issue of spatial relocation of units demonstrates how the integration process of the two organizations became virtually canalized by environmental constraints.

In the face of these results, another aspect of RDT comes to mind: its fundamental doubts regarding the (still) widespread emphasis of managerial discretion and administrative effects as to organizational actions and structures. If the targeted creation of *future* synergies had been more than mere perfunctory political rhetoric, the then prevailing external constraints on the integration process must not have been that obvious. Synergies result from enhanced resource transformation through new binding relations between system components. Setting up new study programs or, admittedly to a much lesser degree, research-related cooperation are facilitated by a common location. A strategic assignment of units relating to content-related complementarities should have been the result.

4.3 Exploring the qualitative pattern relations: three chosen fields of integration

The managerial requirement to protect student interests demonstrated above had been broadly anticipated by political actors within the merging organizations from the very beginning of the integration process (ID1|12; 1–III: 298): "but no permanent changeovers between the sites to attend lectures, that was a primary goal" (1–VI: 135). The founding rectorate, as the main central level political subsystem that encouraged integration, had to encounter further constraining external demands. These were associated with different levels of the organizational environment and were partly in a state of considerable conflict with each other.

To begin with the wider environment, the change process was framed by the general political impetus summarized in 1.1.3. As laid out in the context of the effectiveness-of-coping variables, the demand to deliver strengthened performance indicators within a short period was of special prominence (SP1 07|2005: 5). Although the state ministry made some concessions to the merged university—for example, deficit-related cutbacks had been temporarily reduced for 2004 and 2005 (ID1|11: 1; SP1 17|2004: 7)—a situation of resource scarcity persisted. On the closer federal state level, the disposal of the *Gesamthochschule* model in North Rhine-Westphalia as a state demand has to be added. It expressed a more definite, "pure" university profile in the requirement to advance. This demand corresponded with the budget-effective overall substandard research indicators, like third-party funding and dissertation output (SP1 18|2005: 4).

Two further and more case-specific constraints had their roots in the more direct organizational environment of the merging parties. These first involve the state ministry's strategic interest in seeing the university further develop as a center of teacher training in the western Ruhr area. The reform commission had suggested concentrating the non-occupational teaching degree programs in Essen (CD1|1: 120). In combination with the distance between the two campuses, this settlement was of great significance for integration outcomes (1–VI: 911ff.) and played a decisive role in the post-merger foundation of the Department of Educational Sciences. The second local constraint consisted in the political demand to keep up the quantitative proportions between the two sites (1–II: 498ff.). Since higher education politics in Germany frequently goes hand in hand with the formation and advancement of regional structures, any radical (asymmetric) solution to the problem of unit assignment would thus have caused communal opposition. This indirect (state-mediated) demand regarding merger implementation can be traced in numerous documents and strategy papers on both a central and a subunit level.

Even though ministry officials did not actively intervene in the internal affairs of the merged university, organizational integration of the two merging parties was an important merger objective and can therefore itself be characterized as an external demand. The founding rectorate's strategic guidelines expressed a desire to realize complementary and clear-cut discipline profiles by 2006 at the latest. Due to the many (at least nominal) unit overlaps, this necessarily implied a sizeable integration level being achieved.

The generally constraining demands briefly outlined here joined with the TRU-specific environmental exchange requirements and interacted with them. In the following, Chapter 4 is completed with a compact examination of three integration attempts: the successful establishment of a unified physics department on the one hand, and the failed integration of the social sciences and economics on the other. These three important fields of organizational integration involved ten TRUs, with an overall 50% share of the merged university's student population.

4.3.1 The integration of physics

Both merging universities had included physics departments, which were comparable in size but with varying profile foci. The unit from Essen particularly aimed attention at theoretical physics: quantum optics, quantum statistics, and theoretical surface physics. Its experimental research groups were concerned with surface and ultra-short time physics. In Duisburg, the respective discipline profile was characterized by a stronger emphasis on application-oriented fields of inquiry, like semiconductor physics and gas dynamics (ID1|13: 654ff.)—substantial research cooperation with the local mechanical and electrical engineering units existed. Both physics departments offered traditional diploma as well as several teaching degree programs. The unit in Essen additionally provided an application-oriented program in physical engineering.

The amalgamation of the two physics units into a unified department of physics on the Duisburg campus can genuinely be designated as a paragon of successful integration within the overall merger case. Consensus between representatives of the units regarding the formation of a common department had been found as early as March 2001, shortly after the pre-merger negotiation stage had started (ID1|14: 679ff.). The general agreement as to integration and location on the same campus was confirmed by an external expert-panel in July 2002, which recommended Duisburg as the future site of choice. Plans for internal organization and shared study programs were soon to follow. No doubts about the integration of the two departments whatsoever could be traced in the documents; an interview partner concluded: "it was definitely the area where things proceeded in the most noiseless fashion" (1–II: 738).

In Subsection 3.4.1, we identified qualitative consistencies of organizational interdependence patterns as influential drivers of integration. Paralleling basic founding conditions of organizations, they are a potential source of collectively enhanced reduction of environmental uncertainties. In the case of physics, these qualitative consistencies in the first place were rooted in the research profile complementarity of the two units. The research links with the engineering units in Duisburg especially were seen as pivotal in the decision to locate the new department on the Duisburg campus: "it is a unique combination which is forward-looking and will further bolster the physicists from Essen, with their strong research groups considering laser optics, surface physics, and plasma physics" (ID1|15: 1). The combination of Duisburg's application orientation with Essen's fundamentals researchers was considered the basis of an "attractive focus of natural science-engineering"—the resulting broader profile was also intended to help to make study programs more tempting and counteract low capacity utilization (ID1|13). Numerous new research projects—possible promising common system configurations—from nanobionics to ferromagnetism were foreshadowed; an upsurge in third-party funding for the faculty of not less than 30% was envisaged (ID1|16: 3). Hence, an integrated transformation system was deemed overtly beneficial.

Nonetheless, some qualitative pattern inconsistencies had also existed. They mostly related to the fundamental teaching-supplier function of the physics units on their respective campuses. On the Essen campus, the responsibilities as far as teacher training (technical didactics) was concerned posed a problem, since they were accompanied by larger operating expenses (training in operating experiments). Additionally, medicine, chemistry, and the central systems engineering programs had to be supported. The unit from Duisburg provided services to chemistry, and electrical and mechanical engineering, as well as to the material sciences program(s), amongst others. In either case, locating the faculty on the same campus (in the early stage, both campuses were discussed) would have bound staff and equipment. A further, yet somewhat peripheral category of inconsistencies related to fixed installations in buildings and non-portable laboratory equipment, for example an immovable helium-tube system on the Duisburg campus.

Why did the integrating forces in these parts of the organization prevail so clearly? We have argued that the degree of resource dependence on potentially impaired external interests accounts for integration realization. The rationale for this has been found in the retrospective character of intraorganizational power. Coalitions maintain their stability if they continue to transform and distribute resources from the environment (or even enhance resource acquisition). The impairment of environmental demand satisfaction through integration thus threatens coalitional stability. As regards the two physics units, it therefore first has to be stated that the projected improvement in third-party funding was substantial. In no other unit constellation were prospective advancements in coping with uncertainty that clear-cut. The overall weight of the education-related pattern inconsistencies (EduIM) were merely mediocre (Essen) and low (Duisburg).

However, one thing is of ultimate importance: negotiations had from the outset been backed by strong and reliable financial commitments from the state ministry. Not only could the units realize their preferred faculty headcount and status group composition (ID1|17), but the integration process was fueled by *instantaneous* additional resource inflows. All removal costs were borne by the ministry; the relocation was sweetened through new laboratory and IT equipment, office furniture, and enlarged workshop capacities (also: ID1|13):

> That has to be expressed in a somewhat neutral manner, because nobody ever openly admitted that [...] but it was attractive for the physicists from Essen, because they got furnished anew and got new equipment over there (1–VI: 165).

Bargaining space between the coalitions was further widened through the fact that 50% of professorships had to be reappointed by 2009, which allowed for a broader spectrum of possibilities as to system configurations and further facilitated integration. In brief: the merger in this area was accompanied by a voluminous investment by the state ministry.

If we consider the overall merger, it is important to point out that this kind of commitment was an exception. In many cases, unit relocation was hampered or protracted due to a lack of building capacity. The integration of the Romance studies (Cluster 2) unit from Duisburg into the new Department of Humanities on the Essen campus may provide an example:

> There was so little office space in R12 [Essen, mk] and all of a sudden, four professors had to share one office. This is not an option. Something that is common for undergraduate student assistants is absolutely unacceptable for professors (1–III: 343).

For some units, relocation even led to the temporary deterioration of resource transformation conditions. The physics departments hence represented an exception on multiple counts: clearly identifiable content-related cooperation potential and the limited impairment of external demands in combination with immediate resource inflows effectively fostered organizational integration.

4.3.2 Educational and social sciences

The foundation of the Department of Educational Sciences on the Essen campus in 2004 marked a central moment in the post-merger integration stage. At the same time, it is the story of the failed creation of a large unified department of social sciences. With Essen's pedagogics unit and Duisburg's Department of Social Sciences, two powerful subunits confronted each other during integration negotiations.

At the heart of the respective department in Duisburg had been its political science and sociology TRU (SOCD), which pre-merger had included an Institute for Practical Social Sciences. The department had provided interdisciplinary diploma programs in social sciences with specialization options in one of the three fields of study. Besides that, it had served some subject combination and teaching degree programs (in sociology). The department had also contained the Institute for Pedagogics (PD), and, without their own study programs, the small supportive psychology and geography units (PSYD and GEOD).

On the Essen campus, the respective department profiles had looked different. The strong pedagogics unit (P), as the head of the Department 2, had organized and accompanied the highly pervasive teaching degree programs. It was supplied and supported by sports science (SP) and psychology (PSY). The local social science unit (SOC), originally assigned to the Department of Humanities, had been focused on social work. It provided respective cross-disciplinary subject combination and UAS-level study programs (e.g. "Practical Social Science"), with no distinct program focus.

Integration-related negotiations between the two sides, which had started in early 2001 and further intensified after the merger, had from the very beginning mainly revolved around study program issues (1–V: 65). Essen wanted to preserve its social work program and (in the wake of the parallel Bologna Process) generally voted for cross-disciplinary study programs, while Duisburg expressed a clear preference toward the early separation of sociology and political sciences. Up to a certain point, a consensus on forming an integrated department for social science seems to have existed (ID1|18: 390; 1–V: 262). The founding rectorate, which preferred fewer and cross-disciplinary programs, suggested Duisburg should become the future place of residence for the integrated faculty; teacher training responsibilities should still be assumed in Essen (ID1|19).

However, the pedagogics and social sciences units from Essen quickly vowed to reject these plans. Operative demands of the teaching degree programs were claimed to require the localization of all pedagogics capacities in Essen, including the respective Duisburg-based unit (PD) (ID1|20: 4). Additionally, any transfer or integration of Essen's social work program was denied for three reasons. Firstly, long-term funding relations with the city of Essen called for local structures[33]—about 60 students from the social work program regularly completed a 16-month (three terms) practical study period in city projects (ID1|42). Secondly, a rising political / societal demand to connect teacher training and social work to tackle social inequalities and education deficits better was pointed to. An integrated curriculum of pedagogics and social work was, in this regard, considered a first-mover advantage (ID1|21: 6). Thirdly, the acceptance of Duisburg's diploma degree in practical social sciences within the professional field of social work was deemed to be lower than the state-certified social worker qualification provided in Essen. Disadvantages for future graduates were feared in case of program integration and Duisburg-oriented degree homogenization (*Ibid.*).

The Department of Social Sciences from Duisburg made clear that it was pro-integrationist in principle, but not willing to make any concessions. In a written comment submitted to the founding rectorate, it pointed to its superiority as regards third-party funds and teaching-capacity utilization relative to Essen (ID1|22). Stressing its definite university profile and willingness to compete with other acknowledged institutions, it insisted on plans to install clear-cut bachelor's and master's programs in political science and sociology. Distinct program foci in terms of disciplines were considered to increase graduate employability in highly specialized and project-oriented labor markets (*Ibid.*: 17f.).

In February 2004, the rectorate started a first approach to determine unit allocation; the proposed resolution still envisaged the concentration of social sciences in Duisburg; teacher training and some social work capacities were to remain localized in Essen (ID1|23: 8). On the eve of a decisive senate hearing, it was countered by a concerted initiative of all the units from Essen that were affected, which suggested the local establishment of a department of educational sciences instead (ID1|24). Their argument basically referred to the ideas stated above but had gained momentum—three origins of danger for Essen's teacher training processes were identified by the initiators (*Ibid.*):

33 The city mayor expressed his concerns in a letter (ID1|43).

- It was suggested that the transfer of local administrative capacity and the projected location of an integrated department's dean's office in Duisburg would seriously hamper the management of study programs;
- The looming difficulty of maintaining coordinating subsystems with student involvement to support and inform the dean's office about operative problems (i.e. the danger of fading environmental feedback);
- In an integrated department council, representatives of pedagogics feared they would become structurally dominated by (and thus lose resources to) social scientists with little interest in the non-prestigious teaching degrees: only two of the seven professorial seats on the council would have been allocated to members of their department at the most (ID1|25: 3).

Hence, because of the recommended comprehensive first-order integration and due to qualitative pattern inconsistencies, the units from Essen would have had to face the deterioration of their capabilities to sufficiently handle external demands. Duisburg's Department of Social Sciences, by contrast, was in a different situation. Despite the threat of lower performance indicators, the unit would have instantly improved its resource situation below the line—Essen's political science professorships especially had been of great interest throughout the negotiations (e.g. ID1|26: 5ff.). The council of Duisburg's Department of Social Sciences consequently renounced the establishment of a department of educational sciences and unanimously backed the rectorate's integration plans (ID1|27).

Instead of a large unified department, what was finally realized was a series of small-scale and mostly second-order integration measures. The pedagogics and social science units from Essen had successfully held their ground. The former Department 2 (P / SP / PSY) absorbed the pedagogics unit (PD) from Duisburg, as well as the social work-related parts from Essen (SOC) to form the Department of Educational Sciences a few months later (ID1|28). Duisburg's social sciences department integrated the political science professorships from Essen; only the political science didactics unit remained, as a "satellite" (1-II: 499), localized in Essen. Political science and sociology additionally gained the capacities from Duisburg's former local practical social science institute; the related study program in social work was terminated. Both psychology units remained completely separated and retained their mere supportive status; the unit from Duisburg (PSYD), due to its information science affiliation, became integrated into the Department of Engineering. Geography (GEOD) was moved to Essen and was integrated into the Department of Geography and Biology (B /

GEO), but still had to provide several services for Duisburg's study programs.

In a nutshell, the two main units facing each other, pedagogics in Essen and social sciences in Duisburg, were both heavyweights and owed their power to qualitatively different environmental demands. The potency behind the qualitative inconsistencies claimed was large enough to block the originally planned far-reaching measures. Central level executives could neither dare to risk the continued operation of teacher training, nor the enhancement of the strong social and political sciences in Duisburg[34]. Actual integration outcomes thus represented a political compromise within the organization and further improved the resource base of the powerful units. By balancing some conflicting external demands at the expense of deeper integration, the agreement provided the following benefits:

- The formation of the merged university's focus on teacher training programs was ensured, and demand fulfillment was signaled to the environment through the formal establishment of a specialized department;
- Social sciences (at least nominally) vanished from Essen's campus profile, while its exchange relations with the city were able to go on;
- The strong political science and sociology profile in Duisburg was able to be fostered with some extra faculty positions (ID1|29: 2);
- Quantitative campus proportions remained stable.

Some pro-integrationist voices in the senate criticized the founding rectorate for what was deemed an undue pursuit of compromise (ID1|30). To somehow compensate for the foreseeable low level of integration, a political allocation subsystem without formal responsibilities was claimed to advance coordination between the Departments of Educational and Social Sciences (coordination committee) (1–VI: 633). However, committee establishment was rejected by department representatives from the outset (SP1 1|2004: 5; except. meeting)—actual committee activities are not documented.

4.3.3 Economics

The University of Duisburg–Essen's nowadays two completely separate economics departments still constitute the most obvious reminiscence of its

34 A weak attempt to integrate Duisburg's unit in Essen had likewise failed.

formerly distinct parent institutions. What had originally started with a general consensus (ID1|1) on forming a unified department had quickly turned into hard-bitten integration denial and resource conflicts.

If we consider the system configurations of both units, economics on the Essen campus provided broadly-based training with special emphases on information systems and marketing. Diploma programs in business administration, economics, as well as in information management were offered. A newer development had been the establishment of a bachelor's program in medical management in cooperation with the Department of Medicine. In 2002, Essen's computer sciences unit (I) had been integrated as an Institute for Computing and Information Management prior to the merger.

Duisburg's economics unit had a stronger focus on business administration. (Macro-)economics was secondary as it was regarded as a supporting discipline—its capacities had been significantly lower. Duisburg's business administration study program and research profile were characterized by logistics management, business engineering, and East-Asian business relations (ID1|31). From early 2001 at the latest, the department had been working on plans to form a business school with an even more definite focus on business administration (ID1|32: 3).

The two departments promoted very different organizational arrangements during post-merger integration negotiations:

- Representatives from Essen suggested full integration of all economics capacities into a single department to be located on the Essen campus (ID1|33);
- Duisburg's economists sought a strict division of economics into subdisciplines. They believed that Essen's business administration capacities should be unhinged and incorporated into what was to become the *Mercator School of Management* on campus Duisburg. The study programs in economics and information systems should remain in Essen, where only some basic services in business administration were to be provided (ID1|34).

Essen's unit delineated its sources of qualitative pattern inconsistencies by exposing the effectiveness of its own configuration in an extensive department development plan. Foremost, the city of Essen as a department location was deemed to provide more resources in comparison to Duisburg (ID1|34):

- More and larger potential graduate employers and research and transfer partners in the form of business corporations are situated in the immediate and general vicinity;
- Essen is the hometown and an explicit donation focus of the family-heritage foundation of 20th-century arms and steel industry tycoon *Alfried Krupp von Bohlen und Halbach*. In 2002, three full professorships in the department were granted by the foundation;
- Essen has a larger, younger and faster growing population with a higher proportion of university-qualified school leavers;
- Infrastructure: it has a central campus location and better connections to the public transport system.

Furthermore, the integrative connection between business administration, economics, and information technology was characterized as a demanded and promising strategic form of orientation regarding education and research.

In a direct response (ID1|35) to Essen's vision of integration, the economists from Duisburg laid out their own unit's potential, together with the expected impairments to exchange relations:

- Loss of strategic research opportunities through the damaging of cooperation with the strong Duisburg-based engineering disciplines (e.g. regarding environmental and energy management);
- Advantageous study program interconnectedness with the engineering units, the importance of industrial production and industrial engineering program foci to regional employers;
- Loss of a large student catchment area, while simultaneously creating a situation of intensified competition with the huge University of Bochum (Essen's alleged student abundance was questioned).

The respective written comment also directly addressed the political demand to maintain quantitative campus proportionality. Full integration of economics on campus Essen would have required comprehensive (and likewise disputed) other integration measures to compensate for a more than 25% loss of Duisburg's student population. Duisburg's angst at suffering from unfavorable allocation rules was expressed in its overall insistence on preventing structural council domination by its larger counterpart (ID1|36).

The demeanor of representatives from both sides in the context of central level negotiations and within the senate was generally portrayed in the interviews as confrontational and destructive: "it was oddly aggressive" (1-II: 345). As documented in many accounts and written statements, the respective opposite party was often directly attacked according to its assumed weaknesses—the two units repeatedly accused each other of blocking bilateral consultations. In his report to the founding rectorate, the state commissioner accordingly suggested upholding operative disengagement and separate unit location while, nonetheless, establishing a unified department (ID1|37). The following university-wide planning conference ended up in comprehensive dissent (ID1|38). Representatives from both units eventually arrived at an agreement that settled on the perpetuation of two distinct departments in a state of "fair competition"; both were to be equipped with separate and full allocation responsibilities (*Ibid.*). The rectorate initially adopted this outcome and in its first discipline allocation resolution decided according to the agreement.

As a merger outcome, such permanent separation of economics into two independent subsystems was hard to convey to the public, and the rector's office, in defiance of its initial resolution, wasn't yet ready to accept it. Regardless of the rather inauspicious course of negotiations, a further serious effort to resolve the situation was made in late 2004: the rectorate requested a "certain minimum level of change" (SP 05|2004: 9). Though a wider choice of integration options regarding economics and social sciences had re-entered the agenda, the debate at that time mainly focused on an alleviated version of the solution suggested by Duisburg's economics department (and backed by the rectorate). About half of Essen's business administration professorships was to be integrated into Duisburg's new Mercator School of Management, and the study program in business administration in Essen was to be terminated. Hence, in comparison to many other more far-reaching options, the senate was left to discuss a relatively small-scale first-order integration measure to straighten out campus profiles.

The two parties again brought their control of organizational resources into negotiations and were well able to mobilize their respective environmental exchange partners[35]:

> Both economics departments equally had their city and trade association networks and so on. They had enough to trigger a shitstorm, so the rector had to give in. And the dismay in view of that initiative [...] as I said before, things had been settled for good already in the senate. And why [...] Once he tried to rush something through and failed—my appraisal (1–III: 570f.).

35 A further example is provided by a parliamentary request aimed at the protection of economics in Essen (CD1|2).

A strong internal ally of Essen's unit was the medical department, since the medical management program had been a part of hospital planning agreements with the state. In addition, schedule arrangement complications with the tightly-coupled medicine degree course were apprehended (ID1| 39). Duisburg's position was likewise supported by representatives of its engineering partner units (SP1 05 |2004: 10).

As in the case of the failed creation of a unified department of social sciences, the core arguments hadn't changed over time. The coalition from Essen, which would have been negatively affected by the integration measure advised, in responding to the new initiative tailored its arguments even more explicitly to the looming retrenchment of existing resource flows. Besides the foreseen damages to research and education foci, this especially referred to the uncompensated immediate loss of 2,500 university places and, annually, 100 business administration graduates (ID1|40). It was thought the remaining non-business school professorships, which according to the integration plans should have stayed in Essen, would lose their attractiveness as regards replacement professors due to their isolation (ID1|41: 6).

Organizational integration endeavors regarding the two economics units definitely broke down in December 2004. The senate adopted a settlement that provided for two business administration programs on the two campuses: "it was the argument that we may lose students [...] the sheer number of students which caused us to retain two sites" (1–VI: 603). No common political allocation subsystem whatsoever could be installed; attempts to form an interdepartmental coordination board came to naught.

On balance, and for all the variations of integrating organizational arrangements discussed, proponents again were confronted with the risk of interfering with the respective exchange relations of one of the two successfully existing subsystem configurations:

- either the education immediacy outlier bar none: Essen's integrative approach to economics with its aspiring foci in information and health management;
- or Duisburg's equally promising business school concept, together with logistics management and its well-working ties with the engineering disciplines.

Although the concentration of business administration in Duisburg would have brought about capacity-relevant savings, this and other integration measures would ultimately have resulted in the rather diffuse and prospective strengthening of one of the two profiles. No proper compensation for any imminent losses in resources acquired from the university's environment had become apparent during negotiations.

4.4 Résumé and case-specific study limitations

The first (quantitative) part of the Duisburg–Essen case study was devoted to the subunit level analysis of the organizational interdependence patterns' power dimension. Empirical results back the SCT as an adequate model to that end. The scaling and measurement of intraorganizational power were complemented by the identification of subunit groups with similar power profiles. On this basis, some evidence for our theoretical assumptions regarding the orientation of organizational integration toward the powerful subunits was provided (H3). Post-merger control stays with the powerful, or, in other words, the reduction of organizational differentiation essentially applies to the less potent units. The merger was organized around the organizational pillars of power. Estimating the probability of realizing the integration measures as a function of relevant power profile characteristics subsequently supported the connection between environmental interdependence pattern relationship and overall integration level (H2a / b; H3b).

In the second part (4.3) of the case study, our attention turned to a more detailed examination of qualitative pattern (in)consistencies and the corresponding political positions of subunits (H1) toward integration. Resource transformation-related impairing and / or improving effects of concrete integration measures were considered. Furthermore, post-merger negotiations and integration outcomes were traced for the subunits chosen. The results of structural data analysis were used as background information; the methodical focus was placed on the examination of documents and interviews.

An integrated consideration of the overall explanation complex is also pursued in the following second case study: the incorporation of the former *Hamburger Universität für Wirtschaft und Politik* into the *University of Hamburg* in 2005. Most notably, this case provides a relevant contrast as regards the role of spatial distance in integration outcomes. Spatial distance between the campuses of the two merging parties in the Duisburg–Essen case, though it was sometimes brought forward as a pro-merger argument, emerged as the single most important source of potential environmental demand impairment. Integration-related post-merger negotiations were canalized and influenced by spatial distance in numerous ways:

- Through the necessity to commute between the sites and the connected deterioration of studying and working conditions. Even if spatial detachment of core transformation processes had been kept, the mere operation of integrated political subsystems would, in most cases, have involved considerable costs. Apprehensions regarding the negative effects of first-order integration were fostered by the teacher training service duties of many units.
- In the context of spatial distance (besides the requirements to maintain campus proportionality), all "big hit" integration scenarios were additionally affected by the state ministry's limited willingness to invest. First-order integration proponents had hence been left with the burden of a fundamental lack of credibility regarding the practical accomplishment of unit relocation throughout. The granted removal budget of €57 million had largely been spent on new physics and chemistry laboratory facilities. No removal costs whatsoever had been scheduled for the economics, social sciences and humanities units (SP1 06|2005: 9); unit relocation was declared to be possible only by switching existing building capacities (*Ibid.*). Even in core integration fields like engineering (especially construction engineering), the humanities, and teacher training in Essen, physical unit removal failed or could not be completed until 2009. Office building and lecture room space has remained scarce on both campuses (1–III: 343; SP1 10|2007: 10; SP1 19|2007: 8).

Although these integration constraints were able to be readily captured within the proposed materialist and resource-oriented theoretical framework, some analytical limitations to the consideration of our first Hypothesis ensue. The latter relates to the political positioning of organizational coalitions toward attempted integration measures: qualitative interdependence pattern inconsistencies are suggested to advance disintegrative forces (H1a). It is expected that the negatively affected subunits should reject integration attempts, and seek to impede effective post-merger implementation. Since many integration measures in the Duisburg–Essen case had failed at the bargaining table, and spatial distance has mostly led to clearly separated political subsystems, the analysis and exploration of the intraorganizational handling of integration measures is restricted.

In the context of the following second case study, spatial distance played no role at all. The three merging parties had been situated within walking distance or even within the same building pre-merger. Hence, the central aims of the following fifth chapter will be the exploration and examination of qualitative interdependence pattern aspects beyond spatial distance, as well as the manifold integration-related coping strategies on the subunit level.

5 Case study II: incorporation of the HWP into the University of Hamburg

Chapter 5 proceeds as follows. After a compact introduction of the three merging parties and a synopsis of the pre-merger stage (5.1), the (post-merger) negotiation and implementation of integration measures are considered (5.2). Besides the chronological sequence of events, the potential relative magnitude of resources involved (i.e. potential integration level) in the attempted integration measures in this connection serves as a guiding theoretical classification criterion. We therefore start with the potentially most far-reaching effort in this respect (5.2.1): the attempted elimination of pre-merger department structures in favor of an arrangement according to disciplines. Subsequently, the homogenization of appointment / endowment policies (5.2.2) and the establishment of a common graduate school (5.2.3) are delineated. Sections 5.2.4 and 5.2.5 refer to two education-related regulations: a common dissertation statute and the exchange of teaching activities. In concluding 5.2, I focus on some research (5.2.6) and administration-related measures (5.2.7). Subsequent to a compact account of the faculty's demerger in 2013, Chapter 5 ends with a brief recapitulation of our core insights set against the theoretical background provided.

5.1 Case introduction and background

To understand post-merger integration from a materialist perspective, it is important to be clear about some basic features of the social systems involved. In the following, the systemist CESM framework, as laid out in Section 3.1.2, is taken as a basis. The three merging parties are described and juxtaposed according to their components, important properties (including aspects of organizational structure), their environments, as well as their central transformation processes. Needless to say, it is not my ambition to develop an exhaustive in-depth portrayal of the three units here—I place particular focus on the preeminent and distinctive system characteristics. A first impression of the general pre-merger political positions of the merging units is given in connection with a description of the pre-merger stage (5.1.2). This background information on the case is complemented in 5.1.3

by a tentative account of intraorganizational power relations in the reorganized University of Hamburg.

5.1.1 Outline of the three merging parties

University economics (Dept. 03 / post-merger: DE)

With regard to its composition, structure and processes, the former Department 03 may in many respects be described as a "typical" large university economics department in times of mass higher education. Conforming to the Hamburg's then law on higher education, scholars were organized into institutes and fields of work (instead of chairs) on the subsequent system levels. The overall 37 professorships were assigned to 10 business administration and 7 economics institutes; the department further comprised a research institute devoted to the advancement of the private security industry (FORSI). Professors had gone through the conventional university career stages: dissertation as an assistant, and the postdoc and habilitation stage; appointments occurred according to the typical criteria of universities. The regular faculty division at universities (into professors and non-professorial staff) existed. As far as its education processes were concerned, the Department 03 had provided mostly pre-Bologna study programs prior to the merger. The two largest ones had been typical diploma degree courses in business administration and economics. In addition, three further diploma, three master's and one teaching degree program(s) had, in cooperation with the mathematics, informatics, law, and pedagogics departments, been provided or supplied with teaching capacities. In terms of internal university exchange partners, the latter units represented elements of the economics department's internal environment.

As regards its external environment, the unit was primarily part of the organizational field of university-level economics in Germany. This field mostly consists of other universities' economics departments, chairs, and relevant non- or inter-university research institutions. It is the main source of academic staff (professors, young lecturers), professorial appointments, access to publication networks, journals, conferences, and other forms of academic cooperation. Further elements of the external environment were business firms situated in Hamburg and all over Germany—the industry sectors represented were, for example, banking, telecommunications, security services, and insurance (CD2|1: 90ff.). Resources exchanged with corporations, for instance, typically involved research funds, thesis projects, traineeships for students, dissertation opportunities, or consultancy assignments. Finally, two other important external factors should, of course, not be forgotten: the large (mostly local) student population and the responsible government agency in Hamburg which oversaw the merger.

Hamburger Universität für Wirtschaft und Politik (HWP / post-merger: DEP)

The second merging party, the *Hamburger Universität für Wirtschaft und Politik* (HWP), had been founded as a union academy in 1949 and attained university status in 1991. Its configuration, which in many respects resembled a typical German UAS, can, in its peculiarities, well be portrayed in contrast to the university Department 03. This first and foremost refers to the composition of the former HWP's faculty. Solely 17 out of 44 professors possessed a state doctorate (habilitation); the majority had not undergone a common university appointment procedure. Lectureships had to a large extent (47%) been assigned to salary grades lower than the university norm. Academic staff belonged to one of four fields of work: *business administration*, *economics*, *sociology*, or *law*. As a stand-alone institution, the HWP had a complete administrative apparatus at its disposal, along with a number of supporting units (e.g. international office, public relations unit, computing center). In comparison to a typical university setting, organizational structures were to a lesser extent hierarchical: professors / lecturers regularly had no dependent assistants and no personal secretaries (2–VII: 222).

If we consider its education processes, the HWP had been one of the first institutions nationwide to implement the Bologna guidelines completely. It went into the merger with a large unified Bachelor's program in *Socioeconomics* and six issue-specific graduate programs (e.g. *European Studies* and *Entrepreneurship*). Research activities were conducted by four small research centers, which were in part responsible for the master's programs as well. In addition, the HWP featured an institute of further education (IfW), which on a semi-commercial basis offered vocational courses to externals. Overall, the clear preponderance of education over research processes existed: with the HWP being more like a typical UAS, a large share of its resources was allotted to teaching activities. As regards scientific orientation, both processes were mostly characterized by an interdisciplinary, socioeconomic approach, which stands in explicit opposition to mainstream neo-classical university economics.

The HWP had thus constituted a twofold direct alternative to regular university-level economic sciences. Firstly, the latter's basic assumptions and dominant methods were challenged: social instead of natural sciences were considered the main fundament of economics. Secondly, educational opportunities were more open and easier to access. Besides interdisciplinarity and a significantly lower share of obligatory mathematical subjects, this was achieved with a strong resource focus on education[36]. University-level degrees were provided without the common shortcomings of state-funded university education in times of massification and shrinking budgets: enormous dropout rates, heavily crowded facilities, sparse staff responsiveness, and distinct anonymity.

As regards the comparison of organizational environments, the most striking differences between the HWP and the University of Hamburg relate to their respective student populations. The HWP was characterized by a fixed participation rate of at least 40% of non-traditional students. Most of its graduates (85%) already had a vocational qualification; about two thirds of the latter possessed occupational experience of more than three years. The average student age was around 30 years, and 18% of students had a migration background (ID2|1: 4–5). Since its establishment, the HWP had always been associated with unions and union-affiliated funding agencies. Further resources were acquired from (supra-)governmental and communal agencies like the EU, the city of Bremen, or the German Federal Ministry of Education and Research (ID2|2; Internet archive[37]).

University social sciences (ex Dept. 05 / post-merger: DSS)

The University of Hamburg's former Department (05) of Social Sciences represented the third and smallest of the three merging parties. As a university unit, it shared several properties with the Department of Economics: academic staff had a regular background and, in comparison with the HWP, the student body were younger and more homogenous. According to the five disciplines represented (*sociology*, *political sciences*, *economic history*, *journalism*, and *criminology*), the department was composed of 5 institutes and 6 specific work fields below them. The unit provided several

36 In comparison to the former Department 03, money units spent per graduate were significantly higher (roughly by a factor of 1.7) (ID2|14: 9).

37 E.g. http://web.archive.org/web/20041020041950/http://www.hwp-hamburg.de/5120.shtml.

pre-Bologna study programs (diplomas, magister artium, and state examinations for the teaching profession) in its core disciplines; a graduate program in criminology was offered, along with a corresponding study course for practitioners. The scope of issues and theoretical backgrounds in teaching and research were broad and versatile. Similarly to the HWP, the department's basic orientation was one of interdisciplinary embeddedness: approaches seeking to model economic relations in terms of natural scientific laws were largely rejected. The department had a pronounced research focus, and third-party funding exceeded five million euros in 2005 (ID2|3). Since 2004, research activities had mostly been associated with a departmental research center, the *Center for Globalization and Governance* (CGG). Important environmental actors were funding agencies like the EU, the DFG and several private foundations. The spectrum of project subjects, for example, included issues like family labor division, environmental governance, journalism in Germany and higher education research (ID2|3; ID2|4: 61ff.). As regards the university's internal environment, teaching related connections to the pedagogics and humanity departments existed.

The main configurational differences and commonalities between the merging parties may, in conclusion, be summarized along two main cleavages:

1) Differences between the two university departments (03 / 05) on the one hand and the HWP on the other:
   a) System composition: divergent career backgrounds, qualification levels and remuneration grading of academic staff; the HWP, in contrast to its counterparts, had a complete university administration with typical central level elements;
   b) System environment: a younger, more homogenous and "traditional" student population; more distinct inclusion in established scientific communities and academic fields vs. the HWP's nontraditional students and a stronger socio-political orientation;
   c) Structures and mechanisms: More conventional hierarchical structures existed in the university; stronger focus on research processes; partly fewer, larger, and mostly pre-Bologna study programs.
2) As regards the general scientific orientation in education and research, commonalities between the university's social scientists and the HWP existed. In both units, economic issues were mostly theorized from a cross-disciplinary and socio-scientific perspective of embeddedness; approaching economics in terms of a formal science was rejected or actively criticized.

5.1.2 Pre-merger period and political subunit positioning

Merger plans became tangible as part of the suggestions of an advisory commission on restructuring higher education in Hamburg. The commission, which became known under the label "Dohnanyi-Kommission", had been launched in April 2002 by the right-wing conservative governing coalition. The presentation of the commission's final bulletin in early 2003 marked the beginning of the actual pre-merger negotiation stage. In those parts relevant to the merger, the report, on hardly four pages, touches on a wide range of disciplines and potential activities. Restructuration requirements were generally and exclusively established bearing in mind capacity overload and low student success rates. A unified department of economics and social sciences was to be formed, with the teaching of university economics and the HWP at its core (CD2|2: 77). Especially as regards the basic study programs, the former HWP was pointed to as a blueprint. Entry options for non-traditional students, modularized study programs, and international and practical orientation were valued as innovative approaches (*Ibid.*: 76). The establishment of teaching-related subunits ("schools") was suggested and common undergraduate studies for all three parties pursued.

A rather unspecific recourse to "international and national comparisons" (*Ibid.*: 78) concerning the possible successful cooperation between social sciences and economics was used to establish the involvement of the Department of Social Sciences. For the latter especially, the prospects were bleak: the graduate count was to drop by almost 25%, and the number of first year students was to be reduced by 40% within a decade (*Ibid.*: 79). Members of the commission had publicly doubted the general relevance of sociology as an academic discipline (2–I: 663). Consequently, besides the attempted merger the report had little more to offer than cutbacks and the freezing of already permitted appointments (CD2|2: 79).

All three potential merging parties strongly rejected the merger plans from the outset. Their official political positions, which are expressed in numerous documents, do reveal several sources of qualitative interdependence pattern inconsistencies. Requirements regarding the units' own configurations and resource-related fears as to possible integration measures were repeatedly pointed to.

Response (position) of the Department of Economics (Dept. 03 / DE)

In reference to its (non-)relation to the HWP, the Department of Economics essentially emphasized the importance of an autonomous right to develop its own admittance procedures in a detailed written statement. Particularly in the case of a fixed quota of non-traditional applicants, the DE suspected there would be an ungovernable inflow of unskilled students into its programs. To improve education quality and success rates, it contrariwise sought to reduce capacity utilization (ID2|5: 2). Theoretically speaking, any homogenization of the allocation rule related to admissions toward the HWP was considered harmful in terms of improving compliance with student and state demands. The DE made it clear that it had no interest whatsoever in the HWP's student domain.

The requirement to maintain and strengthen its methodological and content-related orientation dominated the DE's further argumentation. Disastrous effects of organizational integration in terms of the external assessment of publication output, such as low overall rankings, were feared due to the negligible representation of HWP scholars in journals. Difficulties in keeping hold of renowned professors were, in turn, expected to be a consequence of the department's deteriorating reputation. Besides the institution losing its professors, the acquisition of appropriate new ones was deemed at risk as common appointment commissions would have to be formed (ID2|5: 5). It was thought that possible majorities of HWP representatives in these political subsystems would foster detrimental appointments. As a further consequence of the different scientific convictions, growing "disorientation" (ID2|5: 7) among the students was foreshadowed, together with a reduced external acceptance of Hamburg's economics degrees.

Cooperation with the social science department was refused due to the lacking commonalities as regards content. Teaching-related congruencies and functioning exchange relations with mathematics, statistics and jurisprudence were emphasized instead. Finally, a brief hint at true preferences was given, portending the later disintegration of business administration and economics into separate subunits: "This sort of homogeneity is the appropriate conception of focusing"(ID2|5: 8). DE members were also worried about the possible homogenization of allocation rules regarding the proportion between professors and mid faculty staff, which had been considerably better in the DE (2–II: 550; 2–I: 118).

Response (position) of the HWP (DEP)

The misgivings of the HWP manifest themselves in various central level position papers in a more proactive manner and without specific reference to the other merging parties. A large unified undergraduate program for all the units involved was rejected since it was deemed to endanger the HWP's particular study program profile. A possible integrated school should therefrom be subdivided into stand-alone divisions with distinguished "corporate identities" (ID2|6: 4). Generally, the fear of losing the ability to provide arrangements for non-traditional students dominated. This related to the characteristics of study programs, as well as to admission criteria and procedures. It was claimed operative control over education processes would be backed by study program budget autonomy and decisive influence regarding appointments (ID2|7: 4; ID2|6: 5)—no shift in allocation responsibilities would be accepted with regard to these issues. To prevent threatening misappropriations by the university's central political system (ID2|6: 3), the HWP furthermore demanded the retention of its jurisprudence work field, its own administration, service facilities and commercial education activities. In brief: almost any measure that could be associated with a merger was turned down on the grounds of sustaining the HWP's qualities (high success rate, favorable student ratio) as conceded by the reform commission.

Response (position) of the Department of Social Sciences (DSS)

In terms of its positioning, the Department of Social Sciences shared two central arguments with the university's Department of Economics. Firstly, the untypical academic career development of many HWP professors in combination with substandard publication scores and research output were regarded as deleterious to reputation in the merger context. The equal status of representatives in a unified political system was denied (ID2|8: 3). Secondly, and due to the discipline orientation of "large parts" of economics studies, very limited profile-related commonalities with the Department of Economics were stressed (*Ibid.*). From the perspective of social sciences, the complete domination of the merged faculty's profile by business administration loomed (2–III: 868; 2-I 694; 2–IX: 218): the department's comment on the commission report points to an alleged 85% proportion of business study graduates from the HWP. Social science teaching and research were thus expected to turn into a merely peripheral attachment with no profile of their own (ID2|8: 3).

Pre-merger negotiations

Between September 2003 and May 2004, negotiations were institutionalized in moderated talks between the merging partners-to-be. The talks were led by members of a private policy think tank, who had also played a leading role in the drafting process of the Dohnanyi report. However, the overall seven sessions added little to the features of the merger that had been certain already (CD2|3: 11, 26ff.). The retention of the HWP's particular teaching profile was confirmed; the definition of student admission criteria was assigned to the study programs (ID2|9: 4). Participants in the talks agreed on a time schedule and the appointment of an external dean. Decisions as to the creation of an (under)graduate school were postponed, as was the configuration of the new faculty's political system. An initiative of the two university departments to subdivide the new faculty into two departments, social sciences / economics, and assign the HWP faculty accordingly, was blocked (2–VIII: 80–104); HWP representatives had regarded this as an attempted resource-raid (ID2|10: 1). Dissent between the units remained on most relevant issues (ID2|9). Furthermore, the whole pre-merger stage had been accompanied by strong student protests, which were partly associated with a broader movement against the upcoming neoliberal turn in education politics. Protests started in early 2002 and peaked by the end of 2003. Most of the merger-related activities, including demonstrations and the occupation of public buildings had been initiated by students of the HWP (Rogalla & Hauer, 2006). The merger law was nonetheless adopted in February 2004, which carried interorganizational conflicts forward into the following post-merger stage.

5.1.3 Intraorganizational power distribution

The characterization of the three merging parties shall now be complemented by a basic outline of the distribution of intraorganizational power. In line with our preliminary definitions in Section 1.1., the HWP was incorporated by the University of Hamburg. It ceased to exist as a legally independent institution, with the essential allocation responsibilities of its central level political subsystems being shifted to the incorporator. On the other hand, there is a merger perspective in the case—on a department level, the three parties had to arrange a newly founded common faculty. Both perspectives play a role in examining the case: the relation between the former HWP and the central university level, as well as the interaction between the three merging parties within the new faculty. To allow for an (at least superficial) evaluation of the aspect of power in the following, the department level perspective has consequently been chosen.

In the wake of the Dohnanyi reforms, the internal structure of the university had changed considerably. The merged faculty of business, economics and social sciences was just one of six huge new faculties, which had been formed by a series of internal department mergers and incorporations in the summer term 2005:

- *Faculty of Law* (LAW)
- *Faculty for Medicine* (MED)
- *Faculty of Education* (Depts. of Education (EDU); Psychology (PSY); Sports (SP))
- *Faculty of the Humanities* (Depts. of Protestant Theology (TE); Philosophy and History (PHIH); Linguistics, Literature and the Media (LIT); Cultural History and Studies (CULT); Orientalism (Asian–African institute, ORIENT))
- *Faculty of Mathematics, Informatics and Natural Sciences* (Depts. of Biology (BIO); Chemistry (CHEM); Earth Sciences (EARTH); Informatics (INF); Mathematics (MATH); Physics (PHY))

Hence, 18 departments, together with the incorporated HWP, formed the new six-faculty structure. A first impression of the basic quantitative properties of the merging units is provided by the following table:

Pre-merger unit (post-merger unit)	Student count	Professor count	Non-prof. academic staff count	Admin. personnel count
Dept. 03 (university Department of Economics, DE)	5360	37	125	16
Dept. 05 (university Department of Social Sciences, DSS)	2410	22	21	8
HWP (DEP)	2504	41	41	28
Σ	**10274**	**100**	**187**	**52**

Table 5.1: Hamburg merging parties: basic quantitative properties (source: CD2|4: 37 and CD2|4: 93; last two columns: ID2|11)

To approximate relative resource control in the merger year, the following education and research / transfer related indicators were collected for all pre-reform departments (reference year 2002; excluding medicine):

1. Total number of first year students (Doelle et al., 2005: 60f.)
2. Total number of enrolled students (CD2|4: 38)
3. Total number of regular-time (within a certain number of semesters) students (calculated from CD2|4: 38 and CD|2: 5, App. 2: 37)
4. Regular-time students per professor (CD|2: 5, App. 2: 37)
5. Total number of graduates (calculated from CD2|4: 38 and CD|2: 5, App. 2: 37)
6. Graduates per professor (CD|2: 5, App. 2: 37)
7. Total amount of third-party funding (CD|2: 5, App. 2: 30)
8. Third-party funding per professor (CD2|5: 46f.)
9. Total number of dissertations (calculated from CD2|4: 38 and HH 2004: 46f., 2002)
10. Dissertations per professor (CD|2: 5, App. 2: 46f.)
11. Third-party funded staff (headcount) (CD2|4: 50)

Indicators 1–6 refer to *education immediacy* as a power factor; indicators 7–11 are associated with a subunit's *research immediacy*. Just like in the first case study, a figure depicting input-throughput-output in terms of education processes was attempted and efficiency indicators were included as well.

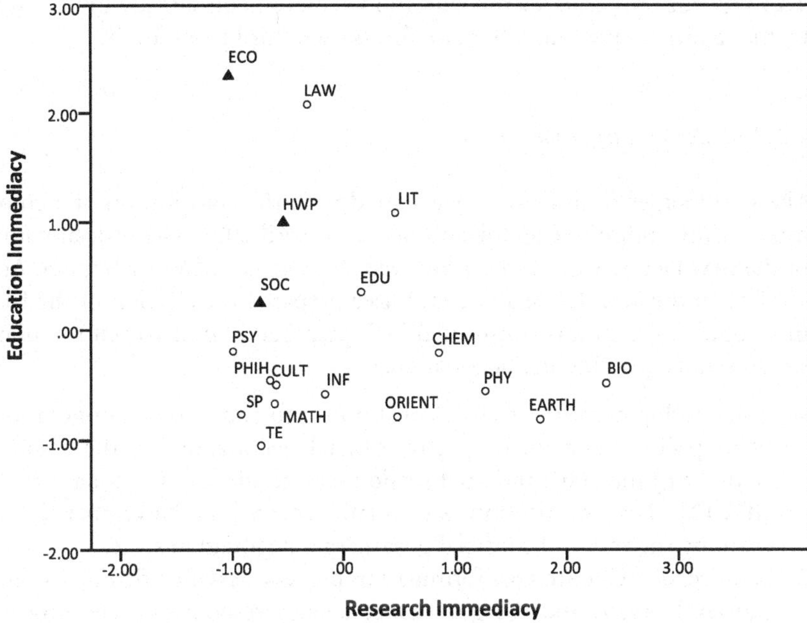

Figure 5.1: Pre-restructuring power distribution of the university departments and the HWP (education and research immediacy)

Figure 4.7 shows a factor-score scatterplot of all university departments based on the two-factor solution of a generalized least square factor analysis (Jöreskog & Goldberger, 1972). Needless to say, it has to be interpreted with considerable care for several reasons. From a theoretical perspective, the representation of subunit power profiles is quite fragmentary: pervasiveness-indicators and coping-indicators have not been included. Due to comparison requirements, the closest possible reference period (year 2002) is still two years before the incorporation. Besides that, the quality of the data is rather modest: some discordance between different sources has to be stated[38].

38 In December 2004, the city senate, for instance, admitted there were huge differences in third-party funding data for the Department of Economics: the numbers

Nonetheless, the scatterplot may serve to underline the fact that, in an overall department comparison, the former HWP wasn't a weak unit at all: it went into the incorporation with a considerable resource base of its own. This was not only true for the education achievements already underlined by the reform commission, but also for its own third-party funds.

5.2 *Post-merger integration efforts*

The post-merger negotiation stage started with the constitution of a common faculty committee and dean's office in April 2005. The official name of the new faculty was: *School of Business, Economics and Social Sciences*. According to the law, the faculty committee prepared the election of the faculty council, which was constituted in September 2005. Two central milestones framed post-merger negotiations:

1) The development of a faculty constitution to codify the configuration of its political system. Respective official negotiations in the council started in June 2007; the final version was decided on in January 2008 (ID2|12). The constitution was finally enacted in November 2008, marking the end of the official post-merger negotiation stage.
2) A university-wide strategy formulation process, as demanded by its central level organs and the governance agency responsible. The process embraced all faculties and had to result in a comprehensive strategy document (*Struktur- und Entwicklungsplan*, ID2|13). The plan was adopted in early 2009 and contained most of the other integration measures.

The order in which the particular integration measures are discussed (see Fig. 5.2) represents a compromise between the theoretical criteria developed in Subsection 3.3.1:

provided by the department's administration itself were three times as high in comparison to university administration numbers (the more conservative estimates of the city's budgeting plan have been used here). According to a parliamentary request (18/4597), the University of Hamburg indicated several reasons for the differences: the existence of some professors' unregistered friends' associations, together with complications in administratively assigning endowed chairs and externally funded research groups to subunits (recall our discussion in 3.2.3).

- The (failed) homogenization of the new faculty's political system according to university standards (5.2.1)
- The homogenization of appointment and endowment policies according to university standards (5.2.2)
- The establishment of a new unified subsystem ("Graduate School") to integrate education processes (5.2.3) (teaching-related integration measures)
- The development of a common dissertation statute (5.2.4)
- Research-related integration attempts (5.2.5)
- Attempts to homogenize administrative and service processes according to university standards (5.2.6)

All of them were first-order integration measures; their arrangement in the section is roughly as follows

a) potential or actual integration level (i.e. the magnitude of resources potentially or actually involved);
b) chronological negotiation order, and
c) the type of basic transformation process involved: *education / research and transfer* and *administration*.

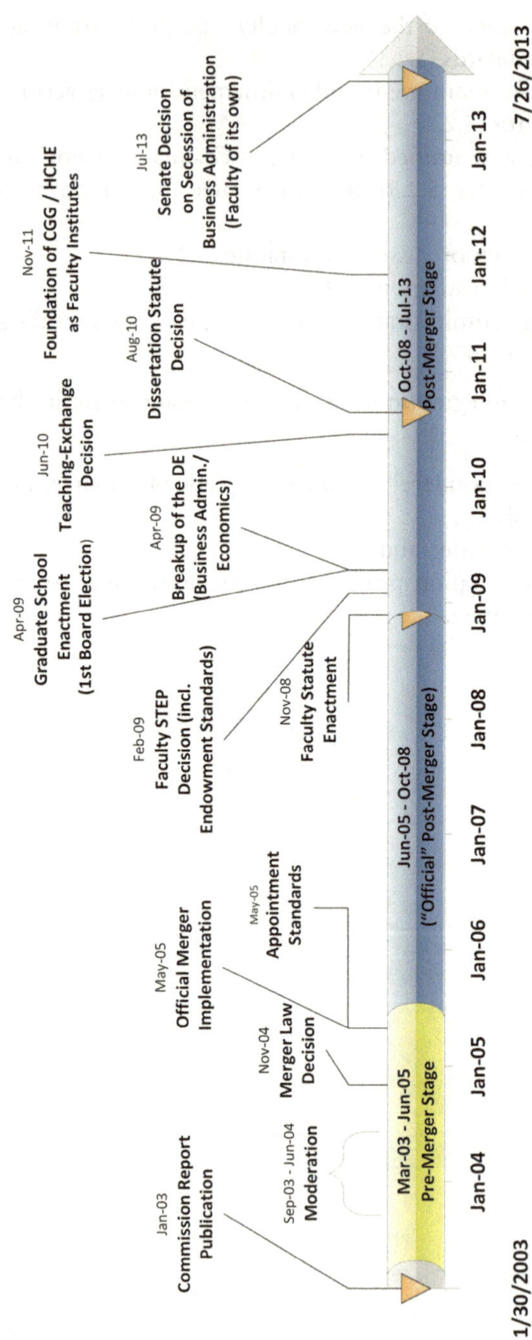

Figure 5.2: Hamburg merger time frame

5.2.1 Basic system structuring—retaining the old parties

The basic configuration of the new organization's political system was the most important bargaining issue in connection with the development of a faculty constitution. In keeping with federal and state laws, the number of political subsystems, and their composition and responsibilities had to be codified.

It had soon become clear that there was no other agreeable option than arranging the political subsystems on a general basis of *equipartition*, using the "old" organizations as a fundament (2–X: 344). The faculty council thus directly represented the three merging parties besides the usual status groups. This was achieved via the establishment of corresponding electoral districts. Only hesitant attempts to restart the pre-merger discussion on a possible form of organization based on two departments according to academic disciplines can be traced in the records (e.g. DP2 80: 1; DP2 72: 1; FR2 14: 7). Oppositional forces against the modification of the provisional department structure remained very strong all the time (2–VI: 216; 2–III: 248). As a consequence of the permanent subdivision of the faculty into three departments, a complete additional level of political subsystems was to persist—all three founding units retained their own management. Department boards were installed promptly after the merger had technically been completed. Consequently, negotiations quickly started to develop parallel to the council, between the department management boards as well as between department executives and the dean's office (II–V: 268–274). In the final version of the faculty constitution, this lineup even became institutionalized in a faculty chamber (ID2|12: § 9).

Allocation rules regarding the composition of the dean's office itself followed the principle of carrying forward the old political systems as well. Members were not (as usual) primarily to be chosen according to transformation processes or basic functions within the faculty (e.g. *teaching* or *equal opportunity*), but according to department affiliation (ID2|12: § 5 Sec. 2). The intended temporary concessions of the pre-merger stage had thus become enduring structures:

> And they make sure that the dean's office is composed of a member of every department. And the informal expectance is, of course, that these members are to represent departmental interests and therefore fulfill an intermediary-interface function (2–III: 234).

How is this development to be assessed in the light of our theoretical framework? We have characterized organizational mergers "by themselves" as the execution of an integration measure: the discrete act of shifting the allocation responsibilities of at least two separate central level political subsystems toward a "new" and unified single one. By providing only a limited shift of resource control, the perpetuation of the old political systems in the form of department boards hence directly charged the technical execution of the merger. Organizing the faculty according to academic disciplines (two departments: social sciences / economics) would have meant more genuine integration in terms of incorporating the HWP. A much deeper level of integration would have been the result. The faculty structure that had effectively been realized instead hence constituted an *organizational anomaly* within the University of Hamburg. Disciplines continued to exist as doubles:

- business administration within the DE vs. business administration within the DEP;
- economics within the DE vs. economics within the DEP;
- sociology within the DEP vs. sociology within the DSS.

The homogenization of faculty allocation rules according to university integration standards thus happened quite cursorily and remained incomplete. Inasmuch as the formal configuration of the faculty's political system often barely reflected actual resource control, the case yields numerous excellent examples of organizational conflict resolution through *decoupling*.

5.2.2 Homogenization of appointment and endowment policies

The emerging long-term arrangement of the faculty according to the premerger organizations represented a serious setback for all the proponents of integration. Professors and study programs remained assigned to the departments. A much higher level of integration was, however, realized as regards professor endowment and appointment rules.

As described in Subsection 5.1.1, the HWP had been different in comparison with university departments as regards the composition of its faculty, the relations of faculty members to each other as well as between the four fields of work. The faculty of the former HWP

1) had largely achieved professor status by other means than appointment criteria that were typical at universities;
2) was in many cases graded below (42%) or far below (12%) university professor standards (CD|2: 5, App. 2.4: 152);

3) did for the most part not have any non-professorial staff, student assistants or personal secretaries and
4) *regardless* of a discipline-related workload had been equally undersupplied (about 75% of HWP graduates had been affiliated to the business administration field of work, ID2|8).

Allocation rule homogenization for all the aforementioned items was imposed according to university standards soon after the merger:

Ad. 1: The ex-HWP (DEP) lost its ability to form appointment commissions and dominate them with its own members: one out of five professorial members had to belong to one of the other departments; two had to be outsiders to be approved by the president of the university (DP2 3: 2f.). The typical appointment criteria for universities had to be applied henceforth, that is, a stronger emphasis was placed on publication output and third-party funding.

Ad 2: Many of the lower graded professorships were combined to form higher graded ones, or were converted into non-professorial positions (DP2 44: 1).

Ads 3 and *4*: What had failed as a generic principle by then—organizing the new faculty according to academic disciplines—was realized regarding the endowment of newly appointed professors. A preexisting Hamburg-wide allocation rule of discipline-related minimum endowment was applied and became codified in the 2009 STEP strategy plan (ID2|13: 21).

How did these integration measures affect the environmental resource-exchange relations between the merging parties? To begin with, the DEP was potentially affected negatively because of its strong focus on education processes and the (long-term) fulfillment of non-traditional student demands:

> Some feared that it won't be enough in the end if you don't have the teaching staff any more that is responsive to these students, teaching staff who knows that they are different students compared to the average school graduate. One has to approach them in a different manner, give them more assistance, more translation services and so on. It calls for a particular open-mindedness toward students. If such openness is not provided, or lecturers even display an openly antagonistic attitude toward such students, our attractiveness will hardly be able to be preserved in the long run (2–IV: 604).

This statement points to the fact that teaching activities in Germany play a minor role in typical appointment-related assessments of candidates at universities. Large parts of teaching and student advice services in state universities are usually provided by temporarily employed assistants under increasing time and publication pressure. This leads to a situation where teaching efforts tend to be punished with poorer academic career prospects on an individual level. By substituting long-term lecturer positions with a teaching focus for fewer, more research-oriented university-style professorships, the DEP threatened to lose its ability to successfully meet the demands of its non-traditional student domain. The former HWP had owed a great deal of its teaching-indicator performance to its specific configuration[39].

As allocation rules were adapted to the requirements of their respective academic fields, the measures were rather advantageous to the other merging parties, especially to the huge business administration faction within the DE. Through the homogenization of endowment and salary grading, it became possible to use DEP resources to acquire professors from the field of university economics (2–VI: 304f.). The end of equal distribution meant a loss for the other fields of work within the former HWP—shifting resources hence (in principle) potentially allowed university economics to be strengthened in the long run *without* additional public spending[40].

From the perspective of our theoretical framework, the question then arises as to why these measures were undertaken despite the considerable relative weight of the impaired external (student) interests. After all, these interests had been enough to preserve the HWP's particular study program and corresponding admission rules (CD2|7 § 10 Sect. (2), (3)). The answer may be found in the long-term time frame of the anticipated negative effects: while, for example, a change in admission criteria would have had an immediate impact, negative consequences due to worsening study conditions were to be expected years later (if at all). Prompt resource losses due to endowment homogenization were furthermore precluded by a highly selective appointment negotiation policy: only newly appointed DEP professors were equipped in line with discipline-related standards (2–IV: 116; DP2 78: 2); hence, all university professors were able to keep their status quo—almost no redistribution toward the DEP occurred (2–VIII: 114; 2–I: 118). In contrast with the looming long-term detriments, the nominal rise

39 As stated by the reform commission, the HWP's student-to-teacher ratio of about 60:1 had been quite advantageous in comparison to its two university counterparts; in 2004 the HWP had provided 96 courses per semester in contrast to 34 (economics) and 36 courses (social sciences) (Source: CD2|4: 67).

40 Probably the main political objective of the merger, see Chapter 6.

in typical university professorships was quickly realized through a series of new appointments in the field of business administration (2–V: 425).

5.2.3 Education-related integration attempts I: the Graduate School

Besides the arrangement of the new faculty according to academic disciplines and the homogenization of appointment and endowment-related allocation rules, a third possible major integration measure soon appeared on the scene: the establishment of a graduate school that was intended to become the faculty's central subunit for managing graduate and doctoral studies in a unified manner. It thus represents a first-order integration measure. Control over subsystems that carry important parts of the involved units' education processes were to be shifted to and concentrated in a new political subsystem on the faculty level. This kind of faculty level homogenization (horizontal shift) of control was discussed only in relation to the graduate programs. Attempts to include undergraduate studies had failed early on during the pre-merger moderated talks (ID2|9: 4f.).

Since the foundation of schools represented an organizational novelty in Hamburg's HEIs, resource-related concerns in the post-merger stage initially occurred on a more general level. Skepticism mostly related to the role and functioning of such a new subsystem within the overall political system of the faculty:

> And this is the point, if the master's programs of a department are not directed by the department but by a faculty body, this certainly means a loss of influence. And this is what we were all afraid of (2–III: 378).

Besides several open questions as regards operating the study programs and accountability (2–IV: 195), ambiguities as to the future assigning of faculty positions prevailed. In the face of the enduring scarcity of state funding, this would have further increased uncertainties for some of the organizational coalitions, for example the DSS:

> [...] because faculty positions have always been negotiated on a department level. And if you wanted a certain position for your graduate program, let's say the criminology of deviant behavior, you were reliant on departmental negotiations concerning its denomination (2–V: 763).

In general, apprehensions relating to the stealthy subdivision of faculty members according to undergraduate and graduate program sections instead of departments were felt (e.g. 2–VII: 512f.). The effect of the Graduate School in constraining departmental elbow room was obvious:

> [...] of course one could say if the study programs are no longer in the departments, what do we need a department structure for—and would the resources which we would have within the department otherwise be in the Graduate School or remain on a department level [...] (2–VI: 501).

Specific qualitative interdependence pattern inconsistencies, for instance, referred to the internal coherence of education processes and shall be explicated in the light of the DE's MBA program properties. A number of common basic methods courses for graduates (e.g. advanced econometrics or linear optimization) formed the basis of the subsequent technically sophisticated and methodologically homogeneous advanced courses. With its curriculum[41], the DE actively positioned itself within the domain of university economics and hence sought to distinguish itself from UAS-level institutions: "This is also what precisely constitutes this MSc—Master of Science" (2–VI: 654). Together with the homogeneous basic curriculum as a demand of the academic field, a multiplicity of focus choices for students in their later studies was thus provided. This facet of program arrangement was again strategically associated with environmental demands: "students are 22 or 23 years old; they do not want to specialize that early" (2–II: 362). One large graduate program instead of several small ones was considered the appropriate configuration to offer particular study profiles (*Ibid.*), and offering these profiles was in turn accordingly identified with adequate resource flows in the interviews:

> Business administration has decided on a large master's program and considers exactly this the USP [unique selling proposition, mk], and this is why students in Hamburg choose our study program. Because they are not ex-ante committed to a single discipline[42], but have the choice and combination options (2–VI: 631).

The DEP was, by contrast, confronted with different effectiveness criteria and thus exhibited a different arrangement of education processes. Due to its heterogeneous student body, its programs had to be more open and accessible instead of methodologically consistent. As the DEP's students were

41 Study program development had been undertaken parallel to Graduate School negotiations (BSc. w. t. 2007-2008 / MSc. w. t. 2009).

42 "Single discipline" here refers to study profile foci like *Accounting* or *Marketing*.

older and most of them had occupational experience, early specialization via program choice wasn't as much of a problem, if not even an advantage.

As an integration measure, the Graduate School hence mainly threatened to impair the resource transformation and exchange processes of the DE. Operating one large graduate program requires considerable communication and coordination between the lecturers involved (2–VI: 513ff.). The master's program handbook (2014) of the DE reveals that only 17% of business administration courses are free from requirements. In about 36% of the cases, completion of corresponding bachelor's or master's courses is presumed to be obligatory, while relevant previous knowledge is recommended for the remainder[43]. Additional coordination with actors from the two other departments in a new political subsystem was anticipated to be accompanied by unduly increased coordination costs. This potential misallocation of resources on the other hand was hardly offset by any perspective in terms of enhanced coping with environmental demands or even making new domains accessible: DE representatives had no interest in any socio-scientific curricula and expected the dilution of their master's program. Both university departments furthermore shared a critical point of view regarding the stronger application-orientation of the extant master's programs of the DEP (2–VIII: 244; 2-I: 269).

The frequently stated pre-merger argument of lacking combination potential returned during Graduate School negotiations and was brought up from different sides:

> The next master's [program, mk], that massively counteracted the development of the Graduate School is an inter-faculty program in media studies, a program having been high in demand of course [...] It addresses communication scientists and humanists, and comprises very little business administration and economics. They had little interest, it was like: 'None of your business administration stuff, we don`t want that at all.' They wanted a journalism program and critical perspectives. They worked against it and always had their representatives within the faculty council (2–V: 781).

In the face of such manifold inconsistencies and doubtful benefits, the question arises as to which actors or coalitions actually advocated and promoted the foundation of the Graduate School. Integration pressures mainly originated in the central governing bodies of the university, particularly the university's chair:

43 My own calculations.

> They [faculty members, mk] in fact didn't want it [Graduate School, mk] to be codified within the faculty constitution. But the dean always said: 'That's not possible. That won't be accepted by the president's office. We are expected to do it, at least the Graduate School must be an achievement of integration' (2–III: 378).

Making the formal implementation of the Graduate School a necessary condition for the approval of the faculty constitution (2–VII: 343) was accompanied by resource-related pressures:

> It was sort of the carrot and the stick: 'You need more appointments and you'll get them because there are many students and the university as a whole needs that to explain itself externally.' On the other hand there were multiple kinds of pressure, where it could be felt that things would change for the worse in the case of noncompliance (2–X: 1048).

Although the opponents of the Graduate School were clearly in the majority, resistance within the faculty wasn't, however, equal across all merging parties. Advocates of an institutionalized form of opening teaching processes could be found within the DEP. Support for organizational integration was thereby linked to a possible instantaneous reduction of resource-related uncertainties: the DEP had to grapple with the appropriation of adequate teaching capacities for its master's programs. This problem, which had already been complained of during accreditation assessments (e.g. ID2|15: 9f.), led to an admissions halt for the "Gender and Work" study program in October 2006 (FP2 10: 9). The Graduate School was thus considered to be a way to act against capacity shortages by some (2–V: 731). Nonetheless, if we look at the faculty as a whole, political resistance clearly remained dominant.

Through the decision by the university presidium to enforce the codification of the Graduate School, the merging parties had to implement a disagreeable political subsystem within the faculty. The organizational solution that was subsequently realized is another useful example of decoupling formal structures and actual activities. The Graduate School was established and neglected at once—it effectively became a mock-up unit. In the dean's office's protocol, its tasks are grandiloquently described as "strategic": "the development of strategic concepts, evaluation and examination of the creation and cessation of programs". All operative tasks—where *operative* refers to designing curricula, teaching capacities and courses—were assigned to the program directors of the departments and accordingly to the respective student office (DP2 146: 1). In the faculty constitution, graduate program-related tasks were assigned to the Graduate school *and* the departments as well (ID2|12: § 7 (4)). The settlement was supplemented with an opt-out rule, according to which the departments could take over operational tasks from the Graduate school (ID2|12:§ 7 (3)): "In particular cases a study program can be assigned to the department, and this exceptional rule is used for everybody" (2–III: 445). Many interview partners openly admitted that relevant responsibilities for the faculty's graduate programs still lay with the departments. The disarming of the new unit was completed by the curtailing of its resource endowment: "[…] €100,000 go to the Graduate School. It thereby becomes apparent that this is a mere bauble" (2–V: 636).

Our first Hypothesis (H1) suggests that qualitative inconsistencies between the merging parties' interdependence patterns should further disintegrative forces within the political system of the merged organization. Disintegrative forces express themselves in activities that aim at the prevention of integration following mergers. The Hamburg merger case shows how this can be achieved by means of all-round organizational decoupling. It was triggered by the university's central level demand to codify the Graduate School (no constitution approval without it), but had been caused by the qualitative pattern inconsistencies that called for detached management of the study programs. Decoupling therefore enabled the formal implementation of the integration measure while simultaneously operating the allocation rules effectively required—"the illusion of satisfaction" (Pfeffer & Salancik, 1978: 98) of integration demands was created.

Various typical elements of decoupling, as stated by Pfeffer and Salancik (1978: 98f.) and Meyer and Rowan (1977: 357), could be found:

- The goals of the Graduate School were made ambiguous and vacuous: the "strategic" tasks were denuded of almost any meaning;
- An informal arrangement of interdependencies gained importance: the formally "exceptional" shift of allocation responsibilities toward the departments became a workaday regularity.

Integration was avoided: the magnitude of resources controlled by the Graduate School was kept small and hence an overall low level of organizational integration as regards education processes was realized.

5.2.4 Education-related integration attempts II: teaching exchange and dissertation statute

After all vital education process-related integration measures had failed up to this point, the department managements and the dean's office finally agreed on a small-scale teaching exchange solution as late as mid-2010. The faculty's professors were formally granted permission to decide to offer teaching in a range of about two semester periods per week in one of the other departments without bureaucratic barriers. Capacity impacts were to be accounted for in terms of future admission numbers—possible net capacity gains thus had to be compensated for (FP2 51: 10). As resource control of the departments was reduced through the implementation of a standardized allocation rule between the parties, the teaching exchange needs to be classified as a first-order integration measure. Control over a small part of the budget was ultimately shifted downwards to individual professors (as against to coequal or superordinate organs)[44]. On closer inspection, the measure was, however, strictly limited (*Ibid.*):

- the receiving department had to consent to the teaching proposal (!);
- the home department was conceded a veto right in the case of unspecified capacity distress;
- teaching exchange that exceeded two semester periods per week generally required approval from the home department;
- there was to be no general opening of lectures with comparable contents.

Additionally, exchange options initially did not apply to assistants who provided tutorials, a corresponding rule was released in December 2012 (FP2 76: 4). Overall, teaching exchange represents another case of integration camouflage. The versatile loopholes made sure that shifting allocation responsibilities for the most part remained fictitious.

The implementation of the integrated education of doctoral students advanced in quite an analogous manner. The relevant responsibilities and procedures are codified in the faculty's dissertation statue, which was adopted in 2010. In line with Hamburg's state laws, formal responsibilities lay with the central dissertation committee, which had to be elected by the council for a three-year term. So again, the right to allocate resources and design the configurations of the transformational system was to be re-

44 This equals organizational integration by *decentralization* and is facilitated by the strong position of professors in German HEIs.

moved from the "old" political subsystems and concentrated in a faculty organ.

A review of the dissertation statute reveals committee composition according to the well-known representation rule of departmental equipartition (FP2 54: AB1). Furthermore, the installation of departmental subcommittees was stipulated. If one considers task sharing between the central faculty committee and the sub-committees, it becomes clear who was actually in control. The central committee's responsibilities were reduced to a minimum, comprising unsubstantial tasks and standard routines like "forwarding of applications" or "Graduate School registration". The decoupling of formal and actual control was this time supplemented with an opt-in rule: dissertation supervisors were enabled to transfer departmental responsibilities to the faculty committee.

Central faculty committee tasks	Department subcommittee tasks
Formal degree award decision	Validity assessment of dissertation program accomplishments (*not* the Graduate School)
Election of faculty committee chair	Admission of dissertation applicants
Transfer of faculty committee responsibilities to chair	Determining terms of admission
Permission of foreign language dissertation procedure	Decision over dissertation admission
Candidate rejection: notice in writing	Explanatory statement in the case of rejection
Graduate School registration of candidates	Assigning advisor
Assigning advisory rights to junior researchers	Extension of dissertation editing time
Appointment of third assessor in the case of "summa cum laude" grading	Determining assessors and board of examiners
Dissertation rejection: notice in writing (extremely rare, mk)	Determining third assessor in the case of co-authorship with advisor
Disputation failed: notice in writing	Rejection of ambiguous evaluations
Forwarding of applications to subcommittee	Determining third assessor in the case of evaluation dissent

Table 5.2: Juxtaposition of chosen dissertation responsibilities (source: after FP2 54, App. B)

Since the validity assessment of doctoral education accomplishments is very important for the overall control of the process, the corresponding regulations were mitigated twice. Besides a number of defined accomplishments like teaching certificates, conference presentations and Graduate School credits, "other forms of scientific achievements or qualification" were accepted as well (FP2 54: App. A)—the ultimate decision-making authority always rested with the subcommittees.

Decoupling and dwarfing faculty organs were linked to environmental demands. As many DEP professors had not supervised any dissertation students (2–IV: 279; CD2|5, App. 24.4: 149), the main cleavages referred to unified procedural quality standards and opened between the university departments. The DSS educated doctoral students mostly for a traditional university career. It therefore feared possible damage to its institutional reputation (2–IX: 530) due to the erosion of quality in paper-based dissertations. Subunit positions in that quality debate and their connection to environmental demands can at this point be further elaborated by us focusing on conflicts regarding co-authorship regulations. In the council protocols, an attempt by the DE[45] to block parts of the dissertation regulations that restrict co-authorship of dissertation assessors is documented (FP2 54: 5). The attempt was rejected with 3 votes for, 10 against, and 1 abstention; it was finally decided that

- at least one of the assessors must not be a co-author of one of the contributions submitted and
- the second assessor can be a co-author of a maximum of 50% of any contributions submitted (FP2 54, App. PromO: § 8 (2)).

To round out the argument, one has to consider the dissertation regulations of the faculty of business administration after the demerger. Almost all restrictions concerning co-authorship have gone, and co-authorship is only denied to the chairperson of the assessment commission (CD2|8: § 7 (1)). Compared to the rules in the merged faculty, it is hence possible that both advisors of a cumulative thesis are co-authors and assessors of all contributions submitted simultaneously. A possible argument used to reject co-authorship restrictions is:

> [...] for example, colleagues who work with huge data sets, who say 'yes, but then the doctoral candidate can never work with that huge data set, because the data set belongs to me, it always did and I maintain it' and so on (2–VI: 740).

45 The DE had meanwhile (August 2010) split up into business administration and macro-economics. For convenience and rigor, the two departments are still labeled "DE".

In disciplines where quantitative analyses are common, data sets can hence be used as resources in environmental exchange relations. Dissertation advisors as holders of data sets may change their use against co-authorship. The homogenization of dissertation regulations that was realized interfered with the external exchange relations of the owners of huge data sets. A limitation of publication output may have been the consequence.

5.2.5 Research and transfer-related integration attempts

Some integration efforts regarding research and transfer, the second major resource transformation process in HEIs, were also undertaken. However, since research activities and resources are, compared to teaching, under the control of single professors to a much greater extent, these attempts were quite restricted from the outset. During pre-merger moderated talks, the three parties had consented on a general level that resources should be devoted to faculty research centers (ID2|9: 6). In the context of the attempted university-wide subunit strategy alignment (STEP), the formation of a common cross-departmental "governance" research focus emerged as the most important post-merger integration attempt concerning this matter. In practice, this was to be achieved by 2012 through the integration of the DSS's *Centre for Globalization and Governance* (CGG) and the DEP's small *Center for International Studies* (CIS) on the one hand and the integration of some relevant economics professorships on the other (ID2|13: 8; DP2 136: 2).

In November 2011, the CGG was elevated to the status of a faculty institute and opened to all faculty members. How should this be characterized as an integration measure? First of all, membership of research institutes of this kind is voluntary. As an important participation condition, full CGG members have to be in control of their own third-party funds (FR2 64 App. 3: § 2 (1)). The center may thus be described best as a communication platform for fund-holders to explore cooperation options[46]: it resembles more an aggregate of single research funds than a resource transforming allocation system in the narrower sense. As a faculty institute, its basic bud-

46 What this could have looked like can be demonstrated by a (failed) unified attempt by CGG and CIS members to acquire a DFG funded collaborative research center (SFB) *Transnationale Normbildungsnetzwerke* in 2005 (DP2 7: 3). If that attempt had been successful, it would have provided a nice example of improving resource acquisition through integration.

get nonetheless stemmed from the pooled resources of all the merging parties, it is hence an example of faculty centralization of (research-related) budget control—a first-order integration measure.

As regards research processes, some interdependence pattern consistencies between the DEP and the DSS existed. Similarities as to potential funding agencies (e.g. DFG, EU) and comparable research orientations, namely a focus on empirical social sciences, can be stated in this regard. Some limited research-related contacts had already existed before the merger (2–IV: 378). However, affinities with the DEP were curbed by the latter's stronger practitioner orientation and the limited internationality of publication output. The aspired integration of the CIS therefore failed (2–IX: 490). Almost no research-related contact points with the DE could be found: a contradictory scientific approach, minor third-party funding and qualitatively different funding partners precluded institutionalized research cooperation (2–IX: 281). A common research profile for the faculty as a whole never emerged (2–VIII: 1071).

Once again, small-scale organizational integration was the result. Council representatives from the DE insisted on capping the CGG's budget (FR2 59: 8). Its resources were kept scarce from the beginning, with little more than €50,000 per annum being guaranteed, while additional grants were coupled to member donations (FP2 64: 8). Furthermore, a look at a mid-2011 list of affiliates (Internet archive, my own calculation) reveals that the center was still clearly dominated by members of the DSS; only 4 of the overall 68 members were affiliated to the university's former economics department, while 8 belonged to the DEP. Noteworthy integration of university economists never happened[47]. Taken as a whole, the establishment of the CGG as a faculty research center had not in itself added much to deepening organizational integration. Reduction of resource control remained very limited and nonbinding in character:

> Yes, members talk to each other for sure. And every now and then, they have a symposium. And there is a small administrative apparatus, too. There is something going on, but in my opinion, it appears somewhat more than it substantially is (2–III: 817).

Additional integration attempts concerning research and transfer processes were undertaken relating to the Institute for Further Education (IFW), a

47 The second faculty-central research center, the Hamburg Center for Health Economics, is not introduced here. It has always been exclusively associated with the university's economics department (DE).

semi-commercial subsystem of the DEP. Some need for action occurred against the background of an existing parallel further education unit within the universities' central administration. The main cleavage thus developed between the DEP and the central administration: shifting control via the IFW toward the central unit was considered. This (option 1) would have meant the reduction of the faculty's resource control (actually: the DEP) in order to homogenize faculty configuration according to university standards.

The IFW had three (ID2|16: 22) positions from the faculty's joint budget at its disposal. Retaining this budget assignment by keeping the IFW under the control of the DEP (option 2) implied the homogenization of allocation rules ("share x of the budget goes to that institute") according to DEP standards. The other departments would have lost control over a small part of their resources in order to support DEP-driven further education on a faculty level:

> After all, there is further education taking place. It is not that one can say there is a budget and nothing happens. [...] But what had been overlooked at the time: they are all on our payroll. If you have certain positions elsewhere [on a central university level, mk], you do not have to pay for them (2–VI: 364–390).

Attempts by the university's central level to exert pressure toward centralization are well documented (e.g. DP2 77: 2 and 78: 3). They obviously failed because the unit responsible didn't manage to come up with a convincing concept of how to carry on with educational programs that were rather atypical of large universities:

> [...] the problem at the time was with the central bureau: who develops the study programs, who decides what we do offer and what we do not offer. Economically, we are virtually acting on a free market. We have to be quick and flexible et cetera. [...] And we were, of course, afraid that the direction would move into the president's office, which pursues interests different from ours (2–VIII: 909).

As with some of its study programs, the DEP was simply too successful in transforming resources and fulfilling external education demands (2–X: 756). Between 2003 and 2004, 286 events had been organized by the IFW with altogether more than 4,000 participants. The revenue generated equaled €770,000 in 2003. All other public HEIs in Hamburg taken together between 2003 and 2004 had realized revenues of €652,000 and had about 2,000 participants in their programs (CD2|9). It is exactly these numbers that awarded the DEP a sufficient potency behind its dismissive position. Integration efforts once more dwindled away as organizational resources were at stake. The institute remained within the faculty and under the control of the DEP—hence, integration option 2 was realized in the end. As with the CGG, some limited cooperation with the DSS developed over time, namely with its criminology further education program (2–X: 67). The involvement of the DE is not reported.

5.2.6 Administration and support-related integration

In concluding the delineation of post-merger integration, I will consider a selection of administration / support-related measures. Most of them display characteristics similar to the attempted centralization of the DEP's Institute for Further Education. As the HWP (DEP) had turned from a standalone institution into a department within a large university faculty, it still had several supportive units post-merger that were fairly odd to be located on the faculty level. Parallel subsystems of facility management, accounting or computing services could, for instance, be found as part of the university's central administration as well. As with the IFW, the choice was between centralization of administrative functions on the one hand, and retaining the DEP's status quo on the other. The shift of control over administrative functions from the DEP toward the university level simultaneously represented the homogenization of allocation rules (regarding faculty configuration) toward university standards.

However, since those standards had often been inferior, integration by centralization was not an easy thing to achieve. The administration of the former HWP had in many respects been more responsive to the demands of the internal and external organizational environment. This may be illustrated by the coordination of procurement. While the DE and DSS had rather patchy processes with either completely decentralized procurement (DE) or a mixture between decentralized and centralized processes (DSS), the DEP displayed more consistent practices. It had already used an IT-based procurement system, had contractual partner management and was able to realize volume discounts by combining orders (ID2|16: 63). Another example are the university's highly fragmented accounting processes that, in certain regards (e.g. document filing), were deemed substandard at the time (ID2|16: 59). In a similar vein, the university's IT services were heterogeneous between the departments and task-division between the central university and department levels was criticized for being ill-defined. The DEP computing center, which was clearly detached from the scientific subsystems it served, had an unambiguous service mandate and was characterized by a greater extent of technological homogeneity (ID2|16: 84–85; 2–X: 237). Hence, many of the university's central administration configurations could not serve as a handy organizational blueprint without revision (at least without jeopardizing certain functions).

In connection with the DEP's administrative resources and responsibilities, some of the few instances of true integration between the departments consequently developed. As, to take a case in point, the DSS had inadequate administrative capacities, cooperation with the DEP became attractive:

> Within the [DSS, mk] department, there were only supportive functions for the presidential administration, which had to administer the budget, do the travel expenses and the student assistant accounting. But they were doing it on a basis where things were quite homespun regarding qualifications—whereas the HWP administration had true professionals, as one would expect from decent university administration (2–I: 84).

In 2007 the DSS handed over some processes to the DEP, namely general and third-party funds accounting and procurement (ID2|16: 56, 64, 76). This meant integration through a horizontal reassignment of functions of supportive subsystems across two departments. For both parties, increased resource-related contingency reduction potential ensued. The DSS was able to benefit from improved administrative efficiency and effectiveness, while the DEP created further dependencies to protect its post-merger atypical subsystems from imminent seizure by the university's central administration.

Support for a more university-centralized solution came from representatives of the DE, who generally feared misallocations due to an improper faculty cost structure (2–II: 661). Just as with the IFW, they hence resisted the pending faculty-level homogenization of administration-related allocation rules according to DEP standards. Little usefulness was expected from the DEP supportive units: "because the economists do not use this international career service that they have over there. These are things which are for the socioeconomics study programs" (2–VI: 401). In 2011, fierce opposition, especially from the Department of Business Administration[48], arose

48 The DE had split up into an economics and a business administration department (April 2009).

against the integration of IT systems into the DEP's IT unit. Once again, an opt-out solution to guarantee separate subsystems and processes prevailed[49] (e.g. FR2 58: 13).

On the whole, a compromise in terms of administration and support subsystems was ultimately realized. The faculty retained its own administration, and a number of parallel subsystems was accepted. Otherwise, considerable DEP capacities were shifted toward the university's central administration. This, among other things, applied to a public relations position (2–X: 256), personnel administration capacities (2–VIII: 773) and facility management (ID2|16: 39). Notably, organizational administration integration on a faculty level, besides the instances described above, occurred in the (already mentioned) arrangement of student affairs offices. By the end of 2008, it was decided that the old examination offices of the DSS and the DE would be converted to form separate offices for student affairs according to DEP standards. These offices carried (and still carry) much of the study program support that had conceptually been foreseen to be managed by the Graduate School (DP2, exceptional meeting, 9-12-2008; 2–III: 423).

5.3 *Demerger, recapitulation and discussion*

In April 2013, faculty demerger through the secession of business administration (a former part of the DE) started to be in the offing. The faculty council initially concerned itself with the issue against the background of a university-wide revision of faculty size. What was originally to be attended to in an unrestricted and wide-ranging course of consideration became a sudden fact only three months later. The university senate had quickly decided to disintegrate business administration to form a self-contained fac-

49 From our theoretical perspective, the question then arises as to why parts of the DE rejected an enormous integration dividend that had been taxed between €166,000 and €600,000 p.a. for the whole faculty (FR2 59, A3: 2). As with the procurement procedures, gains in effectiveness and efficiency should have acted as an impetus to integration. A possible (though somewhat speculative) explanation could be that as late as 2011 business administration members wanted to keep the integration level as low as possible *in principle* to prepare for secession, which had already been underway. Any short-run cooperative advantage would have been overcompensated for by the disintegration costs to come.

ulty[50]. In a brief statement, the faculty council and the dean's office—obviously caught cold at large—condemned what was deemed an inappropriate coup de main (FR2 83: 9). As a reaction to the unilaterally pursued breakup, the board of the DSS decided to cease cooperation with business administration representatives, who for their part conceded to surrender their council decision-making influence (F2 83: 10). Hence, the demerger was ultimately sealed, leaving a faculty for (macro-)economics and social sciences and a business administration faculty.

5.3.1 Recapitulation of integration outcomes

In the course of Chapter 5, the attempted integration measures have been somewhat loosely arranged according to three criteria, namely the potential relative magnitude of the organizational resources involved, the chronological negotiation order and the basic transformation process type. In order to facilitate a conclusive assessment of integration outcomes, it is worth making use of a further distinction.

The *first perspective* on the case concerns the (enduring) integration of the former HWP into the much larger University of Hamburg. Relevant measures have referred to the decision between the homogenization of allocation rules according to university standards on the one hand and the perpetuation of HWP rules on the other. This refers to the homogenization of professor-appointment and endowment rules (5.2.2) as well as to the allocation of administration, support and transfer units (5.2.6 / 5.2.5). The homogenization measures mentioned last simultaneously meant or would have meant a shift in allocation responsibilities from the faculty's center (or rather the DEP) toward the university's center: for instance, the university's center acquired some public-relations capacities (2-X: 256). Though the DE and the DSS were affected and involved, the main negotiation parties were, from this perspective, the HWP (DEP) / faculty dean's office and the university's central political subsystems (chair / central administration).

The *second perspective* is the faculty-central perspective and focuses on the two university departments and the former HWP as major negotiation parties in forming a unified faculty. Measures of shifting control and / or homogenizing rules on the level of departments or within the faculty come

50 The secession was itself reasoned by better profiling of business administration and possible rises in third party funds (FP2 83: 6).

to the fore: the Graduate School (5.2.3) as a fourth (fifth) department focusing on education, teaching exchange and the dissertation statute (5.2.4), as well as the few research-related measures (5.2.5). This second perspective also applies to the failed and potentially far-reaching arrangement of the faculty according to two disciplines pre-merger (5.2.1). Although such a configuration had also been preferred by the university's center (FP2 22: 8), the measure had primarily been negotiated on a department level.

Substantial organizational integration was only able to be accomplished regarding the first of the two perspectives. For the most part, this was due to the homogenization of appointment and endowment rules. Since the expenses for scientific staff covered the lion's share of the DEP' overall input resources, these measures are associated with a high level of integration. In the medium-term, the measure a) led to a considerable adjustment of the former HWP's composition and structures in line with the university and b) stopped the HWP's dominant coalition from reproducing itself. However—and this underscores the importance of our respective conceptual distinction—the homogenization of allocation rules regarding appointments is not to be readily equated with a concentrating shift of control (centralization). Appointment-related and endowment-related measures may eventually well be considered homogenization of HWP rules according to its state-granted university status (using the incorporation as a vehicle). In terms of the desired "true" centralization of the HWP's administrative and support capacities, many concessions had to be made by the university's center. The administrative capacities on the departmental / faculty level remained quite high in comparison to other faculties (FP2 63: 8; FP2 59: 5).

As regards the faculty and department perspective, by contrast, the level of integration had remained very low throughout. Arranging the faculty on a basis of departments that represented the three merging parties was consistently pursued. Virtually no integration occurred with regard to education and research processes: control over graduate and undergraduate programs effectively resided in the departments—programs were mostly introduced and / or developed further apart from each other. The Graduate School and faculty-level dissertation committee ended up as paper tigers; a common habilitation statute could not be realized at all. The situation in terms of research activities was quite similar: aside from some limited cooperation between the DEP and the DSS, no comprehensive faculty research profile emerged. The same is true for inter-department cooperation with regard to administrative services and support processes.

5.3.2 Coping with merger demands (and coping consequences)

In Chapter 5, the focus has specifically been on the diversity of intraorganizational coping strategies concerning integration pressure. Just as in the case of the Universities of Duisburg and Essen, the merger in Hamburg is not to be characterized as an active effort of one of the parties to restructure resource interdependencies in a beneficial manner. The merger, and thereby the pressure to realize some organizational integration, was one substantial environmental demand among several others. Considering the merged faculty's essential transformation processes, I was able to show in the Hamburg case how true integration (would have) interfered with other important external interests. During the course of the merger, almost all the organizational endeavors to manage conflicting environmental demands, as discussed by Pfeffer and Salancik (1978: 98ff.), could be observed:

- *Attempts to control the formation of demands*: the pre-merger stage yielded numerous efforts to affect the very conception of merger demands, particularly by representatives and proponents of the HWP a) on the level of the city's political institutions (e.g. CD2|10) and b) by raising public interest through activities of students as well as the HWP's prominent alumni organization. The post-merger protection of the status quo as regards further education activities (IFW, Subsection 5.2.5) was also associated with the exertion of parliamentary influence (e.g. CD2|11);
- *Controlling the definition of demand satisfaction*: the merger law decidedly (CD2|7: § 9) left the by far largest part of criteria regarding integration outcomes to the three departments, which were for a scarcely specified transitional period explicitly acknowledged as a political subsystem-level within the organization. Codified allocation rules that were relevant to integration were often kept ambiguous (e.g. study program responsibility regulations in the faculty statute, ID2|12 § 7 (4));
- *Reducing the visibility of behavior and outcomes*: the gap between codified structures and actual control had widened; a larger share of decision-making behavior tended to occur behind the scenes (2–V: 256; 2–IX: 981). So, for instance, the technical importance of the department boards was not paralleled by any documentation (2–III: 881); faculty positions to administratively support the department boards (two for each department) were retained against formal rules (FP2 21: 6; FP2 23: 4; DP2 152: 2).

During this chapter, I have repeatedly pointed to decoupling (Pfeffer & Salancik. 1978: 98; Meyer & Rowan, 1977: 357) as an important coping-strategy in merger processes. In important fields of activity, the mere illusion of meeting integration demands was created—unified political subsystems and homogenized sets of allocation rules were implemented and hollowed out at once. Behind that formal integration scenery, large parts of the subsystem-specific technical requirements and strategic decisions to maintain transformation processes were still adhered to. At some points, the protocols show that council members had been well aware of the emptiness of factual integration measures (e.g. FP2 17: 4, FP2 51:8, FP extraordinary meeting 03-04-2013: 3). The realization of decoupling was achieved through various methods:

- Consistently reproducing political-subsystem equipartition according to departmental affiliation (e.g. membership rules in juries and committees);
- (Re)assigning allocation responsibilities or homogenizing allocation rules with little process relevance or even reassigning standard procedures with no discretion at all (e.g. the negligible dissertation responsibilities of the Graduate School);
- Weakening the binding character of integration: opt-out, opt-in, hidden veto-rights or unspecified "exceptional cases" (e.g. the interdepartmental teaching exchange regulations, IT support);
- Dwarfing and capping of pooled budgets (e.g. in terms of faculty-level research activities).

Coping with integration demands in the manner described produced organizational consequences that are in turn (also) associated with the demerger. To begin with, rising complexity and decoupling from a normative (and maybe legal) perspective resulted in the growing dispersion of organizational responsibilities and a lack of transparency. The central level of the faculty had remained weak. It had to share and delegate vast parts of resource control with and to the formally dependent departments beneath it. If we consider the overall political system of the faculty, the congruence of effective discretion with formal control was diminished post-merger.

During the whole period of its existence, the faculty had displayed a lower than usual level of integration. This holds for its relationship with the University of Hamburg as a whole, as well as for its internal organization. Mostly in the context of the elaboration and approval of the faculty's statute, several serious conflicts with the center of the university ensued. After the DE was split into two departments (in 2009), to take a case in point, the faculty tried to install a fourth vice-dean to stick with its departmental representation doctrine (DP2 81: 1). After the university senate had refused to accordingly adjust the superior university statute (DP2 91: 2), the departments established a "gray" co-opted fourth vice-dean, who had no formal vote. Further examples are the informal implementation of assistant positions for the department heads (FP2 23: 4f.) and fierce conflicts regarding the assignment of administrative staff (ID2|17). Disputes with the university's center resulted in further considerable deferment of the difficult post-merger negotiations.

Dogged and time-consuming bargaining was attended by increasing redtapism. Soon after the merger, the looming exuberant staff-intensity of the faculty's self-governance was discussed (FP2 13: 7). Following the rising number of political subsystems, their respective relative discretion had to shrink. Hence, operating an empty faculty-shell, despite its demand-balancing effects, nonetheless coincided with sizable costs. Numerous boards, committees and subcommittees on different system levels had to be regularly staffed; the "gray" political subsystems also had to be managed. Due to the rigid department representation rule, the number of professors in temporal organs (Jurys etc.) had also become larger (e.g. FP2 69: 7). This *inward organizational growth* started to impinge upon workaday life in the faculty: meeting schedules and corresponding streams of documents had swollen (FP2 40: 6). Council members complained about information overflow (e.g. being confronted with a huge number of department-specific study program regulations) and a lack of information on the other hand (FP2 53: 2; FP2 62: 9).

As an outcome of maintaining subunit effectiveness through decoupling, inward organizational growth—which is how it may be summarized —was accompanied by diminishing efficiency. More input resources had to be employed to politically maintain transformation processes as demanded by the external environment. It becomes obvious that lacking organizational efficiency as an internal evaluation standard beyond a certain point stunts effectiveness, too: the resources that went into the growing political system of the faculty were no longer available for education and research processes. The disintegrative forces within the faculty, which had been quite substantial from the outset, were thereby probably further strengthened. The incorporation, at least on a faculty level, had thus created a highly artificial and ultimately unstable organization.

6 Material manifestations of mergers in higher education: conclusion and competing explanations

In Chapter 1, we developed and accessed our research question from several perspectives. Searching for a basic definition, we identified a persistent conceptual contradiction in the extant literature on this subject. On the one hand, M&As have largely been treated as a form of interorganizational relations characterized by having an extreme impact on the interior life of the merging parties. The development of M&A research as a field / subdiscipline in part seems to have been built on that implication. On the other hand, it has become common sense that mergers, in being characterized by a "distinct duality", frequently occur in fewer integrated forms with great local autonomy and the perpetuation of extant structures. In the case of mergers in public HE, we found that implication to be mirrored in the commonly announced political ambitions: mergers and incorporations in themselves are associated with great changes in organizational output (suggesting the measures take a quasi-automatic inward effect). It is also known amongst practitioners that integration frequently fails. From that contradiction, the necessity to analyze post-merger integration as a variable *in its own right* ensues.

Business-related success factor research was identified as the dominant general scientific perspective on organizational mergers. Thorough isolation of M&A research (as a supposed subdiscipline) from organization theory was diagnosed to be the chief source of shortcomings. Within success factor research, the "soft" cultural-cognitive perspective on organizations has become established in research literature as the primary (and de facto only) means of analyzing integration as a variable. In order to overcome the field's deficits, I advocated reconnecting merger analysis to conventional organization theory. Consequently, four adequacy criteria to identify potential organizational theories were worked out: they should display an explicit interest in mergers and IORs; should provide multilevel explanations; be able to conceptualize (post-merger) organizational integration and ultimately should be applied to non-profits. Based on these criteria, I suggested resource dependence theory as the guiding framework with which to investigate post-merger integration in higher education. The discussion of the literature on this subject and the adequacy criteria were supplemented with a materialist and realist meta-theoretical position as opposed to the subjectivist–relativist paradigm underlying the cultural approach.

6.1 Recapitulation of the approach and study results

6.1.1 What have we done?

In Chapter 2, we explicated the potentials and shortcomings of RDT regarding our specific research subject. The potential of the former was mostly found in its attention to mergers and IORs as well as in its multilevel nature. Moreover, during the 1980s, RDT became a key theory in the sociology of higher education; its application in different types of organizations has been manifold. Limitations of the theory's applicability with respect to post-merger integration have been associated with its underspecification of organizational structure. Though RDT seeks to explain both organizational actions *and* structures, its adherents have mostly subsumed the latter under the former. Board composition and interlocks have been the chief research interest; students of intraorganizational phenomena from a resource dependence perspective have paid little attention to structure.

It is at this point important to recall why this asymmetric development of RDT constitutes a deficit. The concept of post-merger integration entails a strong notion of "getting organized". By drawing, for instance, on homogenization, consolidation and coordination, M&A research has gathered many abstractions in its definition attempts concerning organizational integration that could equally well be used to define formal organizations. And, indeed, before it becomes possible to analyze what making one out of at least two organizations might mean, it needs to be understood what constitutes one organization as an integrated and therefore discernible unit. Two organizations becoming integrated refers to getting one / both organized. This is about more than a mere change of ownership: at least two separate units, each of which can be designated integrated and therefore discernible according to a criterion, are deemed to turn into one unit post-merger on the basis of the same criterion. The integration puzzle hence ultimately relates to the question of *what organizations are*. Inasmuch as being structured is a pivotal characteristic of formal organizations as distinct social systems, a structural perspective is also indispensable in any conceptualization effort concerning post-merger integration.

In order to enable such a conceptualization, the definitional basis of RDT was complemented and corroborated in Chapter 3 by Mario Bunge's materialist ontology. Correspondingly, systemism was introduced as the fundamental socio-scientific research approach to flesh out the materialist–realist orientation of the study. The materialist ontology was, in combination with RDT as the complementary system-specific theory, used to characterize organizations in higher education as transformative, distinct and integrated allocation systems. Two system-constituting moments were identified: firstly, some of their subsystems are sometimes functionally related to each other through series of resource allocations (the relevant processes are education, research, and administration); as resource exchange gives rise to power relations, regularities in exchange can be described by power-dependence theory. Secondly, organizations are constituted by discretion-reducing shifts in allocation responsibilities. Resource transformation and exchange are regulated by the political system of the organization. Due to the coalitional model inherent in RDT, the source of regulations that are produced within the political system is ultimately the respective dominant coalition. The conceptual basis for integration was hence essentially found in organizational control over resource transformation processes. Since integration and distinctiveness / differentiation conceptions logically have to build on the same criterion, a system boundary model was borrowed from Bunge (1992) and complemented with RDT propositions.

To lay the groundwork for the general explanation of organizational (dis)integration, a definition of the dependent variable was provided. Organizational integration describes a shift of control to other system components. In doing so, political subsystems of the (emerging) organization are usually reduced, either in absolute numbers or in the respect of decreasing relative resource control. The opposing process of disintegrating / differentiating relates to a rising number of political subsystems and the local disarrangement of regulations. In line with the discussion of organizational boundaries, the level of integration was conceptualized in terms of the relative magnitude of organizational resources involved in integration measures.

In search of essential influence factors on integration, I elaborated the notion of environmental interdependence patterns. According to RDT, organizations face a set of external demands that is characterized by *qualitative* and *quantitative* aspects. The former refers to the quality of how resources have to be transformed to meet the nature of the demand; the latter concerns the relative weight of organizational input resources corresponding to the respective exchange relation.

The interaction of both aspects in turn served to depict the constant presence of counteracting integrative and disintegrative forces in organizations. Environmental demands are regularly in conflict with each other in that they cannot be met simultaneously and often call for different modes of resource transformation. In line with the strategic contingencies' theory of intraorganizational power, a central claim of RDT is that organizations consist of various coalitions: power relations on a subunit level are closely related to the environmental resource interdependence pattern. Integration can be achieved by strong coalitions through consent (side-payments) or force. Conflicts can, however, also be resolved by structural differentiation: qualitatively different environmental demands in the case of sufficient resource bases (power aspect) may lead to separate political subsystems and transformation processes.

This classic interpretation of (dis)integration dynamics subsequently served us as a template with which to derive a specific explanation of post-merger integration depth. The environmental interdependence patterns of at least two organizations suddenly confront each other in a merger situation. They have henceforth to be managed in common central level political subsystems. Organizational coalitions depend on continuous resource inflows to keep their stability: any integration measure, it was argued, will therefore be evaluated by the subunits involved in terms of its effects on resource transformation. The conception of qualitative interdependence pattern (in)consistencies between the parties was used to describe the range of options for the parties to negotiate an at least resource-neutral post-merger configuration of the transformation system. We consequently hypothesized that qualitative pattern (in)consistencies further (dis)integrative forces within the merged organization (H1a / b). While the qualitative relation of patterns to each other should influence (political positioning) the *directionality* of intraorganizational forces (integration vs. disintegration), their quantitative relation determines their *magnitude*. The actual chances of integration measures being realized were hence hypothesized to be a function of the resource weight of the potentially impaired external interests (H2a / b). A third Hypothesis concerned the orientation of post-merger flow of control and the shape of any allocation rule homogenization realized (H3a / b).

6.1.2 Recapitulation of the empirical results

The results of our inquiry *first of all* once more confirm that the focus of analysis of organizations should be on their social context in terms of concrete networks of resource interdependencies. Inter- and intraorganizational negotiations chiefly revolved around the subunit's abilities to continue to acquire critical resources from the environment post-merger—such a contextual perspective's conceptual priority on organizational effectiveness was empirically corroborated in many instances:

- Will we still be able to provide our non-traditional students with adequate learning conditions to sustain the good average duration of our studies, and our graduate and enrollee numbers?
- Will we be able to keep up our ranking positions and reputation to compete for our renowned professors who attract funding?
- Will a broader and more balanced portfolio between application-oriented and theoretical physics in one faculty enable us to acquire a further collaborative research center?
- Will we be able to retain our business engineering students in the long run if the faculty is relocated?
- Will funding agencies and talented students still recognize us as political scientists or will we be dismissed as an unspecific all-round social science department?
- Will there be enough student apprentices in our social work program to fulfill our exchange contract with the city?

Conceptually, the effectiveness criterion in this study relates to the qualitative aspect of environmental interdependence patterns: what needs to be done and in what fashion to maintain the respective exchange relations (and possibly enlarge the input resources acquired from them)?

Secondly, the significance of power-exchange theory (Emerson, 1962; Blau, 1964) as the core social theory with which to explain organizational behavior and structures was underlined with empirical evidence. We have considered mergers as large-scale social experiments; our results support power theory and a power perspective on organizations. The dependence of organizations on external resources is the main source of intraorganizational power: discretionary differentials of subunits and the coalitions beneath them have been demonstrated to correspond with their relative contribution to overall resource-related uncertainty reduction. It has been shown that discretionary differentials were used by the coalitions to create and defend system configurations to perpetuate and enhance the basis of their power (i.e. resource inflows).

In the case of the incorporation of the HWP into the University of Hamburg, the three interdependence patterns were so diverse (and power differentials too small) that almost no integration measures could be effectively implemented on a faculty level. Education and research / transfer processes remained largely independent. With the homogenization of appointment and endowment policies and the shift of some administration capacities, true integration was almost exclusively realized in the central university level vs. the ex-HWP relationship. As for instance discussed for further education activities, looming immediate impairment of working exchange relations in several cases still granted the ex-HWP enough discretion to successfully block centralization attempts.

In the first case study (Chapter 4), for instance, rising values on all the extracted power factors accordingly increased a subunit's chances of preserving its own political subsystem, or, to say it in a different way, it prevented subunits from becoming absorbed. The following analysis of post-merger unit relocation revealed: the higher the relative resource weight of a particular system configuration, the lower the chances that the fulfillment of the associated external interests is hazarded by integration measures.

Moreover, it has become evident that change measures were able to be realized only *with*, but *never* against the potential of huge intraorganizational power—the integration process of the Universities of Duisburg and Essen was largely organized around the interests of the three "pillars of power" clusters. Most of these units were able to hold or even enhance their power position during the process. Mergers and incorporations in higher education were thus depicted as rather conservative change measures. By relating the subunits of at least two formerly separate organizations to each other, mergers challenge intraorganizational power—the search for, and the activation and formation of existing power potential are triggered. The lower the power potential that is associated with a subunit's political position, the easier it is counteracted and overcome. During the Duisburg–Essen merger, internal differentiation became chiefly reduced in those subunit clusters that displayed low power scores. Relative control of material resources and the corresponding power relations hence manifested themselves in organizational structures.

A further aspect of the contextual perspective on organizations therefore became apparent: autonomous managerial decisions and the influence of individual administrators need to be relativized. Level and orientation of post-merger integration are by no means, as for instance suggested by strategic fit approaches to M&A research, to be equated with top management decisions—except if one wants to reinterpret the interests of the strong coalitions as top management goals ex-post. Any flipchart system configuration has to face and make use of intraorganizational power relations rooted in sociomaterial context conditions. In line with the metaphor of a magnetic field (Bunge & Mahner, 2004: 18), networks of power relations are not readily tangible as a whole, but can be partially observed if some (metallic / resource-related) thing is held against them. Internal perspectives on M&A, on the contrary, tend to emphasize top management leadership styles, values and other micro-level characteristics while downplaying constraints on administrative decision-making. However, constraining external demands, thousands of students and heavy teaching supply liabilities are far from being managed or moderated away easily. Managerial discretion being overestimated still doesn't mean that top administrators in higher education mergers are string puppets—but they have to work with what's there, and discretion was fairly limited in the cases under study.

Thirdly and finally, the strategic choice tenet of RDT has become evident: organizations have ways to actively work on, counteract and balance external constraints. The merging parties in both cases tried and partially succeeded in shaping the merger demand itself through political and legal interventions. Particularly in the case of Hamburg, a fascinating multitude of decoupling tactics to buffer and protect the required system configurations against integration attempts were observed. The extant political systems of the merging parties were actively carried forward into the "new" faculty; factual responsibilities were partly disguised by creating gray structures. A pseudo-integration process with little substance but considerable operation costs set in. New faculty-level political subsystems that should have fostered the integration of resource transformation were equipped with ambiguous mandates, insignificant responsibilities and / or a meager budget of their own. In several instances, the coalitions went all out to keep the necessity of actually meeting integration demands to a minimum.

Though I promised not to do so, I will at this juncture take advantage of the recapitulation of the empirical results to conclude it by again briefly theorizing on the political motives underlying the two cases. Instead of relying on officially announced merger goals, in Subsection 1.1.3 I pointed to the general political context of the second merger wave in German higher education. I argued that the mergers conducted were probably considered to at least be largely consistent with the upcoming neoliberal turn by the public agencies responsible. This may be elucidated against the background of the empirical results:

Mergers and incorporations of higher education organizations act as surrogates for direct state interventions and are supposed to bolster other change measures. They potentially increase the discretion of central level organs (chiefly the rectorate) and indirectly of the public agency. In the case of the two formerly independent Universities of Duisburg and Essen, the precarious resource situation of many units besides the legal restrictions additionally constrained their room to maneuver and change the organizations in whatever direction. Let us just pick the two history departments as an example. Both of them were endowed with six professorships and seven assistant positions, which represents the minimum conditions with which to provide a basic study program in history (ID1|44). Any kind of transforming or reducing faculty positions would quickly endanger the operativeness of such a unit. Attempts to increase external control, for example by further stimulating performance based budgeting, would fail to take effect, and financial cutbacks would be factually impossible. Organizational discretion could only be achieved by further public investment. On the other hand, if both units were integrated, the situation could be resolved without increasing the budget. It would, for instance, become possible to cut a professorship, transform a second one into assistant positions and end up with one history unit with ten professorships which are better endowed on average. Political subsystems on higher levels would henceforth better be able to negotiate objectives, pass on altered performance-based funding assignments or handle vacancies. From the public agency's perspective, and under the general condition of sinking budgets, at least two birds are hence killed with one stone: external control attempts are potentiated and the scarcity situation of history as a discipline is partly relieved.

During the Duisburg–Essen merger, the humanities units from clusters one, two and seven indeed seem to have been the main political target. The public agency furthered the integration / relocation of those units pre-merger by discontinuing many of their study programs; they thus reduced their bases of intraorganizational power. Besides the concentration of humanities on the Essen campus, there also seems to have been an early consensus on the realization of an integrated physics department on one of the two campuses. These prospects might already have been enough motivation to push the merger through, ceding supplementary integration outcomes (like a unified economics faculty) to transitional central level management.

The proposed argument applies in a similar way to the second merger case analyzed. Poor studying conditions, particularly in the former Department 03 / DE (university economics), had been closely connected to a student–professor ratio of 188:1; 32 professors had to educate about 6,000 students (ID2|5: 2). The HWP owed its low dropout rate and the favorable duration of its studies to its UAS-like system configuration (focus on education / low "traditional" research output). Improving university education in a stand-alone Department 03 would have called for public investment. Since the latter hadn't been an option due to the general political impetus, and, contrariwise, further budget cutbacks had already[51] been underway, larger units seem to have been considered better able to handle scarcity. Homogenizing HWP and university appointment and endowment-policies made the faculty positions of the former accessible to increased resource maneuvering space in the medium term. Planning to absorb and limit further harm to heavily loaded university study programs and administrative processes could thus be undertaken. In view of the HWP's main student target group, policy homogenization was accompanied by the redistribution of public resources to traditional university students.

6.2 *Idealism and subjectivism in merger analysis*

The story of the intraorganizational consequences of mergers in higher education is first of all to be told in terms of resource interdependencies, configuration requirements and power relations. This is the argument of RDT as the specific organization theory employed in this study. The underlying meta-theoretical core argument is that changes in organizations as material social systems are primarily to be found in the sociomaterial conditions in their environment and (consequently) within them.

Contemporary scholarly debates on the other hand are predominantly based on the meta-theoretical premises of the cultural / linguistic turn, which stands in the long tradition of ideational and subjectivist explanations of stability and change of social structures. The term subjectivism refers to "the philosophical view that the world, far from existing independently, is a creation of the knower" (Bunge, 1996: 330). Ontologically, social systems like business firms or universities are thus mostly conceptualized as collectively shared cognitions or rather conventions with an existence of their own. The analytical relevance of the observer-independent reality of organizations is neglected by and large, the corresponding subjectivist epistemology focuses on elucidating construction processes in terms of a "redescription and reinterpretation" of their contents (Reed, 2009: 434). Idealism and subjectivism stand in opposition to materialism and realism, which we outlined in Chapter 3 as the ontological and epistemological doctrines of systemism as a general scientific approach.

51 These cutbacks of about 18.5 million euros p.a. hit the University of Hamburg in spring 2011.

With regard to specific social theories associated with idealism and subjectivism, in Subsections 1.3.2 and 1.4.1 we first of all introduced the cultural perspective on organizations as the dominating and main rival explanation for post-merger (dis)integration. With the family of neo-institutionalist theories of organization, further specific representatives were briefly addressed in 2.2.1. This was aimed at circumventing RDT and underlining its focus on "the importance of the material conditions of organizational transactions with the environment" (Pfeffer, 2005: 444).

At the risk of unduly oversimplifying the genesis of recent social constructivism, Thomas Berger's and Frank Luckmann's *The Social Construction of Reality* (1967) shall here be referred to as the most common basic social theory. The circular construction process suggested therein comprises the externalization of uncertainty, the reciprocal habitualization and collective institutionalization of a legitimate and therefore objective social reality. Constructed social facts and structures were in turn internalized by individuals as subjective reality; they were for the most part no longer perceivable as human products. The social world and its meaning were reproduced by its inhabitants in a taken-for-granted manner. Hence, the ontological nature of social facts is deemed essentially immaterial (perceptual) instead of material; the function of social systems—if there is a function at all—lies in reducing cognitive uncertainties instead of ensuring control / dominance or granting efficiency.

Though Berger's and Luckmann's (1967) adherence to idealist ontology becomes apparent through their proximity to the phenomenology of Edmund Husserl and Alfred Schütz (Scott, 1987: 495; Bunge, 1996: 293f.), they seem unwilling to engage in meta-theoretical debates. Instead of seeking a dialogue between the philosophy of science and sociology as a discipline, they one-sidedly recommended leaving the decision between "valid and invalid assertions about the world" to the philosophers (Berger & Luckmann, 1967: 2). Likewise, many approaches under the broader umbrella of the cultural linguist turn have remained "ontologically mute" (Reed, 2005: 1624, in referring to Gergen, 1994), simply introduce themselves as anti-positivists or outright declare their specific social theories themselves to be meta-theory (e.g. Thornton & Ocasio, 2008).

Social constructivist subjectivism is always collectivist in nature: the construction of realities takes place in collectives—social facts are facts only relative to the constructing thought collective (Bunge, 1996: 335ff.). Variations of constructivist approaches mainly refer to different kinds of such thought collectives, like larger regions / nation states, groups of organizations, scientific communities, single organizations or tribes. The coming sections examine the explanatory potential of sociological neo-institutionalism and the cultural perspective as regards post-merger integration in higher education more closely and critically. Both groups of theories refer to differently circumscribed thought collectives, yet are quite similar in terms of the mechanism they promote. In doing so, we will again orient our analysis on the theory adequacy criteria derived from the discussion in Chapter 1 (1.3.3).

6.2.1 Neo-institutionalist merger analysis

Sociological neo-institutionalism is the family of possible alternative explanations considered first. The thought collective it regularly refers to is the organizational field[52], which is defined as: "those organizations that, in the aggregate, constitute a recognized area of institutional life: key suppliers, resource and product customers, regulatory agencies, and other organizations that produce similar services or products" (DiMaggio & Powell, 1983: 148). In terms of a "relational space" (Greenwood & Meyer, 2008), it is the main unit of analysis in which the institutionalization process unfolds—Scott (2003: 223ff.) discusses empirical applications of the field concept on different macro-levels of analysis, like communities or nation states. The field concept does not so much refer to concrete relations of resource exchange or competition; the partaking organizations are primarily related to each other in a process of reciprocally "instilling value" (Scott, 1987: 493) to social structures and practices. In the wake of the structuration of such fields, cognitive limits for decision makers regarding how to shape organizations occur. As a consequence, interorganizational homogeneity on the field-level is deemed to increase. According to DiMaggio & Powell (1983), these cognitive limits are spread within a particular field through three ideal type "isomorphic processes" based on *coercion*, *mimicry* and *professionalization*.

52 We limit our considerations largely to the dominant macro-stream of neo-institutionalism. In the work of Lynne Zucker, the relevant thought collectives consist, by contrast, of individuals.

How is the merger-analysis record of neo-institutionalism?

Though networks of interorganizational relations have been at the heart of neo-institutionalism (Greenwood & Meyer, 2008), it has neither figured prominently in merger debates, nor has the phenomenon been a particular focus in foundational writings. Its character as a macro-level theory has become evident in a respective research focus on how M&As are objectified into legitimate change measures on the field-level. In central neo-institutionalist works on mergers, the concept of *institutional logics* (Alford & Friedland, 1991; Thornton & Ocasio, 2008) has been highlighted in particular.

For instance, according to Thornton and Ocasio (1999), merger motives and intraorganizational effects seem to be historically contingent on the particular socially constructed institutional context (logic). In analyzing the higher education publishing industry, they distinguished between *editor logic* with a decision-maker focus on author–editor relationships on the one hand, and *market logic,* which calls for the improvement of market positions on the other hand. It has been argued that during the rule of editor logic, conglomerate acquisitions with low integration requirements were dominant and the executive succession rate therefore remained low. As editor logic was replaced by market logic, related acquisitions became commonplace according to Thornton and Ocasio (1999: 835). Integrating operations on an organization level to enhance the market position was henceforth consistent with the new collective logic and the replacement of executives according to the bidder's interests became more likely.

Several merger studies were undertaken in the healthcare sector (e.g. Kitchener, 2002; Kitchener & Gask, 2003; Chi & Brommels, 2009). Kitchener (2002), to take a case in point, in referring to Friedlander & Alford (1991) and Rueff & Scott (1998) investigated the antecedents, processes and implications of US healthcare center mergers. Internal formal structures of healthcare organizations—professional bureaucracies (Mintzberg, 1979)—are conceived as structural manifestations of professional institutional logic. Mergers as an innovation typical of contradictory managerial logic are deemed to be established as rationality myths (Meyer & Rowan, 1977) by proactive executives. Consultants, local business representatives and the business press were mobilized and constituted a homogenous discourse among healthcare executives. Kitchener (2002: 409ff.) pointed to the negative effects of uncritically adopting mergers as practices pertaining to the new managerial logic. The mixing of different cognitive logics and their structural correlates is seen to result in unstable organizational forms and loose coupling between the different sediments (Cooper, Hinings, Greenwood & Brown, 1996). Recall our argument in contrast: the looming impairment of numerous identifiable material resource exchange relations furthers disintegrative political forces within the merged organization and by extension leads to structural decoupling.

Mergers in higher education have also attracted the interest of macro-institutionalist researchers. Pruisken (2014) compared merger activity in Germany and Great Britain to analyze the influence of global and field-level institutional contexts on merger activity. Furthermore, she partly adopted Kitchener's (2002) framework in a case study (German *Karlsruhe Institute of Technology* merger) to examine (in)consistencies in local and global collective constructions. In a similar research setting—a case study of a large French research institute merger—Barrier (2014) sought to resolve the theoretical contradiction between formal structures being mere myth and ceremony and the fact that they often prove to be quite hard to change in practice (Musselin, 2007). Processes and outcomes of the organizational-level translation and implementation of merger pressures were traced. Barrier (2014) found a high level of second-order integration in one of the parties and reported evidence of structures being more than window dressing. He furthermore sees the connection between symbolic legitimacy and material resource mobilization underlined.

How about multilevel explanations in neo-institutionalism?

A complete explanation for realized post-merger integration on the overall organization level should account for various subunit (and individual) actions and reactions on the system levels below. To what extent has neo-institutionalism been able to provide multilevel explanations of organizational change?

As far as its meta-theoretical premises are concerned, neo-institutionalism is holist, and developing multilevel explanations on its basis is therefore anything but easy. In Chapter 3, holism was introduced as the extreme counterpart of individualism; as a philosophic view it considers society an organic whole that transcends its components (Bunge, 1996: 258ff.). The actions of organizational subunits or individuals within them can only be understood relative to that collective whole; agency is largely neglected (Reed, 2003). All elements within such larger thought collectives constitute a "totality of relevant actors" (DiMaggio & Powell, 1983), who have to be permanently and comprehensively related to each other in a reciprocal (re)construction process. Empirically observable gaps within the totality, like for instance competing interpretations on lower levels, alternative discourses or subunit agency cast doubt on the taken-for-granted nature of institutions (and have always been a gateway for power-exchange arguments). An objectified reality conceived of as "exterior" by lower-level agents depends on institutionalization processes being as comprehensive as possible (Zucker, 1983)—incomplete institutionalization or counter-trend sub-level activities have to be disposed of as temporary phenomena.

As an illustration, one may consider professional logic, which is claimed by Kitchener (2002) to float above a concrete social system of 125 US academic healthcare centers. Subsystems across almost all levels (some agency is conceded to hospital executives) have to take the associated organizational structures and practices for granted, a status that has to be permanently reproduced. In a merger situation, it is said, professional logic was confronted with managerialism, another macro-level form of institutional logic. A holist argument for the (non-)realization of post-merger organizational integration is consequently brought up by referring to Cooper, Hinings, Greenwood and Brown (1996):

> [...] such mixing of logics and structures produces 'unstable' organizational forms in which adopted myths (e.g. merger, PPM) become only loosely coupled to the structural remnants of professional dominance (Kitchener, 2002: 412).

Confronting the field-bound quasi-natural collective scripts and expectations (e.g. decentralized decision-making) with mergers should hence generally lead to unstable and loosely coupled organizations. It follows, then, that any merger case within the field, which features higher integration levels, is at variance with that explanation. Any subunit promoting integration measures to enhance its own resource situation would represent a contradiction. Consequently, considering integration as a variable becomes impossible once more—all subunits and individuals that have internalized "professional logic", which transcends all levels, have to reject it. This is just as doubtful as globally associating mergers with a high level of integration or even equating them with complete cooperation. As a result, neo-institutionalism has failed to provide a multilevel explanation for post-merger integration due to its meta-theoretical premises.

Neo-institutionalism and organizational integration

A third important criterion has been found in a specific theory's capacity to conceptualize organizational integration and differentiation. We have asserted that determining to what extent merging parties become integrated cannot be separated from analyzing the integration of and differentiation between single organizations—there is nothing like a specific merger theory. The conceptualization of integration necessarily requires considerations on what basically constitutes formal organizations and discerns them from other organizations as well as from non-organized parts of society.

In this regard, further doubts can be raised about the potential of neo-institutionalism to analyze intraorganizational merger consequences. As Niklas Luhmann (2000: 36) aptly noted, overall its advocates have added little to the basic (grand) social constructivism as laid out by Berger & Luckmann (1967). The neo-institutionalist program basically consists of a transfer of their arguments on organizations. Instead of individuals in their taken-for-granted *Lebenswelt*, it is now formal organizations which structure their respective organizational fields and mutually convince each other of their existence and rationality. In line with Luhmann, neo-institutionalism is apparently a rollback movement seeking to (re-)dissolve organizations in macro-sociological analysis. The implicit neglect of organizations as distinct social systems in their own right shall subsequently be elaborated against the background of neo-institutionalism's a) shortcomings in analyzing the actual emergence of formal organizations and b) its inadequacy in terms of conceptualizing organizational boundaries.

a) *Neo-Institutionalism and the emergence of organizations* According to Berger and Luckmann (1967: 60ff.), institutionalization begins with reciprocal typifications between individuals. The degree of reification (objectification), that is, the stability of institutions, rises with their transmission over multiple generations. The original argument generally draws very much on family relationships: primary and secondary socialization, significant others, family roles, etc. However, such terminology cannot be smoothly transferred to formal organizations as interacting units and to organizational fields as relational totalities. While childbirth and the existence of some set of significant others may reasonably be assumed for all kinds of human society, the very existence of formal organizations (as phenomena of a particular societal formation) is far from being trivial or universal—it needs to be explained (Türk, 2000: 131).

Within rationalist–functionalist organization theory and its forerunners (see Morgan, 2006: 11ff.), the respective raison d'être is seen in labor division, efficiency and economic selection; as Ronald Coase, eyeing economic institutionalism, put it:

> Adam Smith explained that the productivity of the economic system depends on specialization (he says the division of labor), but specialization is only possible if there is exchange—and the lower the costs of exchange (transaction costs if you will), the more specialization there will be and the greater the productivity of the system (Coase, 1998: 73).

Along the same lines, Mintzberg (1979: 1ff.) described the transition of individual economic activity and the emergence of a business firm by means of supervision and work / output / skill standardization from a contingency theory perspective (neo-institutionalism's initial opponent). Organizations are thus deemed to be rational systems which foster societal productivity.

Power-focused and interest-focused social research has by contrast highlighted asymmetries in exchange relations, and the qualities of formal organizations to deepen, counteract and make use of those asymmetries. Instead of "productivity of the system", resource appropriation and the dominance of single coalitions are the consequence. In Section 2.2, we discussed RDT as a hybrid theory combining both constituting moments of organizations (enhancement of productivity and problem-solving capacity) as well as the sclerotic re-enforcement of power. The creation of organizations (just like their anorganic growth through a merger) is essentially considered a means of reducing competition and / or balancing the concentration activities of other social actors (Pfeffer, 1972).

In contrast, neo-institutionalism has so far hardly been able to provide an endogenous explanation for the very emergence of formal organizations (Türk, 2000; DiMaggio, 1988: 6f.). In line with Meyer and Rowan (1977: 344), formal organizations are "endemic in modern societies" and their source is "the legitimacy of rationalized formal structures" (*Ibid.*: 345). Hasse and Krücken (2005: 244) vaguely circumscribe organizations as the results, medium and multipliers of comprehensive rationalization processes in society. Institutionalization obviously lags behind: to become similar in respect to certain scripts and structures (DiMaggio & Powell, 1983) or allow individual behavior adaption to perceived organizational contexts (Zucker, 1983), formal organizations, as regulatory structures, have to preexist to a certain degree. This forces neo-institutionalists to at least temporarily accept the basic premises of alternative explanations. And this problem has been recognized: Scott (2003: 166) rejects a solution by Zucker (1983; 1987) and DiMaggio & Powell (1983) that admits the productivity effects of formal organizations only in the early stages of institutionalization:

> Although we agree that both technical and institutional processes give rise to organizations, it does not seem obvious that technical forces were dominant in earlier periods and have now given way to institutional forces [...] Both institutional and technical forces appear to be vigorous, to varying degrees, across contemporary organizational domains (Scott, 2003: 166).

However, from a perspective of paradigm competition, it is quite uncomfortable to be partly dependent on premises of theories that were initially intended to be challenged—particularly as regards such fundamental aspects like the origin of one's own research subject. Neither efficiency-oriented nor power-oriented alternative theories have to rely on ideational explanations to the same extent in this regard.

b) *Neo-institutionalism and organizational boundaries:* Difficulties or indifference in terms of conceptualizing the boundaries between organizations as well as between organizations and non-organized parts of society have accompanied all variations of institutionalist theory (Türk, 2000). Neo-institutionalism is holist; organizations and their properties can only be analyzed in terms of the properties of the respective field they are embedded in[53]. Although organizational fields consist of material systems (e.g. evaluation agencies, ministries, student organizations), the analytical focus is on the immaterial joint cognitions that are (re)produced within the field. The corresponding material manifestations of the shared myths, like particular configurations of study programs or funding offices become similar over time. The boundaries of organizational fields hence seem to run where sense-making processes of other collectives start to become more influential. Since material systems can't have immaterial boundaries, neo-institutionalism has actually largely drawn on a field-boundary conception identical to the (equally holist) population ecology approach, according to which populations are characterized by a certain set of "blueprints" (Hannan & Freeman, 1977) or "comps" (McKelvey, 1982). The field-distinguish-

53 Again, I am largely focusing here on the line of research which sees the environment as an institution because it has closely been associated with higher education organizations as research subjects (Meyer & Rowan, 1978; Krücken & Röbken, 2009).

ing criterion thereby is the similarity of properties of the organizations constituting it.

Yet empirically separating organizational fields from each other doesn't help to determine the boundaries of single organizations. Leading institutionalist scholar Richard Scott has sought to solve the problem by declaring boundary conceptualizations arbitrary in general:

> Because of the openness of organizations, determining their boundaries is always difficult and sometimes appears to be a quite arbitrary decision. Does a university include within its boundary its students? Its alumni? Faculty during summer? The spouses of students in university housing (Scott 2003: 89f.)?

The arguments brought forward are well known (*Ibid.*: 146): external actors may temporarily have a voice in the political system of a focal organization, boundaries are not stable over time, subunits may enter or leave the system.

However, such a "pragmatic view" does not solely relate to the boundary decision— the interior and exterior of the system logically have to be declared arbitrary by the same token. Ultimately, to return to Luhmann's (2000) critique, organizations are not treated as distinct social systems but are dissolved within the larger society:

> [...] then it is no longer possible to think of the environment as something 'out there'; its elements are part of the organization, not absorbed by it so that they become separated from the environment but interpenetrating it, infusing it with value, and connecting it with larger systems (Scott, 2003: 147).

Subjectivism and relativism, which are inherent in large parts of neo-intuitionalist theorizing, become acutely obvious at this point. Organizations are not characterized as observer-independent social facts; they exist and can in principle only be analyzed relative to some observer. Their definition is relative to the researcher's subjective (or community-bound) interest (recall Subsection 3.1.1) and so is the conceptualization of their components, environment and boundaries. Their properties, which include their (in)formal structures, can only be understood against the background of the rationality discourse within their respective thought-constructing community. In short, the systematic generation of objective knowledge is deemed largely impossible or irrelevant. Research on organizations is thus considered more an artistic discipline[54] than factual science, an attitude which was typical of the cultural-linguist turn.

In sum then, neo-institutionalism also disqualifies as regards the third criterion. Without an endogenous explanation of why organizations emerge, it is unclear what keeps them integrated and differentiated—without a boundary conception, they cannot be distinguished from other social systems, and their relation to the overall society remains fuzzy. If it is impossible (or unwanted) to discern two organizations from each other and from their environment, the analytical tools needed to analyze post-merger integration are lacking.

6.2.2 Culturalist perspectives on mergers

The second prominent idealist and subjectivist family of theories in merger analysis is commonly grouped under the term *organizational culture*. Though neo-institutionalist and culturalist approaches are often treated separately, their theoretical mechanisms and propositions are basically the same. The main difference lies in the varying thought collectives: the former mostly refers to large organizational fields or society as a whole, while the latter operates on the organizational or subunit meso-level of analysis. In Chapter 1 we introduced organizational culture as the dominant concept in intraorganizational analyses of post-merger integration. It represents the core of the soft paradigm in M&A literature; contributions from the cultural perspective have been manifold. And, indeed, mergers can in this respect rightly be conceived of as test situations of particular relevance: if organizations are primarily to be considered unique thought collectives, this should become particularly apparent in merger situations.

Do culturalist approaches provide multilevel explanations?

Out of the great varieties of cultural approaches, a conception of organizations as phenomena that produce culture (Smircich, 1983: 343) has become an "unrivalled position in the literature on M&A" (Teerikangas &

54 In a later footnote, Scott (2003: 187) denotes novelists as "social analysts" with similar problems in order to discern systems from each other. It is thereby suggested that differences between social scientists and artists are merely of a terminological nature.

Véry, 2012: 408). If we refer mostly to anthropology and cross-cultural psychology, organizations are considered to be all-encompassing and unconscious belief systems of shared symbols, meanings and cognitions (Buono et al., 1985; Buono & Bowditch, 1989; Nahavandi & Malekzadeh, 1988; Cartwright & Cooper 2012), or, as Marks & Mirvis (2010: 14) succinctly put it: "Culture is a lot like breathing: you don't think about breathing, you just do it". In its use as a root metaphor (Smircich, 1983; Morgan, 2006), the cultural approach to organizations is idealist: if organizations *are* cultures, and culture is, for instance, "understood as a system of common symbols and meanings" (Alvesson, 2013: 4), they are studied not as concrete resource transforming systems but as ideas or manifestations of such.

The breathing analogy by Marks & Mirvis (2010) furthermore nicely points to holism, which frequently accompanies idealism, as well as the subjectivist orientation inherent in the cultural perspective. To become taken for granted and coherently guide the behavior of organization members, culture has to be (re)produced within a totality. Subunit and individual behavior is *transcended* by the immaterial body of thoughts; it can only be understood and analyzed relative to the sense-making entirety. Observing and reconstructing such collectively shared social realities has therefore been central to studying organizational cultures (Schein, 1996; Reed, 2009: 434). Mergers have thus been widely conceptualized as whole-on-whole encounters.

Similarly to neo-institutionalists, the proponents of culture hence have to wrestle with how to explain divergent behavior on the subunit and individual levels. Consider the HWP's business administration professors from our second merger case as an empirical example. After the last session of the moderated trilateral pre-merger negotiations, they came up with their own position paper in June 2004 (ID2|18), thereby officially turning against the contra-integration position of their colleagues. While the majority of HWP members had fervently campaigned for the three-department solution based on the old institutions, business administration representatives suggested two alternative configurations of the new faculty:

- A discipline-based three-department "school" solution (business administration / economics / social and political sciences);
- A four-department solution (university and ex-HWP business administration / university economics / university social and political sciences / ex-HWP economics and sociology) (ID2|18: 5ff.).

Both assignments would have led to the secession of HWP business administration members and their integration into the respective university unit.

Why did a single subunit within the HWP break with its parent organization in the critical stage of negotiations? This is hard to explain if mergers are mainly conceptualized in terms of a confrontation of cognitive frames of reference. Had the HPW's organizational culture not been consistent and taken for granted enough? If structural preferences and scripts were closely associated with shared interpretations of the world out there, why was it possible to come to a deviant subunit-specific interpretation?

To understand such situations, it needs to be recognized that organizations and their subsystems are not *primarily* based on shared cognitions, but on resource exchange. Business administration professors within the HWP saw a chance to immediately enhance their social discretion by means of deeper integration. Firstly, since university business administration professors were on average by far the best equipped, their HWP counterparts eyed an increase in their own poor endowment standards (ID2|18: 6). Secondly, and even more importantly, existing HWP allocation rules had enforced resource equality among all lecturers—business administration professors had to attend to the majority of the students but hadn't been compensated adequately (2–IV: 57; ID2|19). For the inferior coalition within the HWP, merging thus provided an opportunity to actually overcome what couldn't be changed within the old boundaries. The looming low level of integration and de facto persistence of the old units did not at all reflect the *material interests* of the HWP's business administration subcoalition.

Further examples could be listed (think of the Graduate School); even in the highly conflict-laden Hamburg merger case, the three parties didn't act as monolithic blocks. In virtually all mergers, comparable instances of divergent subunit and individual actions will be found during negotiations and post-merger integration. Holist perspectives on organizations have not been sufficiently able to analytically embed lower system level behavior.

What concepts of organizational integration does culturalism provide?

Relative to neo-institutionalist theories, the cultural perspective, due to its analytical (meso-)level focus on organizations, offers a more definite integration concept. Since organizations are viewed as shared cognitive frames of reference or embodiments of such, integrating at least two of them refers to arriving at (or actively generating) a unified set of cognitions. The complementary boundary conception consequently centers on immaterial aspects—Santos and Eisenhardt (2005) examine it in terms of an identity boundary, which:

> [...] focuses on the boundary decision as the choice of 'who we are.' It takes a holistic view such that boundaries reflect the inclusion of activities perceived as coherent with organizational identity (Santos & Eisenhardt, 2005: 502).

Organizational boundaries are not considered the consequence of rational decision-making or power struggles, but rather of unconscious cognitive affiliation (*Ibid*.: 500). Hence, in comparison to the materialist system boundary conception discussed in Chapter 3, immaterial representations of the organization rather than subsets of material system components constitute its boundaries.

The culturalist integration concept can be illuminated by an interesting experimental research application provided by Weber and Camerer (2003). In order to investigate the performance effects of post-merger integration, they simulated organizational culture with "a specialized homemade language" (*Ibid*.: 404). Study participants were assigned to two-person teams. Their task was to describe (manager role) and to recognize (employee role) 8 out of 16 similar but not identical pictures chosen by the experimenter. Roles were alternated from round to round and the test persons were compensated according to task completion time. Over 20 rounds, the teams had developed a set of individual codes and metaphors: completion speed increased due to communication efficiency. Afterwards, the acquisition of an organization was simulated by randomly assigning a third teammate from another group. As a consequence, completion of the task took substantially longer in the following post-merger rounds (before the team again developed a shared standard). Furthermore, the experimenters found individuals systematically underestimated post-merger task completion time (prediction accuracy was rewarded). Weber and Camerer (2003: 412) report their results to indicate cultural differences and associated inter-personal conflicts to hamper the performance of merged organizations.

Ultimately, the culturalist perspective's potential to analyze post-merger integration is fairly limited. Material structures—the system-constituting flows of material resources between organizational components—are either overlooked or deemed to simply follow the development of shared cognitions. Besides its ideational conceptions of structures, boundaries and therefore integration, our critique has already highlighted the holist approach inherent in culturalism.

Yet some readers may argue that the pitfalls of holism specifically have been recognized and worked on early on (e.g. Wilkins & Ouchi, 1983; Sackmann, 1992). For example, Nahavandi and Malekzadeh (1988), in discussing their basic and much cited cultural integration typology, have emphasized its multilevel nature: "various subcultures within one organization may be divided along occupational, functional, product or geographical lines". Alvesson (2013: 125f.) claims the monolithic perspective on organizational cultures to have been outworn for quite a long time: organizational cultures were interpenetrated by macro culture on the one hand, and could also conceptually embrace all kinds of (communicating) lower-level subcultures.

However, what seems to be an obvious and proper solution comes at the high price of cutting culturalism's own branch. The explanatory potential and status of the cultural approach as an analytical perspective is deeply interwoven with its holist orientation. Interpreting organizational behavior and structures as manifestations of shared cognitive frames of reference (or outright equating the two) gains plausibility from the latter's totality. The more comprehensive and persuasive a social construction presents itself to the constructors, the fewer alternatives can be thought of and the more important representations become in analyzing organizations. Introducing parallel small-scale cultures nested within several higher-level thought collectives challenges the theoretical basis of social constructivism—still, we are talking about applications of cultural anthropology and macro-sociology. Any kind of lower-level culture produces its own alternative meanings of social facts: numerous institutionalization processes necessarily interfere.

Choosing, for instance, campus cultures as the collective reference with which to analyze post-merger integration in higher education (e.g. Harman, 2003) immediately raises unpleasant questions. What exactly should the totality of relevant actors in a large university be? Everybody who is situated on a campus? What permanent communication processes constitute it? Many university members do not have a clue what goes on in other parts of the organization. Or is it the faculty level? One institute within it? Research teams? Today's highly mobile scholars have often worked in several institutions in different countries; visiting and stand-in professors come and go. Staff below professors is fluctuating; long-term positions are rare. Now, who learns or unlearns whose language? Things are further complicated by considerations of disciplinary cultures (Becher, 1981; 1994), where some hard-to-circumvent national or international disciplinary community constructs cognitions, an idea that is similar to the concept of isomorphism by professionalization (DiMaggio & Powell, 1983). Which of the many collectives suggested forms the relevant scripts, norms and values in a focal organization? Does one dominate? Do they alternate? To what extent and under what conditions? Most of these questions have remained unanswered.

A coalitional perspective on organizations by comparison is built on considering different resource bases, exchange relations and interests on many system levels—as finely grained as data collection allows. If we consider concrete and identifiable resource dependencies instead of fuzzy thought-constructing totalities, the emergence of integrated (sub)systems and new common system boundaries can be explained across an arbitrary number of coalitions with diverging or congruent political positions.

6.3 Conclusion: stuck in the immaterial?

To be clear, my intention is not to discard the role of perceptions and collectively shared cognitions in explaining material outcomes of organizational change across the board. This study has rather aimed at questioning the quasi-imperialist dominance of idealism and subjectivism in post-merger integration analysis, as well as the habitual reference to the unconsciousness of social systems in vast parts of M&A literature.

First of all, it is important to notice that perceptions have been at the heart of power-dependence theory (Emerson, 1962; 1976), and therefore RDT as well. Power bases and alternatives to transacting partners are not perceived automatically and are explicitly subject to political (and faulty) manipulations of all kinds. Interview statements or written subunit responses to announced integration measures are always representations and not social facts in themselves. And, certainly, in a written comment, the editing unit appears to be far more than a faculty of pedagogics: it is the control room of a nuclear plant with the warning lights flashing already. Exchange partners reciprocally delineate and evaluate their respective power potential. When someone is doing research, it is therefore all the more important to safeguard information by comparing multiple sources.

What holds true as regards methodical aspects should apply to the very nature of explanations and causal mechanisms in organization studies, too: challenging idealism and subjectivism is not to say that collective sense-making has no influence on the materiality of organizations. Even though they are of a different ontological quality than material resource-exchange relations, institutions and discourses can objectively be detected on different system levels. Reed (2009: 442) agrees with Fairclough (2001) in that critical realist[55] organization research can benefit from identifying discursive orders. In a similar vein, Bunge (1996: 276f.) asserts that a realistic and complete model of social systems and social change needs to account for the perceptions and beliefs of its agents.

Still that does not imply that organizational practices and structural choices are largely determined by unconscious cognitive frames of reference accessible only relative to some constructing collective. Neither the external constraints of HEIs, nor their system configurations are to be treated as epiphenomena. There is a reality out there. There are social facts, and agents in social systems are to a good degree aware and actively make use of them. There are 3,000 students enrolled in the study programs of a unit or there are just 300. That huge research cluster mentioned on the university's welcome page, doesn't it belong to your faculty? Our successful fuel cell industry cooperation—the mayor himself broke ground on the new building last week. And what about the basic mathematics lectures everybody needs every term? By the way, isn't it the members of our department who run the botanical garden and organize the public guided tours? How about withdrawing them for some project reason? These things can hardly be reduced to ideas or some discursive logic.

As regards the analysis of post-merger integration, the quarrel is hence not with shared perceptions as parts of explanations per se but with the widespread mechanical reference to collective sense-making (Riad, 2005) in connection with marginalizing the sociomateriality of organizations. In practitioner and scientific debates, this has regularly been accompanied by an aesthetic obfuscation of material power-exchange relations in the case of the culture concept. Consider the following interview statement from the Hamburg case:

> [...] due to the common appointment culture which has developed—also by means of the common university-wide appointment regulation—it has become clear that there are unified criteria for appointments, which also led to the necessity of a similar endowment [...] (2–VII: 56f.).

55 Critical realism as delineated by Reed (1992; 2009) is very close to, but not in all aspects identical to Bunge's systemism. A more detailed comparative discussion of philosophies of science, their ontological and epistemological doctrines, would be beyond the scope of this book.

A protocol comment on the negotiations of the dissertation statute reads:

> It is elaborately discussed to determine quality standards. A unified form of determination is, however, impeded by the diverse disciplinary cultures. Deferring quality standard determination to the different departments is suggested (FP2 52: 3).

In both passages, the issues referred to have in fact little to do with unconscious collective constructions in any meaningful sense. The homogenization of appointment regulations was imposed by the incorporating University of Hamburg; there had been no option for the ex-HWP coalition to remain in control of appointments. And, of course, sense-making had only been strong enough to realize minimum endowment standards for newly appointed professors (with few exceptions). As regards the dissertation statute, several clearly identifiable external constraints and related configuration requirements were discussed in Subsection 5.2.4. Regulations followed resource-exchange related requirements and faculty members were well aware of their interests.

Thc popularity of culturalist arguments in managerial talk and their omnipresence in many organizational discourses particularly should spark more scientific skepticism. Alvesson suggests attractiveness for managers to be due to the

> [...] very appealing idea of accomplishing desired outcomes through such inexpensive means as visionary talk and engineered, symbolically loaded events[56] (Alvesson, 2013: 125).

The resource-exchange and power narrative is far less inviting for leaders: changing and divergent interests within organizations, important resources under the control of subordinates, successful resistance by subunits and agency where it was not supposed to occur. A further possible reason for the eager workaday adoption of culturalist terminology may lie in its facilitating effect on communication and negotiation processes in conflict-laden situations. Culture is quite positively connoted—labeling anything that some subunit does in a specific way an aspect of its culture may signal

56 The tale of transcending systems of collective action, operating in a holist top-down manner, and aligning members to the ideas of leaders has accompanied organization theory from the outset and may always find an audience. For example, Chester Barnard (1938: 123f.) discussed the role and suggestibility of "uniform states of minds which crystallize into what we call mores, customs, institutions".

open-mindedness, appreciation of the counterparty's position and the will to maintain organizational peace. Not too bad in a merger situation.

The above-stated examples from a practitioner context reflect a position that has also been backed by scholarly debates on post-merger integration. Despite numerous fruitful contributions, culturalist and neo-institutionalist perspectives have all too often sought to replace one evil with another: global assumptions of an absolute perceptibility of social facts and some quasi-natural system rationality (e.g. contingency theory) have been supplanted by a relativist and equally barren preeminence of the unconscious. Buono et al. (1985: 481), for instance, suggested office-line and assembly-line configurations and car fleet allocation rules in their bank merger study were "(material) reflections of each organization's culture". A "spartan" cafeteria with "a small refrigerator in one of the corners" as well as the "simple, functional appearance" of offices in one of the banks is hence deemed to just reflect shared organizational "values" and a "competitive aura" (*Ibid.*: 489f.).

Explanations focusing on material resources, and power and exchange relations have by contrast largely been crowded out—at least as regards higher education organization sociology and integration-focused M&A research. Taking the development and contemporary role of RDT (as a typical specific social theory) as an example, in Section 2.3 the appraisal of co-founder Jeffrey Pfeffer (2003; 2005) was already pointed to. He deplored the approach for having turned into a merely metaphorical statement, with rather conservative (power-free and often agency-free) social theory having come out on top: "But it is by far best of all to have a theory that, in its fundamental assumptions, is in tune with the times and the political ideas currently in vogue" (Pfeffer, 2005: 455).

In a recent elaborate citation context analysis, Wry, Cobb and Aldrich (2013) were able to confirm Pfeffer's metaphorization credo. More than 80% of the 1,772 journal articles identified in 2011 referred to the *External Control of Organizations* in a merely ceremonial way (*Ibid.*: 449). The authors found substantial citations in RDT to have peaked in the early 1990s, with a following decline in scholarly engagement. Identifying Christine Oliver's (1991) article as a central point of origin, Wry et al. (2013: 462) likewise state "a [sic] deep—if subtle—integration of RD(T) into the canon of institutional scholarship" and provide further reasons for its demise as a sovereign and vital research program:

- Early fragmentation of research into specific lines of inquiry instead of a sustained theory development;

- Comparatively inferior community building (indicated by a low degree of co-citations amongst RDT scholars): "Deprived of followers, it is somewhat remarkable that the perspective has developed *at all*" (*Ibid.*: 461).

A further obstacle to empirical studies in many potential fields of interest has already been hinted at in the study at hand: the immanent tension between scientific transparency requirements and the power sensitiveness of data relevant to RDT itself. Broaching the issues of constraints, resource control, dependencies and power differentials is comparatively difficult—"doing power work" (Clegg, 2009) in organizational research settings is anything but easy. Cohen & Lachman (1988: 380), for example, reported considerable nonresponse issues in their attempt to validate the SCT in Israeli healthcare centers. During their pretest, respondents appeared scared by questions associated with process substitutability. They anticipated cutbacks and other detriments for their subunits; the researchers were therefore forced to use nonobtrusive measures.

However, the triumph of the cultural / linguistic turn goes beyond the dominance of a family of related specific social theories over others. It has entailed the establishment of a wider intellectual milieu, in which some kind of general skepticism as to the role, systematic assessment and evaluation of theories is quite common (Reed, 2009). In their prominent paper on possible conditions and mechanisms beneath the diffusion of social practices from a neo-institutionalist perspective, Strang and Meyer (1993: 493) give a taste of this:

> Theorizing is a strategy for making sense of the world. As such, it is employed in individual-specific ways by the potential adopters themselves. Further, interaction between potential adopters may construct shared theories of the world, the nature of the interacting pair, and the mutual relevance of different practices.

Such kinds of the *new sociology of science* (Bunge, 1991), which in too many cases has silently come to replace an explicit philosophy of science, tends to discourage and harm debates on the actual explanation potential of different theories. Since it considers conceptual content to be largely determined by social context (*Ibid.*: 537ff.), scientific research is deemed to be just one amongst many cultural practices that reduce complexity ("ordinarism"). Not only are organizations to be understood as mere cognitive enterprises, but any scientific endeavor seeking to analyze them is supposed to be a social construction. Theorizing and paradigm building is hence believed to be far more than partly influenced by social contexts: the content and quality of explanations are inextricably bound to the relative rationality of the constructing community. *De gustibus et coloribus non est disputandum*.

Nevertheless, as should have become apparent throughout this volume, idealist and subjectivist social theory has so far not been able to live up to its discursive dominance in terms of factual knowledge generation, at least in consideration of the empirical subjects under study. Can't, however, the promising but forgotten late 1970s debate on structure and budgeting (recall Subsection 2.1.4) provide an excellent example of the underused potential of materialist, realist and power-dependence based approaches, and not only in the sociology of higher education? Particularly against the background of all interim methodological advances and today's options in terms of the availability of structural data in HEIs, didn't it end far too soon? What keeps us from reopening and broadening it?

Annex A (Interview guide and list)

1) Was there any kind of pre-merger contact or cooperation between your organizational unit and its counterpart? If so, please describe.
2) In what fields of organizational regulations has rule adoption or homogenization of rules been pursued post-merger?
   [Examples of rule adoption and homogenization were given: budgeting, examination standards, study programs]
3) What political arrangements were essential to the negotiations of those changes in organizational regulations?
4) What changes (beyond the legally implied), if any, occurred in political arrangements post-merger?
   [Examples: new organs, regular meetings…]
5) Please describe the interests which your unit tried to pursue during negotiations.
   a. What were the essential positions of your unit?
   b. What were the "red lines"; what did your unit fear losing?
   c. What were the ambitions and development options?
6) Have positions within your own unit on how to handle post-merger negotiations been rather homogenous or heterogeneous (Please illustrate)?
7) What other external or internal agents or parties (besides those directly involved in the negotiations) have tried to take up a position or intervene in post-merger negotiations?
   [Examples were given: the city, partner HEIs, industrial partners, the state agency, central administration, other departments…]
8) Could you please identify internal organizational forces that have sought to promote tighter cooperation between the parties post-merger? Based on what arguments?
9) With which (possible) post-merger changes in regulations (questions 2 and 4) did the interests of your unit collide with those of your counterpart / other merging parties during negotiations?
10) Looking back at the pre- and early post-merger stage: what hopes or fears concerning the development of your unit do you think have come true?

Please note that this is a generalized interview guide. Questions varied according to the respondents' role and position. As field research developed, a more distinct focus was placed on specific debates and conflicts (questions 5 and 9 in particular). Respondents were ex-members of the founding senate, internal advising commission and / or former or active organizational executives on the central or subunit levels. My aim was to reflect a broad perspective across all the merging parties. Interviewees were ex-ante issued with a generalized interview guide, and anonymity was guaranteed. The interviews have been transcribed and the cited statements translated.

Interviews are referred to as follows in the text. The first cipher refers to the case studied: 1 for Duisburg–Essen (conducted between 06/2013 and 10/2013), 2 for Hamburg (09/2012–05/2013); the Roman numeral designates the corresponding interview (cited passages are identified with transcript line numbers).

Duisburg-Essen	Hamburg
1-I (49:07)	2-I (01:01:24)
1-II (01:10:20)	2-II (00:45:03)
1-III (01:01:20)	2-III (00:52:08)
1-IV (01:36:50)	2-IV (01:13:40)
1-V (01:06:29)	2-V (00:59:27)
1-VI (01:38:28)	2-VI (00:51:56)
	2-VII (00:51:16)
	2-VIII (phone, 00:50:18)
	2-IX (phone, 00:59:23)
	2-X (01:19:50)

Table A: List of interviews

Annex B (Information on documents)

The document codes are to be read as follows. The first two letters indicate the type of document or protocol:

- CD for context document (mostly publicly available)
- ID for internal document (mostly not publicly available)
- SP for senate protocol (case 1 only, publicly available)
- FP for faculty (council) protocol (case 2 only, not publicly available)
- DP for dean's office protocol (case 2 only, not publicly available)

The first cipher indicates the case: 1/2 for case study 1/2. All protocols are designated in line with the respective organizational standards. Examples:

- SP1 05|2005: 5 → senate protocol case study 1; 5th meeting 2005, pp. 5
- DP2 80 → dean's office protocol case study 2; meeting No. 80

As regards my analysis of the Duisburg–Essen case, a collection of administrative documents for the founding rectorate (handed over in September 2003) has been of particular importance:

"*Bericht des Gründungsbeauftragten für den Gründungsrektor und das Gründungsrektorat*" (a.k.a. "Kleffner Report" [KR], named after state commissioner Heiner Kleffner), consisting of:

- Volume 1 (196 pp.): synopsis and unit-specific recommendations of the founding commissioner;
- Volume 2 (176 pp.): unit comments on Volume I;
- Volume 3 (2 parts, 1370 pp.): administrative materials.

Documents Duisburg–Essen

Code	Date	Title / Description / Source
CD1|1	20-02-2001	Expert Commission final Report (Expertenrat)
CD1|2	01-12-2004	Parliamentary request by liberal representative Ralf Witzel (Landtag NRW 13/ 6320
CD1|3	24-03-2004	Public statement (press release) by student representatives on the future of the humanities and social sciences on campus Essen
ID1| 1	April 2001	Comment Department of Economics Essen on negotiations
ID|2	03-12-2001	Internal bulletin ("Das Rektorat informiert")
ID1|3	30-11-2001	Press release by both universities on negotiation results
ID1|4	30-11-2001	Draft of campus profile Duisburg (fax)
ID1|5	07-12-2001	Senate resolution draft Essen
ID1|6	18-01-2002	Comment by the rectorate Essen on the occasion of a senate hearing
ID1|7	01-03-2001	Protocol of the visit of undersecretary of state Mr. Krebs (KR Vol. 3: 686)
ID1|9	18-10-2002	Press release University of Duisburg senate
ID1|10	11-02-2004	Restructuring recommendations of the founding rectorate
ID1|11	29-01-2004	Letter from the founding rectorate to all unit heads (prospected deficits)
ID1|12	12-2-2001	Memorandum by the rectorate: strategic merger considerations
ID1|13	10-07-2002	Bulletin by the dean of Duisburg's physics unit (unit strategy) (KR Vol. 3: 654)
ID1|14	15-03-2001	Physics: common position of the two units as to merger prospects (KR Vol. 3: 679
ID1|15	26-06-2002	External expertise on the location of a unified department of physics (KR Vol. 3: 667)
ID1|16	28-04-2003	Development plan physics (synopsis) (KR Vol. 3: 652)
ID1|17	29-04-2003	Protocol of consultations between founding commissioner, chancellor and unit representatives of physics
ID1|18	04-06-2003	Protocol of consultations between founding commissioner, chancellor and unit representatives of social sciences (KR Vol. 3: 390)
ID1|19	Sept. 2003	Recommendations of the founding commissioner for the social sciences (KR Vol. 1: 47)

ID1|20	10-10-2003	Dean's office written comment (department 02, Essen) on state commissioner recommendations (KR Vol. 2: 52)
ID1|21	14-10-2003	Dean's office written comment (department 01, Essen) on state commissioner recommendations (KR Vol. 2: 14ff.)
ID1|22	29-10-2003	Comment by the social sciences unit Duisburg on state recommendations (KR Vol. 1: 108ff.)
ID1|23	11-02-2004	Founding rectorate's unit assignment recommendations
ID1|24	19-02-2004	Department 02 position on rectorate's unit allocation recommendations
ID1|25	April 2004	Internal Memorandum: notes as to study programs, personnel and organization of a possible department for educational sciences
ID1|26	24-03-2003	Structural development plan (political science as a discipline) (KR Vol. 3: 448)
ID1|27	10-03-2004	Resolution in support of the rectorate's assignment recommendations (social sciences Duisburg)
ID1|28	08-11-2004	Letter by the dean of the newly found Department of Educational Sciences
ID1|29	December 2004	Senate resolution draft for the second reading on unit assignment
ID1|30	11-03-2004	Senate comment on the protocol SP1 12/2004
ID1|31	10-11-2004	Appendix to a written statement by the dean of Duisburg's economics in anticipation of a senate hearing
ID1|32	16-01-2002	Written synopsis of department statements (Essen) on negotiation situation
ID1|33	28-03-2003	Development plan for economics disciplines (Department of Economics Essen) & materials
ID1|34	02-04-2003	Post-merger reorganization suggestions by Duisburg's economics unit & materials (KR Vol. 3: 492ff.)
ID1|35	31-03-2003	Response of Duisburg's economics unit to Essen's development plan
ID1|36	20-10-2003	Complementary statement by Duisburg's economics unit to state and founding rectorate unit assignment recommendations (KR Vol. 2: 135ff.)
ID1|37	Sept. 2003	Recommendations of the founding commissioner for economics (KR Vol. 1: 49)
ID1|38	17-12-2003	E-Mail from Duisburg's economics dean to members of the founding commission & attached skeleton agreement between both economics units
ID1|39	08-11-2004	Letter from the dean of the Department of Medicine (Essen) to the the head of the Founding Senate
ID1|40	06-12-2004	Open letter by the dean of Essen's Department of Economics on university-wide consequences of business administration removal
ID1|41	09-11-2004	Comment by the Dean of Essen's Department of Economics on reorganization recommendations in advance of a senate hearing
ID1|42	08-10-2003	Comment by the head of the committee on social work and pedagogics study programs as to state reorganization recommendations (KR Vol. 2: 40f.)

ID1|43	10-12-2001	Letter by the Mayor of Essen to the Rector of the University of Essen concerning the integrated social work study program
ID1|44	24-03-2003	Development plan of History as a discipline within the University of Duisburg–Essen (KR Vol. 3: 77f.)

Documents Hamburg

Code	Date	Title / Description / Source
CD2|1	August 2002	Research Report University of Hamburg (1997-1999) (Mitteilungen der Universität 49)
CD2|2	January 2003	Final report of the external reform commission on the reform of higher education in Hamburg ("Dohnanyi-Kommission")
CD2|3	17-06-2003	Guidelines concerning the development of higher education in Hamburg (Senate of the City of Hamburg, doc. No. 17/2914)
CD2|4	14-11-2006	Answer to parliamentary (Bürgerschaft) request (große Anfrage) on higher education in Hamburg (18/5148)
CD2|5	07-08-2003	City of Hamburg: Budget-plan draft 2004 for the Agency of Science and Research (Einzelplan 3.2, Behörde für Wissenschaft und Forschung)
CD2|6	02-02-2005	Parliamentary plenum protocol (Bürgerschaft) (doc. No. 18/23), final debate (foundation of a unified School of Business, Economics and Social Sciences)
CD2|7	08-05-2005	Foundation law of School of Business, Economics and Social Sciences (Fakultät Wirtschafts- und Sozialwissenschaften) (WiSoG, HmbGVBL: 28)
CD2|8	07-05-2014 / 09-07-2014	Dissertation statute of the Faculty of Business Administration (Amtlicher Anzeiger Hamburg, 77: 1816ff.)
CD2|9	14-12-2004	Answer to a parliamentary request concerning further education in Hamburg (doc. No.: 18/1435)
CD2|10	11-05-2003	Parliamentary petition concerning the future of the HWP (doc. No.: 17/2882)
CD2|11	01-03-2001	Senate information for Hamburg's parliament (Bürgerschaft) concerning the HWP's extra-vocational training offers (doc. No.: 18/3134)
ID2|1	07-10-2002	Letter by the president (HWP) to the head of the reform commission (internal HWP information on the reform process, Appendix 9)
ID2|2	01-03-2001	Teaching & research potential analysis by the president (HWP)
ID2|3		Electronic compilation of third-party funded projects (DSS) (project titles, funding periods, funding amount)
ID2|4	December 2005	Research report by the Institute of Sociology Hamburg 2002-2005 (part of DSS);
ID2|5	14-03-2003	Comment by the Departmentof Economics Hamburg on the structural recommendations of the reform commission
ID2| 6	08-05-2003	Second comment (senate resolution) by the HWP on the recommendations by the reform commission

ID2|7	16-04-2004	Masterplan concerning the development of a common faculty (HWP position)
ID2|8	March 2003	Comment by the dean of the university's Department of Social Sciences on the structural recommendations by the reform commission
ID2|9	07-06-2004	Report: results of the moderated negotiations (final session 19-05-2004)
ID2|10	25-05-2004	Comment of the HWP senate on the results of the moderated negotiations
ID2|11	31-10-2003	Internal record: faculty positions overview (functional distribution of personnel)
ID2|12	30-01-2008	Constitution of the School of Business, Economics and Social Sciences (Fakultät Wirtschafts- und Sozialwissenschaften) University of Hamburg
ID2|13	22-01-2009	Structure and Development Plan of the School of Business, Economics and Social Sciences (Fakultät Wirtschafts- und Sozialwissenschaften)
ID2|14	05-12-2000	Report by the president D. Bittscheidt (HWP) to the HWP council
ID2|15	March 2004	Study program assessment (AQUIN) and accreditation proposal for the program "Daten- und Informationsmanagement Master of Arts"
ID2|16	January 2008	"Reorganisation der Verwaltung der WiSo-Fakultät und der zentralen Universitätsverwaltung" Consultancy report (Ramboll Management)
ID2|17	11-07-2005	Letter from the University of Hamburg's vice president to the faculty dean's office concerning the deviation as to central exam administration rules
ID2|18	02-06-2004	Comment by the members of the HWP work field of business adminstration as to the results of the moderated negoriations
ID2|19	03-06-2004	E-Mail response by leading HWP-members to ID2|18

Table B: List of documents

Annex C

Pre-merger departments Univ. of Duisburg (2003)	TRU (No. in dataset)	Student count	Academic personnel count	Integration status (2010)
1. Social sciences	SOCD(30	3085	59	Bidder
	PD (28)	814	25	Target
	PSYD (29)	147	10	Target
	GEOD (37)	77	10	Target
2. Humanities	AD (22)	560	16	Target
	GD (24)	1190	23	Target
	R (26)	263	15	Target
	JAP			Status quo
	TED (27)	51	5	Target
	HD (23)	241	15	Target
	JEW			divested
	PHID (25	164	6	Target
3. Economics	ECOD (10)	4376	82	Status quo
4. Natural sciences	PHYD (34)	364	52	Target
	CD (32)	471	42	Target
	MAD (33)	599	50	Target
5. Engineering	MECD (36)	1003	102	Bidder
	MAT	154	20	Status quo
	ED (35)	1260	88	Status quo
	ID (38)	993	50	Status quo

Table C: Actual faculty organization structure of the University of Duisburg in the merger year

References

Abbott, M. (1996) "Amalgamations and the Changing Costs of Victorian Colleges of Advanced Education during the 1970s and 1980s," *Higher Education Research and Development*, 15:2, 133–144.

Ackroyd, S. & Fleetwood, S. (eds.) [2000] (2003), *Realist Perspectives on Management and Organisations* (London and New York: Routledge).

Albert, A., & Anderson, J. A. (1984) "On the Existence of Maximum Likelihood Estimates in Logistic Regression Models," *Biometrika*, 71:1, 1–10.

Aldrich, H. E., & Pfeffer, J. (1976) "Environments of Organizations," *Annual Review of Sociology*, 2:1, 79–105.

Alvesson, M. (2013), *Understanding Organizational Culture* (Los Angeles: Sage).

Angwin, D. (2007) "Motive Archetypes in Mergers and Acquisitions (M&A): The Implications of a Configurational Approach to Performance," in C. Cooper & S. Finkelstein, *Advances in Mergers and Acquisitions (Vol. 6)* (Bingley, UK: Emerald Publishing Group).

Angwin, D. (2012) "Merger and Acquisition Typologies: A Review," in D. Faulkner, S. Teerikangas & R. J. Joseph, *The Oxford Handbook of Mergers and Acquisitions* (Oxford: OUP).

Ashar, H. (1987), *Internal and External Variables and Their Effect on a University's Retrenchment Decisions: Two Theoretical Perspectives* (University of Washington).

Ashar, H. & Shapiro, J. Z. (1988) "Measuring Centrality: A Note on Hackman's Resource-Allocation Theory," *Administrative Science Quarterly*, 33:2, 275–283.

Astley, W. G. & Van de Ven, A. H. (1983) "Central Perspectives and Debates in Organization Theory," *Administrative Science Quarterly*, 28:2, 245–273.

Astley, W. G. & Zajac, E. J. (1991) "Intraorganizational Power and Organizational Design: Reconciling Rational and Coalitional Models of Organization", *Organization Science*, 2:4, 399–411.

Bacher, J., Pöge, A. & Wenzig, K. (2010), *Clusteranalyse: Anwendungsorientierte Einführung in Klassifikationsverfahren* (München: Oldenbourg).

Barkema, H. G. & Schijven, M. (2008) "How Do Firms Learn to Make Acquisitions? A Review of past Research and an Agenda for the Future," *Journal of Management*, 34:3, 594–634.

Barnard, C. I. [1938] (1968), *The Functions of the Executive* (Cambridge: Harvard University Press).

Barton, A. H. (1955) "The Concept of Property Space in Social Research," in P. F. Lazarsfeld & M. Rosenberg, *Language of Social Research* (New York: Free Press).

Barrier, J. (2014) "Merger Mania in Science: Organizational Restructuring and Patterns of Cooperation in an Academic Research Centre," in R. Whitley & J. Gläser, *Organizational Transformation and Scientific Change: The Impact of Institutional Restructuring on* Universities *and Intellectual Innovation (Research in the Sociology of Organizations) (Vol. 42)* (Bingley, UK: Emerald).

Becher, T. (1981) "Towards a Definition of Disciplinary Cultures," *Studies in Higher Education*, 6:2, 109–122.

Becher, T. (1994) "The Significance of Disciplinary Differences," *Studies in Higher Education*, 19:2, 151–161.

Bengtsson, L. & Larsson, R. (2012) "Researching Mergers & Acquisitions with the Case Study Method: Idiographic Understanding of Longitudinal Integration Processes," in Y. Weber, *Handbook of Research on Mergers and Acquisitions* (Cheltenham: Edward Elgar).

Berger, P. & Luckmann, T. (1967), *The Social Construction of Reality: A Treatise in the Sociology of Knowledge* (London: Penguin Books).

Birkinshaw, J., Bresman, H. & Håkanson, L. (2000) "Managing the Post-Acquisition Integration Process: How the Human Integration and Task Integration Processes Interact to Foster Value Creation," *Journal of Management Studies*, 37:3, 395–425.

Blau, P. M. (1964), *Exchange and Power in Social Life* (New Brunswick: Transaction Publishers).

Blau, P. M. & Scott, W. R. [1962] (2003), *Formal Organizations: A Comparative Approach* (Stanford: Stanford University Press).

Borys, B. & Jemison, D. B. (1989) "Hybrid Arrangements as Strategic Alliances: Theoretical Issues in Organizational Combinations," *Academy of Management Review*, 14:2, 234–249.

Boulding, K. E. (1956) "General Systems Theory: The Skeleton of Science", *Management Science*, 2:3, 197–208.

Bourgeois, L. J. (1980) "Strategy and Environment: A Conceptual Integration," *Academy of Management Review*, 5:1, 25–39.

Braun, D. (1999) "Changing Governance Models in Higher Education: The Case of the New Managerialism," *Swiss Political Science Review*, 5:3, 1–24.

Braun, D. & Merrien, F. X. (Eds.) (1999), *Towards a New Model of Governance for Universities? A Comparative View* (London: J. Kingsley).

Bryman, A. (2009) "Mixed Methods in Organizational Research," in D. Buchanan & A. Bryman, *The Sage Handbook of Organizational Research Methods* (London: Sage).

Bunge, M. A. (1981), *Scientific Materialism* (Dordrecht and Boston: Reidel).

Bunge, M. A. (1996), *Finding Philosophy in Social Science* (New Haven: Yale University Press).

Bunge, M. A. (1998), *Social Science under Debate: A Philosophical Perspective* (Toronto: University of Toronto Press).

Bunge, M. A. (2000) "Systemism: The Alternative to Individualism and Holism," *The Journal of Socio-Economics*, 29:2, 147–157.

Bunge, M. A. & Mahner, M. (2004), *Über die Natur der Dinge: Materialismus und Wissenschaft* (Stuttgart: Hirzel Verlag).

Bunge, M. A. (1979a), *Treatise on Basic Philosophy (Vol IV): A World of Systems* (Dordrecht and Boston: Reidel).

Bunge, M. A. (1979b) "A Systems Concept of Society: Beyond Individualism and Holism," *Theory and Decision*, 10:1, 13–30.

Bunge, M. A. (1991) "A Critical Examination of the New Sociology of Science: Part 1," *Philosophy of the Social Sciences*, 21:4, 524–560.

Bunge, M. A. (1992) "System Boundary," *International Journal of General Systems* 20:3, 215–219.

Buono, A. F. & Bowditch, J. (1989) "The Human Side of Mergers and Acquisitions," *Human Resource Management*, 28:2, 301–304.

Buono, A. F., Bowditch, J. L. & Lewis, J. W. (1985) "When Cultures Collide: The Anatomy of a Merger," *Human Relations*, 38:5, 477–500.

Burrell, G. & Morgan, G. (1979), *Sociological Paradigms and Organisational Analysis* (London: Heinemann).

Burt, R. S. (1980) "Autonomy in a Social Topology," *American Journal of Sociology*, 85:4, 892–925.

Cameron, K. S. (1978) "Measuring Organizational Effectiveness in Institutions of Higher Education," *Administrative Science Quarterly* 23:4, 604–632.

Cameron, K. S. (1986) "Effectiveness as Paradox: Consensus and Conflict in Conceptions of Organizational Effectiveness," *Management Science*, 32:5, 539–553.

Campling, J. T. & Michelson, G. (1998) "A Strategic Choice–Resource Dependence Analysis of Union Mergers in the British and Australian Broadcasting and Film Industries," *Journal of Management Studies*, 35:5, 579–600.

Cartwright, S. & Cooper, C. L. (1993) "The Role of Culture Compatibility in Successful Organizational Marriage," *Academy of Management Executive*, 7:2, 57–70.

Cartwright, S. & Cooper, C. L. (1994) "The Human Effects of Mergers and Acquisitions," in C. L. Cooper & D. M. Rousseau, *Trends in Organizational Behavior* (Chichester: John Wiley & Sons).

Cartwright, S. & Cooper, C. L. (1996), *Managing Mergers, Acquisitions and Strategic Alliances* (London: Routledge).

Cartwright, S., Teerikangas, S., Rouzies, A. & Wilson-Evered, E. (2012) "Methods in M&A—a Look at the past and the Future to Forge a Path Forward," *Scandinavian Journal of Management*, 28:2, 95–106.

Casciaro, T. & Piskorski, M. J. (2005) "Power Imbalance, Mutual Dependence, and Constraint Absorption: A Closer Look at Resource Dependence Theory," *Administrative Science Quarterly*, 50:2, 167–199.

Child, J. (1972) "Organizational Structure, Environment and Performance: The Role of Strategic Choice," *Sociology*, 6:1, 1–22.

Choi, S. & Brommels, M. (2009) "Logics of Pre-Merger Decision-Making Processes: The Case of Karolinska University Hospital," *Journal of Health Organization and Management*, 23:2, 240–254.

Clegg, S. (2009) "Doing Power Work in Organizations," in D. Buchanan & A. Bryman, *The Sage Handbook of Organizational Research Methods* (London: Sage).

Coase, R. (1998) "The New Institutional Economics," *The American Economic Review*, 88:2, 72–74.

Cohen, I. & Lachman, R. (1988) "The Generality of the Strategic Contingencies Approach to Sub-Unit Power," *Organization Studies*, 9:3, 371–391.

Cohen, M. D., March, J. G. & Olsen, J. P. (1972) "A Garbage Can Model of Organizational Choice," *Administrative Science Quarterly*, 17:1, 1–25.

Coleman, J. S. (1986) "Social Theory, Social Research, and a Theory of Action," *American Journal of Sociology*, 91:6, 1309–1335.

Cooper, D. J., Hinings, B., Greenwood, R. & Brown, J. L. (1996) "Sedimentation and Transformation in Organizational Change: The Case of Canadian Law Firms," *Organization Studies*, 17:4, 623–647.

Covaleski, M. A. & Dirsmith, M. W. (1988a) "An Institutional Perspective on the Rise, Social Transformation, and Fall of a University Budget Category," *Administrative Science Quarterly*, 33:4, 562–587.

Covaleski, M. A. & Dirsmith, M. W. (1988b) "The Use of Budgetary Symbols in the Political Arena: An Historically Informed Field Study," *Accounting, Organizations and Society*, 13:1, 1–24.

Covaleski, M. A., Dirsmith, M. W. & Samuel, S. (1996) "Managerial Accounting Research: The Contributions of Organizational and Sociological Theories," *Journal of Management Accounting Research*, 8:1, 1–35.

Cox, D. R. & Snell, E. J. (1989), *Analysis of Binary Data* (London and New York: Chapman and Hall).

Cropper, S., Ebers, M., Huxham, C. & Ring, P. S. (2008) "Introducing Inter-organizational Relations," in S. Cropper, M. Ebers, C. Huxham & P. S. Ring, *The Oxford Handbook of Interorganizational Relations* (Oxford: OUP).

Crozier, M. & Friedberg, E. (1980), *Actors and Systems: The Politics of Collective Action* (Chicago: University of Chicago Press).

Cyert, R. M. & March, J. G. (1963), *A Behavioral Theory of the Firm* (Englewood Cliffs: Prentice Hall).

Datta, D. K. (1991) "Organizational Fit and Acquisition Performance: Effects of Post-Acquisition Integration," *Strategic Management Journal*, 12:4, 281–297.

Davis, G. F. & Cobb, J. A. (2009) "Resource Dependence Theory: Past and Future," *Research in the Sociology of Organizations*, 28:1, 21–42.

Deal, T. E. & Kennedy, A. A. (1985), *Corporate Cultures: The Rites and Rituals of Organizational Life* (Reading, MA: Addison-Wesley).

Deem, R. & Brehony, K. J. (2005) "Management as Ideology: The Case of 'New Managerialism' in Higher Education," *Oxford Review of Education*, 31:2, 217–235.

Demsetz, H. (1967) "Toward a Theory of Property Rights," *The American Economic Review*, 57:2, 347–359.

DiMaggio, P. J. (1988) "Interest and Agency in Institutional Theory: Institutional Patterns and Organizations" in L. Zucker: *Institutional Patterns: Culture and Environment* (Cambridg, MA: Ballinger).

DiMaggio, P. & Powell, W. W. (1983) "The Iron Cage Revisited: Collective Rationality and Institutional Isomorphism in Organizational Fields," *American Sociological Review*, 48:2, 147–160.

Doelle, F., Jenkner, P., Otte, C., Quiram, S., Schacher, M. & Winkelmann, G. (2005), "*Ausstattungs-, Kosten- und Leistungsvergleich Universitäten 2002: Kennzahlenergebnisse für die Länder Berlin, Bremen, Hamburg, Mecklenburg-Vorpommern, Sachsen-Anhalt und Schleswig-Holstein*" (Hannover: HIS GmbH).

Donaldson, L. (1995), *American Anti-Management Theories of Organization: A Critique of Paradigm Proliferation* (Cambridge and New York: Cambridge University Press).

Donaldson, L. (2001), *The Contingency Theory of Organizations* (Thousand Oaks and London: Sage).

Drees, J. M. & Heugens, P. P. (2013) "Synthesizing and Extending Resource Dependence Theory: A Meta-Analysis," *Journal of Management*, 39:6, 1666–1698.

Dunford, R. (1987) "The Suppression of Technology as a Strategy for Controlling Resource Dependence," *Administrative Science Quarterly*, 32, 512–525.

Eastman, J. & Lang, D. (2001), *Mergers in Higher Education: Lessons from Theory and Experience* (Toronto: University of Toronto Press).

Eisenhardt, K. M. (1989) "Agency Theory: An Assessment and Review," *Academy of Management Review*, 14, 57–74.

Elsass, P. M. & Veiga, J. F. (1994) "Acculturation in Acquired Organizations: A Force-Field Perspective," *Human Relations*, 47, 431–453.

Emerson, R. M. (1962) "Power-Dependence Relations," *American Sociological Review*, 27:1, 31–41.

Emerson, R. M. (1976) "Social Exchange Theory," *Annual Review of Sociology*, 2:1, 335–362.

Emirbayer, M. (1997) "Manifesto for a Relational Sociology," *American Journal of Sociology*, 103:2, 281–317.

Evan, W. D. (1966) "The Organization-Set," in J. D. Thompson and V. H. Vroom, *Organizational Design and Research: Approaches to Organizational Design* (Pittsburgh: University of Pittsburgh Press).

Fairclough, N. (2001), *Language and Power* (Harlow: Longman).

Fama, E. F. & Jensen, M. C. (1983) "Separation of Ownership and Control," *Journal of Law & Economics*, 26:2, 301–325.

Faulkner, D. (2012) "M&A Motives, Definitions and Defining Characteristics," in D. Faulkner & S. Teerinkangas & R. Joseph, *The Oxford Handbook of Mergers and Acquisitions* (Oxford: OUP).

Finkelstein, S. (1997) "Interindustry Merger Patterns and Resource Dependence: A Replication and Extension of Pfeffer (1972)," *Strategic Management Journal*, 18:10, 787–810.

Fournier, V. & Grey, C. (2000) "At the Critical Moment: Conditions and Prospects for Critical Management Studies," *Human Relations*, 53:1, 7–32.

Friedland, R. & Alford, R. R. (1991) "Bringing Society Back In: Symbols, Practices and Institutional Contradictions," in W. W. Powell & P. J. DiMaggio, *The New Institutionalism in Organizational Analysis* (Chicago: University of Chicago Press).

Frost, P. J., Moore, L. F., Louis, M. R. E., Lundberg, C. C. & Martin, J. E. (eds.) (1985), *Organizational Culture* (London: Sage).

Furobotn, E.G. & Pejovich, S. (1974), *The Economics of Property Rights* (Cambridge, MA: Ballinger).

Galaskiewicz, J. (1985) "Interorganizational Relations," *Annual Review of Sociology*, 11:1, 281–304.

Gärditz, K. F. (2009), *Hochschulorganisation und verwaltungsrechtliche Systembildung* (Tübingen: Mohr Siebeck).

Geraldi, J. & Teerikangas, S. (2015) "Integration in the Study of Organizations—A Lack of Integration?" *75th Annual Meeting of the Academy of Management*.

Gergen, K. (1994), *Realities and Relationships: Soundings in Social Construction* (Cambridge: Cambridge University Press).

Gerpott, T. J. (1995) "Successful integration of R&D functions after acquisitions: An exploratory empirical study," *R&D Management*, 25:2, 161–178.

Giddens, A. (1979), *Central Problems in Social Theory: Action, Structure, and Contradiction in Social Analysis* (London: MacMillan).

Glaser, B. G. & Strauss, A. L. (1967), *The Discovery of Grounded Theory: Strategies for Qualitative Research* (New York: A. de Gruyter).

Goedegebuure, L. C. & Meek, V. L. (1991) "Restructuring Higher Education—A Comparative Analysis between Australia and the Netherlands," *Comparative Education* 27:1, 7–22.

Goedegebuure, L. C. (1992), *Mergers in Higher Education: A Comparative Perspective* (Utrecht: Lemma).

Goodman, P. S., Atkin, R. S. & Schoorman, F. D. (1983) "On the Demise of Organizational Effectiveness Studies," in K. S. Cameron & D. A. Whetten, *Organizational Effectiveness: A Comparison of Multiple Models* (New York: Academic Press).

Gort, M. (1962), *Diversification and Integration in American Industry* (Princeton: Princeton University Press).

Green, C. & Johnes, G. (2009) "Economies of Scale and Mergers in Higher Education," in M. Tight, K. H. Mok, J. Huisman & C. Morphew, *The Routledge International Handbook of Higher Education* (New York and London: Routledge).

Greene, J. C., Caracelli, V. J. & Graham, W. F. (1989) "Toward a Conceptual Framework for Mixed-Method Evaluation Designs," *Educational Evaluation and Policy Analysis*, 11:3, 255–274.

Greenwood, R. & Meyer, R. E. (2008) "Influencing Ideas: A Celebration of DiMaggio and Powell (1983)," *Journal of Management Inquiry*, 17:4, 258–264.

Greenwood, R., Hinings, C. R. & Brown, J. (1994) "Merging Professional Service Firms," *Organization Science*, 5:2, 239–257.

Hackman, J. D. (1985) "Power and Centrality in the Allocation of Resources in Colleges and Universities," *Administrative Science Quarterly*, 30:1, 61–77.

Haleblian, J., Devers, C. E., McNamara, G., Carpenter, M. A. & Davison, R. B. (2009) "Taking Stock of What We Know About Mergers and Acquisitions: A Review and Research Agenda," *Journal of Management*, 35:3, 469–502.

Hall, A. D. & Fagen, R. E. (1956) "Definition of System," *General Systems*, 1:1, 18–28.

Hannan, M. T. & Freeman, J. (1977) "The Population Ecology of Organizations," *American Journal of Sociology*, 82:5, 929–964.

Harman, G. & Harman, K. (2008) "Strategic Mergers of Strong Institutions to Enhance Competitive Advantage," *Higher Education Policy*, 21:1, 99–121.

Hargadon, A. B. (2003) "Organizations in Action—Reprinted Edition ASQ Book Review Symposium," *Administrative Science Quarterly*, 48:3, 498–509.

Harman, G. & Meek, V. L. (1988), *Institutional Amalgamations in Higher Education: Process and Outcome in Five Countries* (Armidale, NSW: University of New England).

Harman, G. (1983) "Research on Institutional Amalgamations in Tertiary Education: Concepts, Classificatory Schemes and Relevant Literature," *Journal of Higher Education Policy and Management*, 5:2, 113–129.

Harman, G. (1986) "Restructuring Higher Education Systems through Institutional Mergers: Australian Experience, 1981–1983," *Higher Education*, 15:6, 567–586.

Harman, G. & Harman, K. (2003) "Institutional Mergers in Higher Education: Lessons from International Experience," *Tertiary Education and Management*, 9:1, 29–44.

Harvey, D. (2005), *A Brief History of Neoliberalism* (Oxford: OUP).

Haspeslagh, P. C. & Jemison, D. B. (1991), *Managing Acquisitions: Creating Value through Corporate Renewal* (New York and London: Free Press).

Hasse, R. & Krücken, G. (2009) "Neo-institutionalistische Theorie," in G. Kneer & M. Schroer, *Handbuch Soziologische Theorien* (Wiesbaden: VS Verlag für Sozialwissenschaften).

Hauer, D. & Rogalla, B. (2006), *HWP in Bewegung: Studierendenproteste gegen neoliberale Hochschulreformen* (Hamburg: VSA).

Hay, D. & Fourie, M. (2002) "Preparing the Way for Mergers in South African Higher and Further Education Institutions: An Investigation into Staff Perceptions," *Higher Education*, 44:1, 115–131.

Henning, C., (2013), *fpc: Flexible Procedures for Clustering*, R package, vers. 2.1–7.

Hickson, D. J., Hinings, C. R., Lee, C. A., Schneck, R. E. & Pennings, J. M. (1971) "A Strategic Contingencies' Theory of Intraorganizational Power," *Administrative Science Quarterly*, 16:2, 216–229.

Hillman, A. J.; Withers, M. C. & Collins, B. J. (2009) "Resource Dependence Theory: A Review," *Journal of Management*, 35:6, 1404–1427.

Hills, F. S. & Mahoney, T. A. (1978) "University Budgets and Organizational Decision-Making," *Administrative Science Quarterly*, 23:3, 454–465.

Hinings, C. R. & Tolbert, P. S. (2008) "Organizational Institutionalism and Sociology: A Reflection," in R. Greenwood, K. S. Anderson, C. Oliver & R. Suddaby, *The Sage Handbook of Organizational Institutionalism* (London: Sage).

Hinings, C. R., Hickson, D. J., Pennings, J. M. & Schneck, R. E. (1974) "Structural Conditions of Intraorganizational Power," *Administrative Science Quarterly*, 19:1, 22–44.

Homburg, C. & Bucerius, M. (2006) "Is Speed of Integration Really a Success Factor of Mergers and Acquisitions? An Analysis of the Role of Internal and External Relatedness," *Strategic Management Journal*, 27:4, 347–367.

Hubbard, N. & Purcell, J. (2001) "Managing Employee Expectations During Acquisitions," *Human Resource Management Journal*, 11:2, 17–33.

Huck, S., Konrad, K. A., Müller, W. & Normann, H. T. (2007) "The Merger Paradox and Why Aspiration Levels Let It Fail in the Laboratory," *The Economic Journal*, 117:522, 1073–1095.

Humpal, J. J. (1971) "Organizational Marriage Counseling: A First Step," *The Journal of Applied Behavior Science*, 7:1, 103–109.

Jacobs, D. (1974) "Dependency and Vulnerability: An Exchange Approach to the Control of Organizations," *Administrative Science Quarterly*, 19:1, 45–59.

Jemison, D. B. & Sitkin, S. B. (1986) "Corporate Acquisitions: A Process Perspective," *Academy of Management Review*, 11:1, 145–163.

Jensen, M. C. & Meckling, W. H. (1976) "Theory of the Firm: Managerial Behavior, Agency Costs and Ownership Structure," *Journal of Financial Economics*, 3:4, 305–360.

Jolink, A. & Niesten, E. (2012) "Recent Qualitative Advances on Hybrid Organizations: Taking Stock, Looking Ahead," *Scandinavian Journal of Management*, 28:2, 149–161.

Jolliffe, I. T. (1986), *Principal Component Analysis* (New York: Springer).

Jöreskog, K. G. & Goldberger, A. S. (1972) "Factor Analysis by Generalized Least Squares," *Psychometrika*, 37:3, 243–260.

Kanter, R. M. & Brinkerhoff, D. (1981) "Organizational Performance: Recent Developments in Measurement," *Annual Review of Sociology*, 7, 321–349.

Katz, D. & Kahn, R. L. (1966), *The Psychology of Organizations* (New York: John Wiley & Sons).

Kaufman, L. & Rousseeuw, P. J. (2005), *Finding Groups in Data: An Introduction to Cluster Analysis* (Hoboken: Wiley Interscience).

Kavanagh, M. H. & Ashkanasy, N. M. (2006) "The Impact of Leadership and Change Management Strategy on Organizational Culture and Individual Acceptance of Change during a Merger," *British Journal of Management*, 17:S1, 81–103.

Kavanagh, M. H. & Ashkanasy, N. M. (2012) "Individual Values and Organizational Culture during a Merger: Immovable Objects or Shifting Sands?" in Y. Weber, *The Handbook of Research on Mergers and Acquisitions* (Cheltenham: Edward Elgar).

King, D. R., Dalton, D. R., Daily, C. M. & Covin, J. G. (2004) "Meta-Analyses of Post-Acquisition Performance: Indications of Unidentified Moderators," *Strategic Management Journal*, 25:2, 187–200.

Kitchener, M. (2002) "Mobilizing the Logic of Managerialism in Professional Fields: The Case of Academic Health Centre Mergers," *Organization Studies*, 23:3, 391–420.

Kitchener, M. & Gask, L. (2003) "NPM Merger Mania Lessons from an Early Case," *Public Management Review*, 5:1, 19–44.

Klumpp, M. & Zelewski, S. (2012) „Economies of Scale in Hochschulen – Das Beispiel der Hochschulfusion Duisburg-Essen," *Hochschulmanagement*, 7, 47–52.

Krücken, G. & Röbken, H. (2009) „Neo-institutionalistische Hochschulforschung," in S. Koch & M. Schemmann, *Neo-Institutionalismus in der Erziehungswissenschaft* (Wiesbaden: VS Verlag).

Kyvik, S. (2002) "The Merger of Non-University Colleges in Norway," *Higher Education*, 44:1, 53–72.

Lachman, R. (1989) "Power from What? A Reexamination of its Relationships with Structural Conditions," *Administrative Science Quarterly*, 34:2, 231–251.

Lang, D. W. (2002) "A Lexicon of Inter-Instituional Cooperation," *Higher Education*, 44:1, 153–183.

Lang, D. W. (2002): "There are Mergers, and There are Mergers: The Forms of Inter-Institutional Combination," *Higher Education Management and Policy*, 14:1, 11–50.

Larsson, R. & Finkelstein, S. (1999) "Integrating Strategic, Organizational, and Human Resource Perspectives on Mergers and Acquisitions: A Case Survey of Synergy Realization," *Organization Science*, 10:1, 1–26.

Larsson, R. & Lubatkin, M. (2001) "Achieving Acculturation in Mergers and Acquisitions: An International Case Survey," *Human Relations*, 54:12, 1573–1607.

Lawrence, P. R. & Lorsch, J. W. (1967) "Differentiation and Integration in Complex Organizations," *Administrative Science Quarterly*, 12:1, 1–47.

Lazarsfeld P. F. (1937) "Some Remarks on the Typological Procedures in Social Research," *Zeitschrift für Sozialforschung*, 6:1, 119–39.

Leblebici, H., Salancik, G. R., Copay, A. & King, T. (1991) "Institutional Change and the Transformation of Interorganizational Fields: An Organizational History of the US Radio Broadcasting Industry," *Administrative Science Quarterly*, 36:3, 333–363.

Levy, D. L., Alvesson, M. & Willmott, H. (2003) "Critical Approaches to Strategic Management," in M. Alvesson & H. Willmott, *Studying Management Critically* (London: Sage).

Lloyd, P. J., Morgan, M. H. & Williams, R. A. (1993) "Amalgamations of Universities: Are There Economics of Scale or Scope?" *Applied Economics*, 25:8, 1081–1092.

Locke, W. (2007) "Higher Education Mergers: Integrating Organisational Cultures and Developing Appropriate Management Styles," *Higher Education Quarterly*, 61:1, 83–102.

Lueken, G. L. (1992), *Inkommensurabilität als Problem rationalen Argumentierens* (Stuttgart: Frommann-Holzboog).

Luhmann, N. (2000), *Organisation und Entscheidung* (Opladen: Westdt. Verlag).

Maechler, M., Rousseeuw, P., Struyf, A., Hubert, M., & Hornik, K. (2013), *Cluster: Cluster Analysis Basics and Extensions*, R package, version 1.15.2.

Mangham, I. L. (1973) „Facilitating Organizational Dialogue in a Merger Situation", *Interpersonal Development*, 4:3, 133–147.

March, J. G. & Simon, H. A. (1958), *Organizations* (New York: John Wiley & Sons).

March, J. G. (1962) "The Business Firm as a Political Coalition," *The Journal of Politics*, 24:4, 662–678.

March, J. G. & Olsen, J. P. (1976), *Ambiguity and Choice in Organizations* (Bergen: Universitetsforlaget).

Marks, M. L. & Mirvis, P. H. (2010), *Joining Forces: Making One Plus One Equal Three in Mergers, Acquisitions, and Alliances* (San Francisco: Josey-Bass).

Martin, J. (2002), *Organizational Culture: Mapping the Terrain* (London: Sage).

Marx, K. & Engels, F. [1932/1947] (1970), *The German Ideology* (New York: International Publishers).

McKelvey, B. (1982), *Organizational Systematics. Taxonomy, Evolution, Classification* (Berkeley: University of California Press).

McKelvey, B. (1978) "Organizational Systematics: Taxonomic Lessons from Biology," *Management Science*, 24:13, 1428–1440.

McKinley, W. & Mone, M. A. (2003) "Micro and Macro Perspectives in Organization Theory: A Tale of Incommensurability," in H. Tsoukas & C. Knudsen, *The Oxford Handbook of Organization Theory* (Oxford: OUP).

Meek, L. (1994) "Higher Education Policy in Australia," in L. Goedegebuure, F. Kaiser, P. Maassen, L. Meek., F. van Vught & E. de Weert, *Higher education policy: An international comparative perspective* (Oxford: Pergamon Press).

Meglio, O. & Risberg, A. (2010) "Mergers and Acquisitions—Time for a Methodological Rejuvenation of the Field?" *Scandinavian Journal of Management*, 26:1, 87–95.

Meglio, O. & Risberg, A. (2012) "Are All Mergers and Acquisitions Treated as If They Were Alike? A Review of Empirical Literature," in C. Cooper & S. Finkelstein, *Advances in Mergers and Acquisitions (Vol. 10)* (Bingley, UK: Emerald).

Meilă, M. (2007) "Comparing Clusterings—an Information-Based Distance," *Journal of Multivariate Analysis*," 98:5, 873–895.

Ménard, C. (2004) "The Economics of Hybrid Organizations," *Journal of Institutional and Theoretical Economics*, 160:3, 345–376.

Meyer, J. W., Ramirez, F. O., Frank, D. J. & Schofer, E. (2007) "Higher Education as an Institution," in P. J. Gumport, *Sociology of Higher Education: Contributions and Their Contexts* (Baltimore, ML: Johns Hopkins University Press).

Meyer, J. W. & Rowan, B. (1977) "Institutionalized Organizations: Formal Structure as Myth and Ceremony," *American Journal of Sociology*, 83:2, 340–363.

Meyer, J. W. & Rowan, B. (1978) "The Structure of Educational Organizations," in M. W. Meyer, *Environments and Organizations* (San Francisco: Josey Bass).

Ministerium für Wissenschaft und Kultur Niedersachsen (2009), *Empfehlungen zur zukünftigen Hochschulentwicklung im nordwestlichen Niedersachsen* (Hannover: MWK).

Mintzberg, H. (1979), *The Structuring of Organizations: A Synthesis of the Research* (Upper Saddle River: Prentice-Hall).

Mintzberg, H. (1990) "The Design School: Reconsidering the Basic Premises of Strategic Management," *Strategic Management Journal*, 11:3, 171–195.

Mirvis, P. H. & Marks, M. L. (1992) "The Human Side of Merger Planning: Assessing and Analyzing 'Fit,' *Human Resource Planning*, 15:3, 69–92.

Mizruchi, M. S. & Fein, L. C. (1999) "The Social Construction of Organizational Knowledge: A Study of the Uses of Coercive, Mimetic, and Normative Isomorphism," *Administrative Science Quarterly*, 44:4, 653–683.

Mok, K. H. (2005) "Globalization and Educational Restructuring: University Merging and Changing Governance in China," *Higher Education*, 50:1, 57–88.

Morgan, G. (1980) "Paradigms, Metaphors, and Puzzle Solving in Organization Theory," *Administrative Science Quarterly*, 25:4, 605–622

Morgan, G. [1986] (2006), *Images of Organization* (London: Sage).

Morgan, G. & Spicer, A. (2009) "Critical Approaches to Organizational Change," in M. Alvesson, T. Bridgman & H. Willmott, *The Oxford Handbook of Critical Management Studies* (Oxford: OUP).

Musselin, C. (2007) "Are Universities Specific Organizations?" in G. Krücken, G. Kosmützky & M. Torga, *Towards a Multiversity: Universities between Global Trends and National Traditions* (Bielefeld: Transcript).

Nahavandi, A. & Malekzadeh, A. R. (1988) "Acculturation in Mergers and Acquisitions," *Academy of Management Review*, 13:1, 79–90.

Napier, N. K. (1989) "Mergers and Acquisitions, Human Resource Issues and Outcomes: A Review and Suggested Typology," *Journal of Management Studies*, 26:3, 271–290.

Nienhüser, W. (2008) "Resource Dependence Theory – How Well Does It Explain Behavior of Organizations?" *Management Revue*, 19:1/2, 9–32.

Nienhüser, W. & Jacob, A. K. (2008) „Changing of the Guards – Eine empirische Analyse der Sozialstruktur von Hochschulräten," *Hochschulmanagement*, 3, 67–73.

Norgård, J. D. & Skodvin, O. J. (2002) "The Importance of Geography and Culture in Mergers: A Norwegian Institutional Case Study," *Higher Education*, 44:1, 73–90.

Oliver, C. (1991) "Strategic Responses to Institutional Processes," *Academy of Management Review*, 16:1, 145–179.

Olsen, J. P. & Maassen, P. (2007), *University Dynamics and European Integration* (Dordrecht: Springer).

Ortmann, G. (2004), *Als ob: Fiktionen und Organisationen* (Wiesbaden: VS Verlag).

Orton, J. D. & Weick, K. E. (1990) "Loosely Coupled Systems: A Reconceptualization," *Academy of Management Review*, 15:2, 203–223.

Pablo, A. L. (1994) "Determinants of Acquisition Integration Level: A Decision-Making Perspective," *Academy of Management Journal*, 37:4, 803–836.

Pablo, A. L. (2016) "Deconstructing M&A Research—Paradigm Progress," in A. Risberg, D. A. King & O. Meglio, *The Routledge Companion to Mergers and Acquisitions* (London and New York: Routledge).

Peteraf, M. A. (1993) "The Cornerstones of Competitive Advantage: A Resource-Based View," *Strategic Management Journal*, 14:3, 179–191.

Pfeffer, J. (1972) "Merger as a Response to Organizational Interdependence," *Administrative Science Quarterly*, 17:3, 382–394.

Pfeffer, J. (1978), *Organizational Design* (Arlington Heights, Ill.: Harlan Davidson).

Pfeffer, J. (2003) "Introduction to the Classic Edition," in J. Pfeffer & G. Salancik, *The External Control of Organizations: A Resource Dependence Perspective* [1978 reprint] (Redwood, CA: Stanford University Press).

Pfeffer, J. (2005) "Developing Resource Dependence Theory: How Theory is Affected by its Environment," in K. G. Smith & M. A. Hitt, *Great Minds in Management: The Process of Theory Development* (Oxford: OUP).

Pfeffer, J. & Davis-Blake, A. (1987) "Understanding Organizational Wage Structures: A Resource Dependence Approach," *Academy of Management Journal*, 30:3, 437–455.

Pfeffer, J. & Davis-Blake, A. (1992) "Salary Dispersion, Location in the Salary Distribution, and Turnover among College Administrators," *Industrial & Labor Relations Review*, 45:4, 753–763.

Pfeffer, J. & Moore, W. L. (1980) "Power in University Budgeting: A Replication and Extension," *Administrative Science Quarterly*, 25:4, 637–653.

Pfeffer, J. & Salancik, G. R. [1978] (2003), *The External Control of Organizations: A Resource Dependence Perspective* (Redwood, CA: Stanford University Press).

Pooley (2013) "Substantialist and Relationist Approaches to Spacetime," in R. Batterman, *The Oxford Handbook of Philosophy of Physics* (Oxford: OUP).

Pruisken, I. (2014), *Fusionen im institutionellen Feld "Hochschule und Wissenschaft"* (Baden-Baden: Nomos).

Ranft, A. L. & Lord, M. D. (2002) "Acquiring New Technologies and Capabilities: A Grounded Model of Acquisition Implementation," *Organization Science*, 13:4, 420–441.

Ranft, A. L., Butler, F. C. & Sexton, J. C. (2010) "A Review of Research Progress in Understanding the Acquisition Integration Process: Building Directions for Future Research," in P. Mazzolo & F. Kellermans, *Handbook of Research on Strategy Process* (Cheltenham, UK: Elgar Publishing).

Rashdall, H. (1895), *The Universities of Europe in the Middle Ages: Salerno-Bologna-Paris* (Oxford: OUP).

Reed, M. I. (2003) "The Agency / Structure Dilemma in Organization Theory: Open Doors and Brick Walls," in H. Tsoukas & C. Knudsen, *The Oxford Handbook of Organization Theory* (Oxford: OUP).

Reed, M. I. (2005) "Reflections on the 'Realist Turn' in Organization and Management Studies," *Journal of Management Studies*, 42:8, 1621–1644.

Reed, M. I. (2006) "Organizational Theorizing: A Historically Contested Terrain," in S. R. Clegg, C. Hardy, T. B. Lawrence & W. R. Nord, *The Sage Handbook of Organization Studies* (London: Sage).

Reed, M. I. (2009) "Critical Realism: Philosophy, Method, or Philosophy in Search for a Method?" in D. A. Buchanan & A. Bryman, *The Sage Handbook of Organizational Research Methods* (London: Sage).

Reus, T. H., Ellis, K. M., Lamont, B. T. & Ranft, A. L. (2012) "Placing Process Factors Along with Contextual Factors in Merger and Acquisition Research," in Y. Weber, *Handbook of Research on Mergers and Acquisitions* (Cheltenham: Edward Elgar).

Riad, S. (2005) "The Power of 'Organizational Culture' as a Discursive Formation in Merger Integration," *Organization Studies*, 26:10, 1529–1554.

Risberg, A. (2016) "Qualitative and Longitudinal Studies of Mergers and Acquisitions: A Reflection of Methods in Use," in A. Risberg, D. A. King & O. Meglio, *The Routledge Companion to Mergers and Acquisitions* (London and New York: Routledge).

Risberg, A. & Meglio, O. (2012) "Merger and Acquisition Outcomes—Is It Meaningful to Talk about High Failure Rates?" in Y. Weber, *Handbook of Research on Mergers and Acquisitions* (Cheltenham: Edward Elgar).

Sackmann, S. A. (1992) "Culture and Subcultures: An Analysis of Organizational Knowledge," *Administrative Science Quarterly*, 37:1, 140–161.

Salancik, G. R. & Pfeffer, J. (1974) "The Bases and Use of Power in Organizational Decision-making: The Case of a University," *Administrative Science Quarterly*, 19:4, 453–473.

Salancik, G. R., Staw, B. M. & Pondy, L. R. (1980) "Administrative Turnover as a Response to Unmanaged Organizational Interdependence," *Academy of Management Journal*, 23:3, 422–437.

Salancik, G. R. (1984) "A Single Value Function for Evaluating Organizations with Multiple Constituencies," *The Academy of Management Review*, 9:4, 617–625.

Santner, T. J., & Duffy, D. E. (1986) "A Note on A. Albert and J. A. Anderson's Conditions for the Existence of Maximum Likelihood Estimates in Logistic Regression Models," *Biometrika*, 73:3, 755–758.

Santos, F. M. & Eisenhardt, K. M. (2005) "Organizational Boundaries and Theories of Organization," *Organization Science*, 16:5, 491–508.

Saunders, C. (1990) "The Strategic Contingencies Theory of Power: Multiple Perspectives," *Journal of Management Studies*, 27:1, 1–18.

Saunders, C. S. & Scamell, R. (1982) "Intraorganizational Distributions of Power: Replication Research," *Academy of Management Journal*, 25:1, 192–200.

Schein, E. H. (1985), *Organizational Culture and Leadership* (San Francisco: Josey Bass).

Schein, E. H. (1996) "Culture: The Missing Concept in Organization Studies," *Administrative Science Quarterly*, 41:2, 229–240.

Scherer, A. G. (1998) "Pluralism and Incommensurability in Strategic Management and Organization Theory: A Problem in Search of a Solution," *Organization*, 5:2, 147–168.

Scherer, A. G. (2003) "Modes of Explanation in Organization Theory," in H. Tsoukas & C. Knudsen, *The Oxford Handbook of Organization Theory* (Oxford: OUP).

Scherer, A. G. & Dowling, M. J. (1995) "Towards a Reconciliation of the Theory Pluralism in Strategic Management-Incommensurability and the Constructivist Approach of the Erlangen School," *Advances in Strategic Management*, 12 A, 195–247.

Schick, A. G. (1985) "University Budgeting: Administrative Perspective, Budget Structure, and Budget Process," *Academy of Management Review*, 10:4, 794–802.

Schimank, U. (2005) "'New Public Management' and the Academic Profession: Reflections on the German Situation," *Minerva*, 43:4, 361–376.

Schoonhoven, C. B. (1981) "Problems with Contingency Theory: Testing Assumptions Hidden Within the Language of Contingency 'Theory'," *Administrative Science Quarterly*, 26:3, 349–377.

Schuetz, A. (1971) "Über die mannigfaltigen Wirklichkeiten," in A. Schuetz: *Gesammelte Aufsätze I: Das Problem der sozialen Wirklichkeit* (Amsterdam: Springer).

Schweiger, D. M. & Very, P. (2003) "Creating Value Through Merger and Acquisition Integration," in C. Cooper & S. Finkelstein, *Advances in Mergers and Acquisitions (Vol. 2)* (Bingley, UK: Emerald).

Schweiger, D. M., Csiszar, E. N. & Napier, N. K. (1993) "Implementing International Mergers and Acquisitions," *Human Resource Planning*, 16:1, 53–71.

Schweiger, D. M. & Goulet, P. K. (2000) "Integrating Mergers and Acquisitions: An International Research Review," in C. Cooper & S. Finkelstein, *Advances in Mergers and Acquisitions (Vol. 1)* (Bingley, UK: Emerald).

Schweiger, D. M., Ivancevich, J. M. & Power, F. R. (1987) "Executive Actions for Managing Human Resources Before and After Acquisition," *The Academy of Management Executive*, 1:2, 127–138.

Scott, W. R. (1987) "The Adolescence of Institutional Theory," *Administrative Science Quarterly*, 32:4, 493–511.

Scott, W. R. (2003), *Organizations: Rational, Natural and Open Systems* (Upper Saddle River, NJ: Prentice Hall).

Sehoole, M. T. (2005): "The Politics of Mergers in Higher Education in South Africa," *Higher Education*, 50:1, 159–179.

Shenhav, Y., Alon, S. & Shrum, W. (1994) "'Goodness' Concepts in the Study of Organizations: A Longitudinal Survey of Four Leading Journals," *Organization Studies*, 15:5, 753–776.

Sherer, P. D. & Lee, K. (2002) "Institutional Change in Large Law Firms: A Resource Dependency and Institutional Perspective," *Academy of Management Journal*, 45:1, 102–119.

Singh, A. (1971), *Take-Overs: Their Relevance to the Stock Market and the Theory of the Firm* (London and New York: Cambridge University Press).

Skodvin, O.-J. (1999) "Mergers in Higher Education—Success or Failure?" *Tertiary Education and Management*, 5:1, 65–80.

Smircich, L. (1983) "Concepts of Culture and Organizational Analysis," *Administrative Science Quarterly*, 28:3, 339–358.

Stahl, G. K. & Voigt, A. (2008) "Do Cultural Differences Matter in Mergers and Acquisitions? A Tentative Model and Examination," *Organization Science*, 19:1, 160–176.

Starbuck, W. H. (2003) "The Origins of Organization Theory," in H. Tsoukas & C. Knudsen, *The Oxford Handbook of Organization Theory* (Oxford: OUP).

Steers, R. M. (1975) "Problems in the Measurement of Organizational Effectiveness," *Administrative Science Quarterly*, 20:4, 546–558.

Stevenson, W. B., Pearce, J. L. & Porter, L. W. (1985) "The Concept of 'Coalition' in Organization Theory and Research," *Academy of Management Review*, 10:2, 256–268.

Strang, D., & Meyer, J. W. (1993) "Institutional Conditions for Diffusion," *Theory and Society*, 22:4, 487–511.

Suchman, M. C. (1995) "Managing Legitimacy: Strategic and Institutional Approaches," *Academy of Management Review*, 20:3, 571–610.

Teerikangas, S. (2007) "A Comparative Overview of the Impact of Cultural Diversity on Inter-Organisational Encounters," in C. L. Cooper & S. Finkelstein, *Advances in Mergers and Acquisitions (Vol. 6)* (Bingley, UK: Emerald).

Teerikangas, S. P. & Joseph, R. (2012) "Post – Deal Integration: An Overview," in D. Faulkner, S. Teerikangas & R. Joseph, *The Oxford Handbook Mergers and Acquisitions* (Oxford: OUP).

Teerikangas, S. P. & Very, P. (2012) "Culture in Mergers and Acquisitions: A Critical Synthesis and Steps Forward," in D. Faulkner, S. Teerikangas & R. Joseph, *The Oxford Handbook Mergers and Acquisitions* (Oxford: OUP).

Thanos, I. C. & Papadakis, V. M. (2012) "The Use of Accounting-Based Measures for Measuring M&A Performance: A Review of Five Decades of Research," in C. L. Cooper & S. Finkelstein, *Advances in Mergers and Acquisitions (Vol. 10)* (Bingley, UK: Emerald).

Thomas, H. (2000) "Power in the Resource Allocation Process: The Impact of 'Rational' Systems," *Journal of Higher Education Policy and Management*, 22:2, 127–137.

Thompson, J. D. (1967), *Organizations in Action: Social Sciences Bases of Administrative Theory* (New York: McGraw-Hill).

Thornton, P. H. & Ocasio, W. (1999) "Institutional Logics and the Historical Contingency of Power in Organizations: Executive Succession in the Higher Education Publishing Industry, 1958–1990," *American Journal of Sociology*, 105:3, 801–843.

Thornton, P. H. & Ocasio, W. (2008) "Institutional Logics," in R. Greenwood , K. S. Anderson, , C. Oliver, & R. Suddaby, *The Sage Handbook of Organizational Institutionalism* (London: Sage).

Tichy, G. (2001) "What Do We Know About Success and Failure of Mergers?" *Journal of Industry, Competition and Trade*, 1:4, 347–394.

Tolbert, P. S. (1985) "Institutional Environments and Resource Dependence: Sources of Administrative Structure in Institutions of Higher Education," *Administrative Science Quarterly*, 30:1, 1–13.

Tosi, H. L. (2009), *Theories of Organization* (London: Sage).

Trautwein, F. (1990) "Merger Motives and Merger Prescriptions," *Strategic Management Journal*, 11:4, 283–295.

Türk, K. (1997) "Organisation als Institution der kapitalistischen Gesellschaftsformation," in G. Ortmann, J. Sydow & K. Türk, *Theorien der Organisation: Die Rückkehr der Gesellschaft* (Opladen: Westdeutscher Verlag).

Umbach, I. & Palsherm, D. C. (2003) "Fusionen und Auflösungen von Universitäten und Fakultäten nach Länder- und Bundesrecht," in W. Knippel, *Verfassungsgerichtsbarkeit im Land Brandenburg* (Baden-Baden: Nomos).

Überla, K. (1971), *Faktorenanalyse: Eine systematische Einführung für Psychologen, Mediziner, Wirtschafts- und Sozialwissenschaftler* (Berlin: Springer).

Van de Ven, A. H. & Poole, M. S. (2005) "Alternative Approaches for Studying Organizational Change," *Organization Studies*, 26:9, 1377–1404.

Venkatraman, N. & Camillus, J. C. (1984) "Exploring the Concept of 'Fit' in Strategic Management," *Academy of Management Review*, 9:3, 513–525.

Vögtle, E. M. (2014), *Higher Education Policy Convergence and the Bologna Process: A Cross-National Study* (Basingstoke: Palgrave Macmillan).

Wan, Y. & Peterson, M. W. (2007) "A Case Study of a Merger in Chinese Higher Education: The Motives, Processes, and Outcomes," *International Journal of Educational Development*, 27:6, 683–696.

Weber, R. A. & Camerer, C. F. (2003) "Cultural Conflict and Merger Failure: An Experimental Approach," *Management Science*, 49:4, 400–415.

Weick, K. E. (1979) "Cognitive Processes in Organizations," *Research in Organizational Behavior*, 1:1, 41–74.

Weick, K. E., Sutcliffe, K. M. & Obstfeld, D. (2005) "Organizing and the Process of Sensemaking," Organization Science, 16:4, 409–421.

Weick, Karl E. (1969), *The Social Psychology of Organizing* (Reading, MA: Addison-Wesley).

Wernerfelt, B. (1984) "A Resource-Based View of the Firm," *Strategic Management Journal*, 5:2, 171–180.

Wilkins, A. L. & Ouchi, W. G. (1983) "Efficient Cultures: Exploring the Relationship Between Culture and Organizational Performance," *Administrative Science Quarterly*, 28:3, 468–481.

Williamson, O. E. (1975), *Markets and Hierarchies: Analysis and Antitrust Implications: A Study in the Economics of Internal Organization* (New York: Free Press).

Williamson, O. E. (1981) "The Economics of Organization: The Transaction Cost Approach," *American Journal of Sociology*, 87:3, 548–577.

Williamson, O. E. (1985), *The Economic Institutions of Capitalism—Firms, Markets, Relational Contracting* (New York: Free Press).

Williamson, O. E. (1991) "Comparative Economic Organization: The Analysis of Discrete Structural Alternatives," *Administrative Science Quarterly*, 36:2, 269–296.

Williamson, O. E. & Ouchi, W. G. (1980) "The Markets and Hierarchies Program of Research: Origins, Implications, Prospects," *IIM Discussion Papers (Vol. 72)* (Berlin: Internationales Institut für Management und Verwaltung).

Wilson, T. (1991) "The Proletarianisation of Academic Labour," *Industrial Relations*, 22:4, 250–262.

Witte, J. K. (2006), *Change of Degrees and Degrees of Change—Comparing Adaptions of European Higher Education Systems in the Context of the Bologna Process* (Enschede: University of Twente).

Wry, T., Cobb, J. A., & Aldrich, H. E. (2013) "More Than a Metaphor: Assessing the Historical Legacy of Resource Dependence and Its Contemporary Promise as a Theory of Environmental Complexity," *The Academy of Management Annals*, 7:1, 441–488.

Yang, R. (2000) "Tensions between the Global and the Local: A Comparative Illustration of the Reorganisation of China's Higher Education in the 1950s and 1990s," *Higher Education*, 39:3, 319–337.

Zald, M. N. (2003) "Preface to the Transaction Edition," in J. Thompson, *Organizations in Action: Social Sciences Bases of Administrative Theory* [1967 Reprint] (New York: Transaction Publishers).

Zucker, L. G. (1983) "Organizations as Institutions," *Research in the Sociology of Organizations*, 2:1, 1–47.

Zucker, L. G. (1987) "Institutional Theories of Organization," *Annual Review of Sociology*, 13, 443–464.